WILDERNESS MAN
The strange story of Grey Owl

BOOKS BY **Lovat Dickson**

Wilderness Man: The Strange Story of Grey Owl   1973
H. G. Wells: His Turbulent Life and Times   1969
The House of Words   1963
The Ante-Room   1960

LOVAT DICKSON

WILDERN

ESS MAN

The strange story of
Grey Owl

Atheneum
New York 1973

Library of Congress catalog card number 73-81707
ISBN 0-689-10580-0

Manufactured in Canada by
Hunter Rose

Designed by Robert Burgess Garbutt

FIRST AMERICAN EDITION

ILLUSTRATIONS

Archie Belaney in Canadian army uniform. (*Ontario Archives*)

Trapper's cabin in winter. (*Peter Davies Ltd. Collection, Ontario Archives*)

Archie Belaney and Charlie Duval on the fire-range. (*Ontario Department of Lands and Forests*)

Ne-ganik-abo, one of the old-time Indians. (*Jack Woodworth Collection, Ontario Archives*)

Alex Espaniel, Archie's best friend in Bisco. (*Ed Sawyer Collection, Ontario Archives*)

Archie Belaney, a friend, and Jim Espaniel. (*Vince Crichton Collection, Ontario Archives*)

between pages 144 and 145

Anahareo at Wabikon Camp on Lake Temagami. (*Ontario Department of Lands and Forests*)

Archie before a cabin at Marquis River, Abitibi. (*Grey Owl and Anahareo Collection lent by Dawn Bruce, Ontario Archives*)

Archie and Anahareo near Doucet (*Bill Cartier Collection, Ontario Archives*)

Grey Owl and a beaver. (*Peter Davies Ltd. Collection, Ontario Archives*)

Grey Owl and Jelly Roll at Métis, Quebec. (*Peter Davies Ltd. Collection, Ontario Archives*)

Dave White Stone, who lived with Archie and Anahareo at Birch Lake. (*Grey Owl and Anahareo Collection lent by Dawn Bruce, Ontario Archives*)

Grey Owl, 1931. (*Ontario Archives*)

"Beaver Lodge" on Lake Ajawaan. (*Ontario Archives*)

Grey Owl feeding a beaver kitten.

Inside "Beaver Lodge", Grey Owl's cabin on Lake Ajawaan. (*Margaret Winters Charko Collection, Ontario Archives*)

Grey Owl and daughter Dawn. (*Ontario Archives*)

Grey Owl on snowshoes at Lake Ajawaan. (*Grey Owl and Anahareo Collection lent by Dawn Bruce, Ontario Archives*)

Grey Owl canoeing (*Margaret Winters Charko Collection, Ontario Archives*)

Anahareo canoeing with daughter Dawn (*Margaret Winters
Charko Collection, Ontario Archives*)
Anahareo, photo inscribed by Archie.
Grey Owl, portrait by Karsh. (*Copyright by Karsh of Ottawa*)

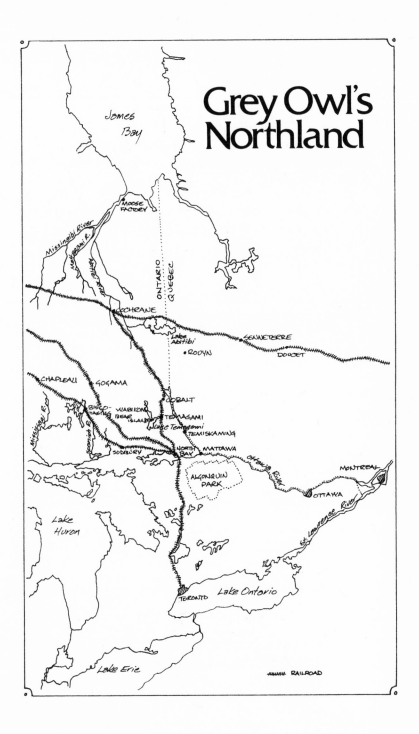

Grey Owl's Northland

James Bay

Missinaibi River

Mattagami R.

Abitibi R.

MOOSE FACTORY

ONTARIO

QUEBEC

COCHRANE

Lake Abitibi

SENNETERRE

ROUYN

DOUCET

CHAPLEAU

GOGAMA

BISCO-TASTING

WABIKON

BEAR ISLAND

COBALT

TEMAGAMI

Lake Temagami

TEMISKAMING

Mississagi R.

SUDBURY

NORTH BAY

MATTAWA

Ottawa River

MONTREAL

ALGONQUIN PARK

OTTAWA

Lake Huron

St. Lawrence River

TORONTO

Lake Ontario

Lake Erie

++++++ RAILROAD

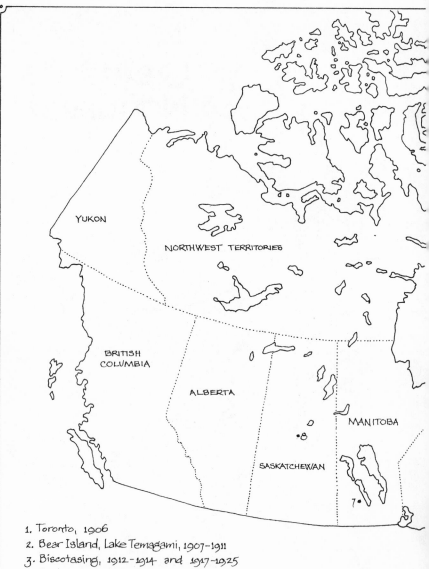

YUKON

NORTHWEST TERRITORIES

BRITISH
COLUMBIA

ALBERTA

SASKATCHEWAN

MANITOBA

•8

7•

1. Toronto, 1906
2. Bear Island, Lake Temagami, 1907–1911
3. Biscotasing, 1912–1914 and 1917–1925
4. Digby, 1915
5. Doucet, Abitibi, 1926–1928
6. Cabano, Temiscouata, 1928–1931
7. Riding Mountain National Park, 1931
8. Prince Albert National Park, 1931–1938

Grey Owl's Canada

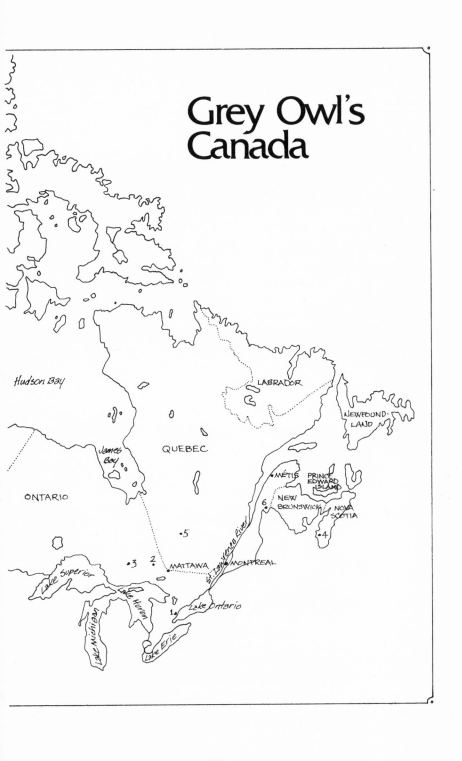

Hudson Bay

LABRADOR

NEWFOUND-
LAND

James
Bay

QUEBEC

MÉTIS

PRINCE
EDWARD
ISLAND

ONTARIO

• 6   NEW
BRUNSWICK

NOVA
SCOTIA

• 5

• 4

• 3   2
•   MATTAWA   MONTREAL

St. Lawrence River

Lake Superior

Lake Huron

1 •   Lake Ontario

Lake Michigan

Lake Erie

WILDERNESS MAN
The strange story of Grey Owl

CHAPTER 1

SOMETIMES when I return to London, a piece of the past
swings into view, like a bit of the horizon caught in
one of those telescopes or view-finders you sometimes
find placed at look-out points on scenic drives, which revolve
on their bases to take in a 180-degree view. I never know
what it is that prompts the view-finder to stop at a particular
point: the amount of force your finger gives to it, or inscrutable fate. But there it is, and when you apply your eye,
suddenly revealed before you is another and yet a familiar
world, separated by the glass of the telescope and a space of
unbridgeable miles.

This is a universal experience and hardly worth mention-
ing, except that when this shifting of focus in the small
business of our lives brings back some vision of the past,

1

it is as though one caught one's breath sharply with the pressure of passing backwards through time; the blood surges again through arteries worn by the struggle and turmoil of life since then. Suddenly we are back where we were.

I, for instance, am young again, and in the heat of the battle. Also he is alive again, not dead these thirty-five years; caught in this strong reflow of memory in London is the cause of all the excitement, Archie Belaney himself, Wa-Sha-Quon-Asin as the Ojibways called him, He-Who-Flies-By-Night, Grey Owl.

I am forced to intrude for a moment with the bare bones of a *curriculum vitae*, so that you will know who it is that is bearing witness about Belaney.

I had been teaching English in a Canadian university in my home province of Alberta. Chance, the merest chance, gave me the opportunity to become assistant editor of an ancient magazine in England, then tottering towards its grave after a long and honourable life. I crossed to London in my twenty-fifth year, and the effect on me was overwhelming. I became a bookman. I had always been an avid and indiscriminate reader, and now I began to make friends with young authors of my own age: Richard Church and Charles Morgan, Evelyn Waugh and his dear brother Alec, Victor Pritchett, Clifford Bax, Francis Watson, A. D. Peters the literary agent, a dozen or so others. I started writing book reviews for *The Fortnightly*. An American publisher visiting London asked me to find books for his firm and offered to pay me a modest retainer. Luck and my friends helped me to find what he wanted. I made up my mind, my friends concurring in the opinion, that I had the touch. With insufficient capital but an excess of confidence, I threw up my job on *The Fortnightly* and set up the publishing business in London called Lovat Dickson Limited.

My friends kept me going for two years with their books, and others they introduced, and sometimes with small draughts of their exiguous capital. We had some moments of glory. But there were some anxious, careworn moments too, when I was summoned from time to time by my local bank manager, who had heard of best-sellers, and thought a young fellow who had been fishing for them for two years without getting a bite ought to think of dismantling his rod and taking what he called a "regular" job.

And then, not from Oxford where I was spending occasional hilarious weekends with fledgling dons, nor from Bloomsbury where we had glorious nights of talk when ambition soared and hopes had strong pinions, but from the adjoining province to mine in Canada, Saskatchewan, came a manuscript that was indirectly to make my fortune and change the whole course of my life. The script was *Pilgrims of the Wild*, by a self-declared half-breed calling himself Grey Owl; it was this that sent my life spinning through a period of action and high drama which I can never recall without that familiar surge in the blood that makes old men turn giddy, and young men strong and brave. This was how it happened.

Grey Owl had always said little about his origins. All he had let drop were a few principal details. He said that his father, a Scotsman named George MacNeill, had been an Indian scout in the wars against the Indians in the southwestern United States in the 1870s. His mother had been Katherine Cochise of the Jacarilla band of the Apache tribe.

As Grey Owl told the story, MacNeill had been a friend of Colonel Bill Cody, the Indian fighter, and he and his Indian wife had joined the first show which Buffalo Bill had brought over to England for Queen Victoria's Jubilee in 1887. Grey Owl said that his parents had returned to the States "on my appearance threatening to become imminent", and declared himself to have been born in Hermosillo, Mexico, in 1888.

The family had subsequently made its way up through the unsettled west to near the Canadian border. At some point, when he was about fifteen, Grey Owl had gone on alone, earning a living as a packer and guide. He had been drawn to Northern Ontario by the silver strike at Cobalt in 1903 and by the subsequent construction of the new Northern Ontario Railway. He had got as far as Temagami, thirty miles south of Cobalt, in 1906, and there had begun his long and colourful career as trapper, riverman, and interpreter of nature which was to make him famous.

3

He was something more in the beginning than all these things. He was a hard-living man whose hand was often on his knife, a skilful woodsman but a dangerous man to have as an enemy. He had had one or two brushes with the police. The offences were not serious; they seemed more often to have arisen out of an excess of animal vitality than from a desire to do damage to someone. But when violence intruded, he had to escape to the woods to avoid justice.

In 1925, when he was thirty-seven, Grey Owl was in flight and Inspector Jordan was on his way down from Chapleau to Biscotasing to serve a warrant on him for pasting the station agent, Joe Bolton. Just before this time, Grey Owl had met at Temagami a beautiful young Iroquois girl called Gertrude Bernard, who was to bear the Indian name Anahareo, with whom he had fallen desperately in love. He disappeared, but he urged her to follow him. She did, and the story of *Pilgrims of the Wild* which dropped into my lap told of their flight together across two thousand miles of Northern Canada, of how she sickened of the hunt and pressed him to give it up, of how he resisted her pleas until they captured two beaver kittens whose mother had been drowned in Grey Owl's trap, and of how these beaver released a spring in him that firmly closed him from his past.

The story is beautifully told, without sentimentalism or false emotions of any kind. He had a genius for describing animal life, and the joint struggle of these two humans to survive without any means of livelihood seemed to combine the best of Thoreau with the best of Robinson Crusoe.

I had a strong feeling, after seeing many pictures of him and reading this wonderful account of the transformation of a killer of wild animals into a protector of them, that this romantic figure would appeal enormously to the instincts of the animal-loving British public, and his appearance on platforms, if I could arrange it, would be worth many columns of paid advertising in the *Observer* and the *Sunday Times*. I suggested to him that he should come; he hesitated, then came, clad in buckskin jacket and fringed leather pants, wearing moccasins, his long black hair hanging in plaits to his shoulders. His appearance in London in October 1935 created a sensation. Not only did he look

4

romantic, he spoke pure romance. His thrilling voice brought the wilderness and its inhabitants, animal and Indian, alive to his audiences. He won the hearts of everyone from the monarch to the smallest child who heard his stories and saw the films which the Canadian government had made of his cabin in the woods and of the animals who lived in and around it with him.

It was the mid-thirties when Europe was stumbling towards another war. This voice from the forests momentarily released us from some spell. In contrast with Hitler's screaming, ranting voice, and the remorseless clang of modern technology, Grey Owl's words evoked an unforgettable charm, lighting in our minds the vision of a cool, quiet place, where men and animals lived in love and trust together. So great was the demand for his healing presence that we had to bring him back in 1937 for a second tour. He ended this at Christmas, and started immediately on a lecture tour throughout the United States.

The strain was more than anyone could bear. Suddenly, on April 13, 1938, at the age of fifty, he died; and as though they were waiting for him to be gone, within twenty-four hours there began an outburst of revelations.

Grey Owl, it was said, was not an Indian. His real name was Archie Belaney, and he had been born in Hastings, England, in 1888, the son of George Belaney and Katherine Cox. Archie Belaney had arrived in Canada on April 7, 1906, and that same summer had appeared in Temagami in Northern Ontario. The young Englishman had begun to wear his hair long, and wore buckskin clothes and moccasins. He identified himself from the beginning with the Indians, and gave the same account, whenever he had to, of his birth in Mexico and of his Scottish-Indian parentage. The Temagami band of Ojibways to which he quickly attached himself may have had other ideas. But if so, it was of no importance to them. They taught him nearly everything he was to know about trapping, woodcraft, and Indian lore.

Voices from out of the forest, woodsmen and guides who had known him in the North in the early days as a young Englishman, encouraged by interviewers, were destroying the whole myth on which his appeal to the English public had been based. Cries of "fraud" and "hoax" headlined stories in the press, and his claim to have had Indian blood was ridiculed, as one might laugh at a grown man playing childish roles. Even his morality was suspect. It appeared that he had had several wives, that he had been the trouble-maker in the small Northern Ontario settlement of Biscotasing which had been his headquarters as a trapper, that on at least two occasions warrants had been sworn out for his arrest and he had escaped gaol only by taking to the woods.

The saint was fast being turned into a mountebank. I had so long been devoting myself to this man and his books that automatically I began to spend as much time in defending him as I had done in promoting him. I became his sole champion. I could not believe that he had deceived me. I thought that the story of his having had an Indian mother must be true. As to the tales of his wild behaviour in Bisco, I knew from experience how narrow-minded and puritanical the Ontario small-town mind could be, and to what extravagances of behaviour the sheer boredom of such surroundings can drive an active, life-loving man. Besides, all these reports referred to the period between his return from the First World War in a state of almost suicidal dejection, and his meeting with the Iroquois girl, Anahareo, in 1925, when he had turned from killing animals to protecting them. And, after all, there was nothing inherently impossible in being born in Hastings of an American Indian mother. Perhaps his father, George Belaney, had masqueraded somewhere as George MacNeill; not even masqueraded: perhaps the well-dressed young planter reported in some of the interviews to have been seen strolling restlessly around Hastings streets and the Parade, wearing a sombrero-type hat and exhibiting the air of one who felt himself superior to his surroundings, might, in the course of a career that was to turn out on investigation to be curious and secretive, have been an Indian scout, and his mother, Katherine Cox, a woman with Indian blood, whose real name was not the Anglicized Cox but the Spanish Cochise.

To the anxious scrutineer, looking back over the mists

of sixty years, it sometimes seemed as if there were two men, both called Archie Belaney; the one half-Indian, exotic, dark, mysterious; the other fresh-faced, cultured in manner and voice, passionately interested in his new surroundings, but with his roots firmly fastened in the educated English world.

I had to fight to establish that it was the Indian who was the genuine figure, and that the Englishman, if he did exist, was a coincidence. So while I was finding out what I could about the Belaney family, I went to Hastings to call on the two aunts, who on Grey Owl's death had come very prominently into the papers, asserting that he was none other than their nephew Archie, whom they had brought up since babyhood, and who had emigrated to Canada when he was eighteen. With no such intention, and with a desire only to establish the truth, these two blessed old ladies were making Grey Owl seem to have perpetrated a deliberate fraud on the public.

The aunts knew that in press interviews I had been contradicting the claims they had made, and they received me very frigidly in their home, wearing hats and carrying their gloves in Edwardian fashion to show that my call was to be brief, as they were on the point of going out.

Miss Ada, the younger sister, dominated the conversation. She was tall, firm-jawed, robust in build: what one would call a commanding woman. Probably handsome once, for the blue eyes were very fine, the features were even, and the skin was soft and well-coloured. Miss Carrie was thinner, smaller, had a prominent nose, and was nervous and confused.

It was plain that Ada prided herself on her ability to crush people; her answers to my nervous, probing questions were brief and contemptuous, and the blue eyes were cold and unfriendly. But I wasn't prepared to be dismissed. I stuck obstinately to the point that there might easily have been two Archie Belaneys, her nephew and my Grey Owl, and nothing so far, except her own assertions, indicated that the two were one and the same. But she insisted that they were. And then suddenly, as though pandering to a persistent child, she went on to reveal to me much more about Archie than she had done to the reporters. He had come to convalesce at their home when he was on leave from hospital in the First World War. She showed me a photograph of a tall, lean soldier, with the clipped head of a First War warrior, standing in the garden of a house. He had married his childhood sweetheart, Constance Ivy Holmes, from their house in 1917. I said, had they not known that at the time he was married to an Indian woman, and the father of two children? She said, no, not at that time. He had told them later, but the Indian marriage, in any case, was not legal; it was a common-law association.

Pride in him, and a perfectly understandable reluctance to reveal family skeletons, fought with each other in Ada's narrative. She had begun by bullying me, and now, half an hour later, she was acting like a mother defending her child from undeserved accusations. He had been such a clever boy, and had always been mad about Indians and about animals. Ada led me to a glass-fronted bookcase, one shelf of which appeared to be filled with books written by earlier generations of the family. Grey Owl's four books, *The Men of the Last Frontier*, *Pilgrims of the Wild*, *The Adventures of Sajo and Her Beaver People*, and *Tales of an Empty Cabin*, stood cheek by jowl with his grand-uncle's *The Massacre of The Carmes*, his grandfather's *The 100 Days of Napoleon*, and another grand-uncle's *The Steeplechase* and *A Treatise on Falconry*. Evidently there was a strong literary bent in the family. Side by side with these were touching souvenirs of the past in the shape of a number of handsomely bound prize books from Hastings Grammar School, and a number of boys' novels and the paper-covered penny dreadfuls of the day, these being chiefly stories about Red Indians which had had a great success with boys in the early years of this century. Nearly all these much-used books were inscribed with his name in his writing, and some had in the margins ink drawings he had made of Indians fighting against the white man. One very good ink sketch caught my eye. It was of an Indian in fringed buckskins, wearing one feather. It might have been a drawing of Grey Owl himself as I remembered him standing on the lecture platform, hand raised, saying

8

in that haunting voice: "I am Wa-Sha-Quon-Asin, Grey Owl. I come in peace. . . ."

But it was to the prize books that she was drawing my attention. "He was such a clever boy," she was saying. . . . Suddenly I saw it all, or thought I did. This woman, young at the time when he first came into her life, perhaps twenty-eight or thirty, handsome, bossy, the sexual fire within her screened from the casual eye by the repressive manners of the time, cruellest of all to young women of her class. No man had probably ever touched her. What visions and dreams she must have had of joys she would never know. How she must have envied her brother his sexual liberties. Then this child, his offspring, presented to her, just when she must have realized she would probably never have one of her own.

Her love for him had become fierce and possessive. I wondered if he had been aware of it, troubled by it, but responsive to it. I remembered that *The Men of the Last Frontier* had been dedicated "as a tribute to an aunt whom I must thank for such education that enables me to interpret into words the spirit of the forest, beautiful for all its underlying wildness."

One had thought then, reading this dedication, of some clay cabin in an Indian encampment in Mexico, an old woman under the shade of a tree, teaching a brown little boy his letters. One had not thought of an English spinster in this middle-class villa in a small seaside town, and the little boy in a sailor cap whose framed photograph she now handed to me. She had taught him not only his letters, but carpentry and music. She took him for all his early walks, and explained about trees and forest undergrowth, wild flowers, birds, insects, and creepy-crawlers to him. The love of nature was born in him, and she first gave it form and names.

When he was eight, she sent him to a church school, so that he might make other friends, and then at eleven he had entered the Grammar School.

A writer has to beware of seeing all imagined situations in dramatic terms. That is to say, the situation along with the pressures that created it, and the denouement that eventually results, all in one. The writer's mind jumps to give artistic form and completion to everything that forces itself on his attention, demanding cohesion instead of disorder, explanation in place of enigma.

I had already accepted, although I had not admitted it to her, that Grey Owl had been Archie Belaney and had been brought up in England. The complete drama demanded that he should be just as genuinely Grey Owl, the half-breed whom I had known, as he had once been Archie Belaney, the little English boy who lived with his grandmother and his two aunts in a large house in Hastings. I knew about Grey Owl: she knew about Belaney. I was begging for facts which would explain that transition without making him out a fraud and a hoax.

I wanted to know what his father and mother had been like, what had brought them together, and what had later separated them. I wanted to know about his grandfather, Archibald, and his grandfather's brothers, and where the family had come from; whether earlier members of it had shown the same desire to escape narrow, conventional life as Grey Owl and his father had done; and whether the special understanding and sympathy with the world of nature had revealed itself in any of Grey Owl's immediate ancestors.

But from these questions she shied away until, in exasperation at such damnable determination not to help, I said that all this could be found out by a determined researcher. She was simply making things more difficult and perhaps leaving open the way to wrong interpretations.

Yes, but why go back into private family history?

Because I had to show what made him adopt a different identity. Why did he turn his back on the white world? You tell me that he led a perfectly normal life as an English boy, but within a few months of leaving England he had cast in his lot with the Indians. He wasn't, forgive me, your child to begin with, and he left you as soon as he could. Was he repeating a family pattern? Was there some strain in him, and in his father, that drew them both to the wild?

Absolutely none. There isn't a trace of foreign blood in our family. Our grandfather Belaney was born in Scotland.

On my mother's side—she was a Jackson—we are pure English.

But Archie's mother. Your brother's wife?

She was an American.

Why was Archie left to you to bring up?

There was a slight pause, almost imperceptible, and I thought—or perhaps I imagined it—that the two sisters exchanged glances.

"My brother and his wife separated. He went back to America where he died twenty years later. Before they parted they had had a second child, a boy called Hugh. Kitty took Hugh with her when she went to live in London after my brother's departure for America. Subsequently she married again. She could not manage both boys, so my mother undertook to pay for Archie's education, and he came to live with us when he was four."

CHAPTER 2

THERE ARE few Belaneys left now in Britain, where they had been settled from time immemorial in Berwickshire. Those Lowlands of Scotland produced a curious and admirable type of mind around the end of the eighteenth and the beginning of the nineteenth centuries. The people seemed to have kept some of the poetic effusion which came from their share of Celtic blood, and yet to be vigorous men of the fields who loved the wooded hills and meadows of their countryside. Nearly everywhere, in farm-houses and cottages, the Bible was read morning and evening, and the work of the great poets recited, except on the Sabbath. In this way the cadences of literature were knitted into the familiar everyday speech. Robert Burns was the genius, but not an isolated figure.

They were by no means quaint rustics with a little learning, but broad-muscled, ambitious men who in the nineteenth century were to spill out of over-large rural families
into the professions, taking with them often the liking for
sport and the open air which had been bred into them
through generations of country life.

At the beginning of the nineteenth century, John Belaney
had been a prosperous farmer, and the father of a large
family of ten children. Two at least of his sons went to
university, James to Medical School at Edinburgh University, and Robert, his older brother, to Cambridge University. A third and younger son, Archibald, went into business
in the city of London and became the father of George,
and thus the grandfather of Archie born in 1888 in
Hastings.

These three Belaney brothers all wrote, not for private
pleasure but for publication. James was first off the mark
with a long poem in heroic couplets, published in 1837,
entitled *The Steeplechase*. His next book won him quite
extensive fame. *A Treatise on Falconry* appeared in 1841.
He had been fond of this sport since boyhood. It is evident
in reading this book that James Belaney had an unusual
affinity with animals, and lived with them on terms of
affection which he describes fully.

One hawk in particular, a female bird, travelled with
him everywhere "by steamboat, post-chaise, gig, omnibus,
van, on foot or horseback she sat upon my hand. If I happened to sleep beyond my usual rising hour, she would
leave her block, fly into the bed and take me gently by the
ear."

He goes on to say that if he was out for an evening she
would wait by his bedroom door, from which no one could
entice her away. When he returned, she would fly to his
arm, get upon his shoulder, and rub her beak against his
cheek, showing every sign of gladness at his return.

James Belaney, who in the preface to *A Treatise on Falconry* described himself as "a true-born bachelor" and a
very happy one, married in 1843 a young woman half his
age with whom he appeared to be greatly in love. But perhaps solitude is essential to animal lovers. He seems, on

the evidence available, and there is a great mass of it, to have suffered very soon from domestic claustrophobia. First his mother-in-law, in whose house the couple came to live, and then his wife died suddenly. The autopsy showed that his wife's stomach contained a quantity of prussic acid. There was a perfectly valid excuse for James having this in his possession. Taken in mere pinches, prussic acid can relieve indigestion, and he could prove that he had been taking this for years.

James Belaney was arrested and charged with the murder of his wife. The case attracted wide attention and was reported fully over several days in the *Times*. There seemed no motive for James Belaney's alleged crime, of which the jury found him not guilty. But as the judge, Baron Gurney, reminded the jurors in his summing up, we cannot dive into the heart and ascertain motive, and sometimes a great crime might be committed without a clear motive for it being found.

But if he were guilty, as the *Times* and other leading commentators assumed, why was he the kind of man he was—a lover of the open air, vigorous and violent in his manner, but otherwise attractive to those whom he met? Was he, like the animals with whom he established immediate empathy, intolerant of restraint? Were these traits inherited? Was there a persistent Belaney factor which might be found in other members of this family in subsequent generations, which would explain oddity of conduct? Was George Belaney, Archie's father, prompted by some of the same pressures that had affected his uncle James? George seemed to love mystery, and sometimes gave ordinary matters a conspiratorial semblage when it wasn't in the least necessary. Could these factors explain the apparent mystery of Archie Belaney's life?

People of this sort, unfortunately, make more interesting subjects than the blameless amongst us. They burn with some kind of inward energy which, like the principle on which the internal combustion works, propels them forward explosively, and makes their lives eventful.

The two Belaney brothers who also wrote turned out better. The Reverend Robert Belaney led a blameless life, and the list of his published books, which are concerned with the burning ecclesiastical questions of the day, occupies half a column in the British Museum catalogue. Archibald Belaney published a book of verse, *The 100 Days of Napoleon*, dedicated it to Queen Victoria, who acknowledged the dedication and thanked the young poet in a letter from Windsor Castle, lovingly preserved thereafter by the family.

After Archibald had laid aside poetry and overcome the extreme sensibility of his feelings about everything, he turned out to have quite a hard nose for business and became a prominent ship's broker. He married a young heiress, Juliana Jackson, who presented him with three children: a son George, and the girls Caroline and Adelaide, who as aunts Carrie and Ada were to dominate the life of George's son, Archie.

The family had moved from Upper Montagu Street in London as the children grew and needed country air. Langton House on Crescent Road in Dagnall Park, Croydon, was built for the Belaneys. There were then only three other houses on the Crescent, and the gardens were large and the surroundings, unlike today, very rustic. The Belaneys lived here for twenty years. Archibald Belaney had died in the first year that he lived in the house, but Mrs. Belaney had her own fortune and she recovered her marriage settlement, so they were able to continue living on a very comfortable scale.

At eighteen, on leaving school, George had been put into the long-established tea- and coffee-importing business of his mother's cousin, Sir Frederick Huth. He had found the daily railway journey up from Croydon to London Bridge tiring, so rooms were taken for him in Notting Hill Gate, and he went home at week-ends. Being on his own in London was too much for a boy who had never left home before, and Mrs. Belaney blamed the long office-hours and the journey down to the city every day by the new sulphurous underground railway for George's pallor and the lines about his eyes. George played up this factor too. Only his outspoken sister Ada, whom he had never liked, asked in that rude, cold voice of hers if it was dissipation, not hard work, which left its mark on his face.

After two years, George complained to his mother that

he was tired of being an underdog, and he painted a picture of an overbearing office manager, and the cousin-owner who "didn't seem to like him", and asked him very seldom to his house. He declared himself deeply interested in the tea- and coffee-importing business, and persuaded his mother that, given a chance, he could go it alone. She attributed to pride and independence of spirit what Ada said was self-indulgence; he wanted to be his own master, said Ada flatly, so that he could allow himself more time off. Mrs. Belaney said this was unkind, and commanded Ada to say nothing if she could not say anything charitable; and she arranged with her solicitors to sell some of her capital, and to form the company which was opened soon afterwards as George Furmage Belaney & Co., tea and coffee merchants, with premises only a few yards from the old-established and prosperous Huth & Co. at 2 Talbot Court, off Gracechurch Street in the City of London.

Then George had "a wonderful chance" to go big-game shooting in East Africa, with a rich young contemporary who would pay all expenses. He was away the better part of half a year, and the new business languished, not to say nearly expired, for want of attention and activity. Returning, George brought with him a black servant, much to the perturbation of his mother and sisters, for George could not keep him in London, and the ladies did not want him in Croydon. George went off in February to visit friends and do some rough shooting in Suffolk. He remained a month, returning in mid-March to face the liquidation of his business, and to hang moodily around home while fresh plans were engendered for his employment.

He had not been home more than a few weeks when he returned to Suffolk to stay with the same friend, representing to his mother that a prospect of employment for him had arisen in that part of the world through a connection of his friend's father. He drew from her £50 so that he could keep his "end up". But he had more serious business to deal with than employment, and this his friend had lost no time in imparting to him. While on the earlier visit, he had got the daughter of a woman who kept a tavern a mile from the great house pregnant, and Mrs. Elizar Hines, the tavern-keeper, a woman of determination, had demanded flatly to know what the young gentleman was going to do about it, and threatened trouble unless he presented himself forthwith.

On April 13, 1881, without telling his mother of the step he was being forced to take, George, who was twenty-one, married Rose Ethel Hines, aged fifteen, in the Baptist Chapel at Diss, Norfolk, twenty miles from Botesdale in Suffolk where George had been staying with his friend. It must have been a sad little ceremony. The marriage certificate shows the youthful George describing himself "Bachelor and Independent Gentleman, formerly Tea Merchant", and the witnesses to the marriage, Thomas and Mathilda Turtle, who, like the bride, could not write, signing the Register with an "X".

On December 9, a little girl, christened Rose Ethel Belaney, was born at her grandmother's public house in the village of Mellis, near Botesdale. I think that by then George had already abandoned his wife. He was certainly not there when eighteen months later the child died. The death was registered by Elizar Hines, describing herself as "grandmother". Report had it that the mother, Rose Ethel Belaney, had left the district and had gone to Derbyshire, where she was reported to have married again. But I was not able to find any record of divorce proceedings, nor of her subsequent death. She simply disappeared from the scene.

Before George, always an impetuous man, got into trouble with Rose Ethel, he had met and fallen in love with Elizabeth Cox. George had introduced her to his family with a view to getting his mother's approval to a marriage. But Mrs. Belaney told Elizabeth that George could not marry until he had made some sort of career for himself, as she could not provide for him and possibly for a family later on.

Soon after he abandoned Rose Ethel, George and Elizabeth Cox departed together from England. They went first to Tampa in Florida, and then made their way down the Gulf coast to Key West, where Elizabeth was delivered of a girl baby who was christened Gertrude. George was very keen about game-shooting, and his chief interest in this was as an amateur taxidermist. He made and mounted a considerable collection of animal and snake skins in Florida between 1882 and 1883, but then had to return to England with Elizabeth who was seriously ill. The illness turned out on examination to be arsenical poisoning, and this was due to helping George with his hobby, arsenic being used in taxidermy. They brought their collection back to England with them, and George gave his mother a great many specimens, some of them extremely lifelike such as a rattlesnake coiled and ready to strike.

His relationship to Elizabeth was not revealed to his mother. It was impossible while Rose Ethel lived for George to marry Elizabeth, and he still had no income other than the allowance which his fond mother gave him, supplemented by a small income which Elizabeth had just inherited on her grandmother's death.

George now persuaded his mother to let him return to Florida and take up some land near Bridgeport, on the banks of the River Charles. Here he was to grow oranges, and he painted to his mother a bright picture of his prospects. Once again she yielded, but this, she insisted, would be the last time.

They took passage on the *Sydian Monarch*, bound from London for New York, sailing on November 18, 1885. Accompanying them was the child Gertrude, and Elizabeth's twelve-year-old sister, Katherine. Kitty had been a delicate child, with a history of chest weakness, and it was thought that American air would be helpful. The party travelled under the name of Barry, giving out to the other passengers that they were going west to take up land. They arrived in New York on November 28, spent a few days sightseeing, and then made their way directly to Bridgeport, Florida, where Mr. Belaney, as Mr. Barry immediately became on landing in New York, had purchased through the Florida Development Company a parcel of land on the banks of the River Charles.

Within a year of their settling in Florida, Elizabeth died at Voss's Hotel in Florida, on her way back from New York where she had been to consult a specialist about a stomach ailment. A year after that, in November 1886, George married Katherine Verona Cox, her sister, then aged thirteen.

In June 1888, he suddenly sold up his land, left his daughter Gertrude, then a little girl of three, with a neighbour, and took ship with his pregnant child-wife to England.

In 1885, when George had departed a second time for America, for good so it seemed, Mrs. Belaney and her two daughters had purchased 52 St. Helen's Wood Road in Hastings, a large, commodious house on the edge of St. Helen's Woods, looking down over the town to the sea.

Mrs. Belaney was by no means as pleased as she might have been when she had a letter from George to say that he had married an American girl, who was about to make her a grandmother; that he had sold his property in Florida and was returning to England in order that his child might be born there.

Mrs. Belaney hurried up to London. She knew from experience that when George turned up unexpectedly he was in need of money. Five years before, when he had decided to buy an orange grove in Florida, she had advanced the capital on the understanding that this must be the last time. Now here he was again, not only with a wife, but with a baby about to make its appearance.

She called on them in their hotel, found the bride "a frightened little thing" but otherwise very pretty and rather pathetic. George was as handsome and as elegant as ever; she never could ultimately resist his requests. Ada, the younger of her daughters, was highly critical of George. When Mrs. Belaney had Ada beside her she could face up to her son with a show of firmness at least, but alone with him she was always won over. She agreed that they should come to Hastings, but with the baby coming, she could not have them in her own home. She would take a furnished house for them for a few months, during which time George could look around and find suitable employment.

At first all went well. The Belaney girls were delighted at the thought of a child in the family, and busied themselves with preparing an elaborate layette. Kitty, George's wife, was an endearing child, much younger and more unsophisticated than they had expected. George said she was eighteen, but it was hard to believe: she seemed in many ways very childlike. He also told them her maiden name was Morris.

George's search for suitable employment was not very vigorously pursued. He hated England, and despised office work. He could not bear this little town of Hastings. The family home they had had when he left for America was in Croydon, and before that, in his father's lifetime, they had lived in the centre of London. Hastings seemed to combine the worst aspects of both places, the remoteness from the centre that made Croydon intolerable, with the boring snobberies of town social life that made London unlivable. Aware that he was the cynosure of curious local eyes, George walked up and down the Parade every day, a tall, elegant figure, wearing a large sombrero-type hat, looking out sombrely over the shingle beach and the slapping waves, and longing to get away from it all.

In the early hours of the morning of September 18, 1888, a boy, Archibald Stansfeld Belaney, was born to George and Katherine.

I have been writing about the father of the man who is to be the central figure of my story, and I have built up a picture of a vain, lazy, spoilt, impetuous failure, who loved only one thing, hunting the animals whose living images he then recreated in their own skins, posed in natural attitudes. Archie Belaney, who became Grey Owl, was to give quite a different account of his father than the one I have given here.

But my account is based on documents—birth and marriage certificates, land deeds in Florida, shipping lists, what I could find out about the whole Belaney family for a century back—and on what George's surviving wife and his two sisters told me when I had several long interviews with them in 1938.

For it was Kitty herself who told me this, thus supporting the documents. Fifty-three years later, here was that girl of thirteen, grown into a little old woman of sixty-five, with a large stepson escorting her. She approached me following the death of Grey Owl, at a time when the papers were in full cry against the man who had deceived the public. She affected an air of mystery she must have copied from George. She even began with an alias.

"I am a relative"—she paused—"an aunt."

Having come with the express purpose of supplying me with information, she became, after taking her seat, maddeningly reticent, and when she did speak in more than monosyllables, aimlessly discursive. Then she suddenly edged forward on her chair and said, "I am Grey Owl's mother."

I suppose I looked incredulous, for the stepson, who had said little, now said, "That's right."

So this was Kitty Cox or Kitty Cochise; this had been the girl George had brought back from Florida, this little atom of intense respectability. She was dressed entirely in subdued black, the black which was almost a uniform worn by the elderly poor in those days, faded a little with long exposure to the sun and frequent ironing so that it had a rusty tint woven into the black.

"I am prepared to swear anything," she said, "as long as they don't look into the past. He was an Indian; he thought so; why cannot they let him remain so? Why must everything be looked into and gone over again?"

She could not remember where she had been born. Elizabeth had been her sister but more like a mother to her. George had insisted on her telling Mother (Mrs. Belaney) that her name was Morris, not Cox, because he did not want Mother to know that she was Elizabeth's sister. Elizabeth had come into considerable money from their grandmother, and half, if not all, the property in Florida had belonged to her. They had had a nice house there, and three estates adjoining, all stocked with orange trees.

George had begun to drink there, as though drowning some secret grief. Then he got delirium tremens, and had to be taken away to hospital. Then a priest took him in hand, but it was all to no purpose. This all happened upon Elizabeth's death. He would say to Kitty how sorry he was to have landed her in this situation, and blame his mother, whose fault he said it was. She should have made him work.

Then he pleaded with her to marry him, and she agreed. George and she had been very happy together, but he was hopeless about money. They came back home when the baby was going to be born. He hated England, and could

21

not wait to get away. He wanted all the time to go west, but with a wife and two children, for Hugh was born two years after Archie, he could never get away.

Then the "bombshell" fell, and scattered them, altering all their lives.

Mr. Brace, one of Mrs. Belaney's trustees, and a representative of the family's solicitors came to see them with a document which George was persuaded to sign. It was to everybody's benefit, including his own, that he should go into exile. He would be allowed a small income on condition that he never set foot in England again. The document also required Kitty's signature. She must undertake never to see George again, or even to communicate with him. She would be allowed a comfortable income for life, enough to bring up the two boys.

And so they parted. Archie was four years old at the time, and he and George had become very good friends; Hugh was too young to understand. But Archie was affected by George's tears, and could understand that he was going away and that he might never see him again.

George departed, still wearing his foreign-looking sombrero. "Goodbye, Little Hat," he said to Archie. It was the pet name he had invented for him, and Archie, moved by the solemnity and drama of this moment, screamed out and would not be comforted by his mother.

George appealed to his wife for money once or twice after that, but she did not see him again, although she sent the money. Then, twelve years later, she heard of his death in Mexico, and she married a Mr. Scott-Brown. By the time I got to know her, her second husband was dead, and she was poor and old, and working at some domestic job. The Belaneys had long ago cut off her income when they discovered that she had sent money to George. They had taken Archie from her and brought him up so that he could lead a good life. She had had rather a hard time at the hands of the Belaney family, and one could not help feeling sorry for her.

What a mother for a romantic dreamer to have! To turn this retiring, rusty little figure in black into a woman of the Apache tribe, and poor George into one of Buffalo Bill's friends, a doughty fighter in the pacification of the West: what dreams must have illuminated the mind of a little boy surrounded by ultra-respectable, middle-class English-women, who were shamed by the failure of the man of the family, and determined that the little boy should not go the same way.

I make only reasonable assumptions, and as few of these as possible, and I bring all this unpalatable evidence for-ward because sons do bear some resemblance to their fathers, and to penetrate the mystery of Archie's life I had to consider what mental and physical traits he might have inherited from his immediate ancestors.

That Grey Owl's statements about his origins were un-true the documents proved beyond a doubt. Yet how near the truth they were. Just skirting it.* Why did he romance about his birth long before he became famous? A little exaggeration about one's ancestors is permissible, is even devout. What you are trying to do is embellish their dull images. But to claim to be an Indian in Canada early in this century, where it was only too plain to see that Indians enjoyed no perceptible benefit from the state, to endure the hardships and impress no one except maybe a few summer visitors to the district, argued an unusual state of mind, and demanded a close look at his ancestry. George had mismanaged his life; he had had to give up his son to be brought up respectably and stiffly in a good, solid, English middle-class home, as he, George, had been. From this, as soon as he was able, the boy broke out, to repeat in many particulars his father's wayward conduct. But at

---

*Grey Owl wrote to Anahareo: "Two old maiden ladies living in some part of Scotland have written me through Country Life, and claim to be first cousins, or some kind of cousins of my father's side of the family. . . . They have a letter from Buffalo Bill which they treasure very much in answer to an enquiry as to his (my father's) where-abouts time he was in the old show, in which he speaks very highly of my dad. Gee, I must get that letter of old man Cody's about him, or a photograph. . . . Funny how things turn out. No doubt we will find that you have inherited your war-like spirit from the Duke of Buckingham. Perhaps our daughter is the rightful Queen of Scotland, or an Apache Princess. Who knows what next will be heard?" The letter is undated, but probably October 1932. The Belaney family tree shows two Miss Falconers, still living in Berwickshire in that year.

the same time to remind us all that the clean world of
nature still exists, and awaits us like an empty paradise,
where all can begin again. What Archie had, which his
father and grand-uncle did not have, was a poet's imagination. His reticent grandfather Archie, after whom he was
named, may have passed that on to him.

CHAPTER

3

H ASTINGS was once a small fishing village set in a cleft
of rocks which formed a natural harbour, and protected the cluster of houses from the boisterous
channel winds. The village has spread out during the last
hundred years.

Above the town are the remains of a Norman castle, now
inevitably floodlit at night. Down below, stretching from
East Hill to St. Leonard's in the west is the Grand Parade.
Hastings Pier juts out from the centre, and White Rock
Pavilion, the home of local entertainment, where Grey Owl
came to lecture, stands on Grand Parade just opposite the
Pier. The sea-front is ugly, as it is in most English seaside
towns, a mixture of shops and tea-rooms, hotels and board-
ing-houses, filled with happy and raucous visitors in the

25

summer, and deserted, dreary, wet, and cold in the English winter.

But when you stand with your back to the sea, and look up above the roofs and the thousand English chimney-pots of the lower town, the beauty of the situation of Hastings is immediately apparent. It rises in terrace after terrace to the South Downs. Up there, where tourists rarely tread, there is a pleasantly laid-out town, with ample public gardens, preserved woods, nice houses, trim gardens, and trim citizens. Over to the east lies the Old Town, with the great chasm of the Bourne running down its centre to the shore, where the fishermen's boats lie bobbing at anchor or pulled up on the shingle, while fishing nets are stretched out to dry. In the streets of the Old Town there are porti-coed Georgian houses where Nelson's captains lived, even a few diamond-paned, old rough-stone houses from which Elizabethan captains emerged to answer the call to ship when the Armada turned to come up channel.

It was a good place for a boy to grow up in, especially a solitary one who loved nature. Grandmother Belaney and the aunts had moved from St. Helen's Wood Road in 1895 to 36 St. Mary's Terrace. A few minutes away was the grassy slope of Castle Hill. From here he could cross the Old Town to East Hill, and walk for miles along the Cliff walk, looking out over the English Channel towards France, and on his return, facing west, imagine North America, the land of the Red Indians, hidden behind three thousand miles of tossing ocean.

Northward from St. Mary's Terrace lay St. Helen's Woods. This large tract of woodland had been given to the town by a wealthy citizen, and today it is as unspoilt as it must have been in William the Conqueror's time. The paths are Victorian additions. They lead out in various directions, as though at random, and in late spring and early summer the woods are rich with blossom and loud with birdsong. Here boys from the Grammar School played all through the last century and still play today, although the old Grammar School has been pulled down, and something a good deal more efficient and hygienic, if less poetical in appearance, has been erected in another place.

No boy was wholly solitary when Archie was growing

up. Children seemed more numerous, even if statistics did not bear out the overpowering assumption which noise and the ubiquity of the species flatly affirmed. Children were thrown back on themselves for entertainment, and the mania for organized sport as distinct from impromptu games had not yet filtered down to them.

It was an age in which children's magazines proliferated and adventure stories in weekly serial form were followed with fascinated interest. From 1870 onwards the opening up of the American West provided the plots for hundreds of these stories. The struggle between Indian and white man for supremacy, the cruel treatment of the Indians, their fierce and relentless methods of making war: all these stimulated the imaginations of young readers. Chiefs' names like Sitting Bull, Cochise, Standing Bear, White Eagle, Big Elk, were familiar to every growing boy, and the names which Indians had given to individual white men who were prominent as commanders of the white troops used against them, or as agents appointed by the government to deal with them on their Reserves, were equally familiar.

The passionate interest in these matters was not confined to children. Red Indians, to use the name current then, had been a feature of theatrical shows long before Colonel Bill Cody capitalized on all this and brought Buffalo Bill's Wild West Show to London, in the year before Archie was born. A mid-Victorian theatrical poster announces in a profusion of emphatic capital letters

> At the Egyptian Hall, Piccadilly, at 2 o'clock in the afternoon and eight in the evening: JUST AR-RIVED, ELEVEN NATIVE NORTH AMERICAN INDIANS, OF THE OJIBWAY, ODELAU-WAN, and MIS-SIS-SAGEE tribes of INDIANS, from the Western Wilds of NORTH AMERICA, HEADED BY TWO CHIEFS. A GRAND INDIAN COUNCIL in front of the Wigwam, when the whole party will appear in FULL NATIVE COSTUME, displaying all the Implements of War. A FACSIMILE of the OPERATION OF SCALPING! Never before at-tempted in this country, followed by the WAR

DANCE, in which the Indians will give a true
specimen of the Furious Rage with which their
feelings are Aroused against Their Adversary at an
approaching Conflict.

By re-enacting scenes from the lurid history of the subjugation of the American West, Buffalo Bill was simply
building on what had already been started.

After the fashion set by Buffalo Bill's show at Olympia,
where there was much firing of guns, dust, and the din of
battle, the attacks of boys storming imaginary palisades in
St. Helen's Woods were noisy. Bloodcurdling yells rent the
air, scalps were taken, and there was general rack and ruin
enjoyed by all.

Young Belaney scorned such theatricals. He was a loner,
an odd chap, and the boys laughed at him behind his back
but never to his face. The school history, written in the
tongue-in-cheek style much favoured by authors of such
works, has a picture of him at the time he joined the
school, when he was eleven years old.

A third eccentric joined the School that September
[1899]. This was Archie Belaney. He did not conceal firearms in his pockets, but just as likely
might produce from them a snake or a field-
mouse. Born eleven years before, and living at 36
St Mary's Terrace, he was a delicate boy but full
of devilment; and fascinated by woods and wild
animals. . . . What with his camping out, his tracking of all and sundry, and wild hooting, he was
more like a Red Indian than a respectable Grammar School boy.

It was perverse of the historian to refer to his "wild
hooting". Belaney was as little likely to be caught doing
this as Queen Victoria, and that is why his friends laughed
a little uneasily, for they felt his intense concentration to
be a reproof to the general hullaballoo of their own performances. He always played the Indian scout, and they
were familiar enough with such a figure from their serials.
Silent tracking was his hobby: to move unobserved, using

28

the woods as a cloak, and to read what lay there plain to the curious eye in crushed bracken fronds, disturbed leaves, bent grass. He tracked animals, imagining himself an Indian in the forest, feeling his way forward, every sense alert to betraying noise, crack of stick, the hushed warning call of an animal, or the sudden cessation of birdsong as, heads to one side, disturbed birds listened for confirmation or denial of what had alarmed them.

Another world was visible to him as he crawled forward, close-pressed to the earth, matching the silence of the insects. It was a world alive with small, palpitating, fearful life, revealing itself in the protruding eye of a panting, momentarily frightened frog, in the sight of startled rabbits, of squirrels poised in shock, their thudding heartbeats almost audible as they watched alarmed at this unaccustomed human presence—one that was not upright and threatening but bent to their world. It thrilled him beyond measure to find their fear turning slowly to tremulous trust. It was a submissive act of love that sent a sensuous shock through his body to feel them, if he were patient and still, climb on to his hand, or lie there palpitating while he touched them. It made up for something missing in his life which he wasn't really aware was missing until the animals told him that it was: tactile love. Nobody ever caressed him, and kisses were brisk and dutiful.

There was no doubt that he had an unusual touch with wild animals; they seemed not only entirely without fear of him, but to enjoy being handled by him. One snake he picked up and took home became his devoted pet. He called it Rajah, and it nearly frightened the life out of his mother when she came to stay at St. Mary's Terrace one summer when he had been dangerously ill with pneumonia.

Archie, like everyone else in the family, thought Kitty constitutionally a silly woman. He knew that as his mother she had some claim to authority over him, but he saw her only twice during his boyhood for extended periods, the summer when he had pneumonia, and another summer just before he entered Grammar School when he joined her and Hugh, his younger brother, for a holiday at Worthing. He used these periods to try to pump her for information about his absent father. He did not consciously miss his father, in fact he thought about him very rarely. But other boys asked where he was and what he was doing, and it was embarrassing not to be able to make a reply. When he complained about this to Ada, she said sharply: "Tell them it is none of their business."

Then she added, being a sensible woman, "No, of course you can't say that. Just say that he is in America, and you don't know when he will be coming back."

Ada dominated his life. She became both mother and father to him, and he never knew whether he feared her or loved her. She bathed and dressed him when he was too young to do these things for himself; she taught him his prayers, read him stories, tucked him up and kissed him goodnight. But her wrath was terrible when it was kindled; she was the only one who ever punished him, and so was the only one he ever wanted to please and impress.

He responded so intelligently to everything that she taught him about books, nature, and music that she perhaps pressed him a little too hard. Music became one of his enthusiasms, and he practised the piano for hours on end. By the time that he was twelve, he could play with confidence whenever he was invited to do so when calling on friends with his aunt. But these disciplines nettled him, for they restricted his liberty. Ada the benevolent became Ada the terrible when he wandered off without telling anyone where he was going and returned sometimes at the end of the day, having eaten nothing. Or when, soaked with rain, he tramped out of the woods and into the house, without any explanation of where he had been or what he had been doing. The more they demanded to know, the less he was willing to tell them. Punishment followed his obstinate silence. Then he hated Aunt Ada, and made up his mind that he would kill her and leave home for ever. The gust would pass, but the resentment would leave a scar which was still with him many years later.

Carrie was Ada's shadow, a constant, muffled echo. Although she was the older sister, she must very early in life have yielded to Ada's domineering character. Habit now made her seem to walk always a shade behind Ada; her step appeared to be hesitant and uncertain, while Ada's was aggressive. Ada was the more attractive of the two physically. Her skin was smoother and pinker, and her eyes a piercing blue. Although she was firm and direct in manner, everyone, but especially the tradesmen, respected her. Her neighbours bowed to her, and were bowed to in return.

But the Belaney ladies rarely entertained. The notion got about that they considered themselves rather a cut above local society, and local society felt resentful, and experienced an urge to find fault with them. But their lives were blameless, and their manners, while not warm, were correct. After a time speculation ceased on what there might be in the Belaney family history that made them show such little amiability, and have on their hands a boy whose father and mother never appeared.

Mrs. Juliana Belaney was the dead spit and image of the gracious Queen. So were nearly all ladies of her age then living in England. Widowhood, by royal example, was long, mournful, and almost totally incapacitating, as far as physical activity was concerned. Mrs. Belaney dressed always in black, wore a white cap, and sat with her hands folded in her lap in the drawing-room, in which the blinds were never more than half-raised, excluding both the sun and the curious gaze of neighbours. Those admitted to the drawing-room reported that Mrs. Belaney was a very fine-looking woman, and must once have been beautiful. She was said to speak in the cultivated voice of a member of the upper middle class, a quite distinctive intonation rather than accent, accorded respect by all those who did not have it.

This was the occasional visitor's view. Archie adored his grandmother, which must mean that she adored him too. She left the management and upbringing of him entirely to Ada, and she provided the gentle affection, the outward manifestations of which were excluded in Ada's practice. In much the same way Juliana Belaney must have adored her son George once, before George dissolved the bond between them by continual and bitter disappointments. The boy was his father over again, but seemed to have more determination in his character.

Archie responded by giving his grandmother all the love in his heart. He was in constant fear of her dying, for then he would be left alone with the terrible-tempered Ada. If only Ada would die instead, and leave him alone with Granny. Once when he was nine he tried to bring about this longed-for conclusion. In Highbury Villa on St. James's Road, a larger house to which they had moved in 1899, Granny's bedroom was on the ground floor, opposite the dining-room. The drawing-room was in the front of the house on the second floor up, a not uncommon feature of houses built in the early nineteenth century when there were servants to run up and down with coal-buckets and tea-trays.

This arrangement meant that the upper hall was rather a grand place, at the head of the stairway, and was often furnished with a sofa and an armchair, for the large window gave a view, in the case of Highbury Villa, of the sea, and in the case of other houses, of the front ornamental garden and of approaching visitors.

The furnishings of the upper hall at Highbury Villa included a bust of someone who might have been Beethoven, or merely a local stonemason's image of a learned man. Archie's bedroom was on this floor, as were those of his aunts, and he often took a swipe at the head as he ran upstairs or down. He knew that it was a little loose on its base. Once, sent upstairs by Ada as a punishment, he knelt with murder in his heart waiting for her to come out of the servants' daily room and cross to her mother's room. He had shoved and worked at the head while he was waiting until it was really loose, and when he saw Ada come out he timed his great push with the precision that he was going to display later on in throwing knives, and sent it crashing to the floor below. It missed Ada by inches. Terrible were his fears in anticipation of the wrath about to fall on him. But he was not punished for this. Ada told her mother and her sister that it was an accident. She then came and sat on his bed and reasoned with him, trying to win back his trust and affection.

Thirty years later, as an unknown Métis, on sending the manuscript of *The Men of the Last Frontier* to the editor of *Country Life,* he wrote:

I do not know if it is still the custom to dedicate a book to some person or another. I have done so, but maybe this is irregular. My own mother I unfortunately never knew. An aunt took her place, and it is to her that I must give the credit of the ordinary education that enables me to interpret into words the spirit of the forest, beautiful for all its underlying note of wildness, and to tell of ways and means that better men have taught me.

In *Pilgrims of the Wild*, published thirty years after this time, comparing his own kind of education with Anahareo's more practical kind, he wrote: "In my young days I had received some pretty extensive home tuition from an ever-blessed aunt, but had shown little aptitude save in geography, history and English."

And yet to Anahareo he confided:

"I hated her guts. She was a good-looking woman, always primped and starched, a snob and a perfectionist to a T. All she lacked was a human heart."

Anahareo remembered Archie imitating his aunt for her by piling his long hair on top of his head and altering his voice to that of a scold, and lecturing her on some imagined misdemeanour.

"She tried to make some kind of a genius out of Archie," said Anahareo. "But he said all she succeeded in doing was turning him into a devil. And a real bad one at that."

Mr. Overton, handsome and jaunty still at the age of eighty, who has spent all his life in Hastings, was a few years younger than Belaney, but he remembers him at school very well. Belaney was a lone wolf. He was mad about Indians, and he used to go wandering about farmers' fields by himself, or spend the day among the scrub on the cliffs at Pett, or in St. Helen's Woods. Mr. Overton says he was tall for his age, dark-complexioned even to the point of being swarthy. Years later, when his skin was already burnt dark brown by exposure summer and winter, he would use artificial means to darken it even more, and perhaps already he was buying cheap dyes with his pocket money, just as he was beginning to tell stories about his mother and father living in the far western states whom he was to join as soon as he left school. The other boys laughed uncertainly and were impressed. Everybody by this time was beginning to take Belaney's mania as seriously as he did himself.

But he was not without affectionate companions. There was a large family consisting of twelve children, by name McCormick, who lived in a house called Preston Lodge on Quarry Road, adjoining St. James's Road; the gardens of the two houses were separated by a pedestrian passage. "Jolly" is the word Mr. Overton constantly uses about this family, and one hears in his anecdotes laughter continually ringing out in this great jumble of a household, headed by two easygoing parents who welcomed their children's friends to the house. Two of the McCormick boys, George and Jim, had a job what to make of Belaney, who used to visit their house a lot.

Both house and garden were big and rambling. Archie built a wigwam in the garden. The frame of wood was covered with painted blankets, which gave it a very realistic effect. Here they camped out all night, the McCormick parents genially approving, and Archie cooked their supper in a frying-pan over a fire built between stones.

One of the sisters, Margaret, remembered the first night he had met them all. It was when the Belaneys had moved to Highbury Villa and had thus become neighbours. The McCormick children were all busy at their "prep" one evening, while outside a wild sou'-wester was raging up the Channel and the rain was slashing down.

Suddenly from outside there came the melancholy hooting of an owl, repeated two or three times. George, who attended the Grammar School, said "That's old Archie," and rushed out to a door that led to the garden. He returned accompanied by a tall, slim boy, strikingly handsome, with the acquiline features and high cheekbones of the North American Indian. His lank, dark hair, soaked with rain, completed the resemblance.

Gradually he introduced an element of the unexpected and of adventure into this laughing household. He would arrive sometimes in the boys' bedroom before dawn, having clambered down the wall of Highbury Villa over the

34

tradesmen's entrance, climbed over a low roof, and made his way up the tiles to the open window, and awaken the McCormick boys with the soft call of the owl.

Then he and George would set off for a walk along the cliffs, returning an hour or two later when the sun was up and the house was in turmoil with twelve children and two parents rising for the day. Sometimes the boys brought back with them a basket of mushrooms collected, dew-fresh, from a farmer's fields. It must have been with envy that on their return Archie would watch George entering his front door without care, to be greeted no doubt by shouts, nobody condemning him, all inquiring out of the warmth of the family nest what he had seen and done and what Archie had told him. Archie had to climb the wall of his house again, to avoid Ada's reproving eye, while all around him would be the heavy silence, punctuated by thumps, of three elderly ladies reluctantly preparing to meet the onslaught of another day.

He could ask his friends back into his own home only singly, and then he had to take them up to the "menagerie" which, after a struggle, he had been allowed to establish in an attic room. The struggle arose when Grandmama and the aunts realized that nothing would prevent him from bringing what they called pests into the house. These would be found in his bedroom, on the stairs, and, it was gloomily prophesied, would soon be in the drawing-room. Ada, as usual, was sensible, firm, practical, and unsympathetic. She brushed aside objections and laid down regulations, and the menagerie was established, but so hedged about with rules and regulations that some of the joy of it was dimmed.

But here he was allowed to keep his animals, and here, alive in hutches and boxes, or dead and preserved in spirits of wine, were his "friends", collected in St. Helen's Woods or along the grassy cliffs as far as Rye. Snakes were his particular pets. He would take them out and place them on sheets of glass, and there play with them affectionately, to the eye-popping excitement of any friend he took up there.

One snake in particular, an adder whose fangs he had removed, used sometimes to accompany him to school, coiled inside his shirt. Once at an "At Home" at the Mc-

Cormicks', the children were commanded down to the drawing-room to meet the guests. Archie came in with them, and one of the lady callers shrieked as she saw this strange boy nonchalantly stuffing a snake back into his trousers' pocket.

He had a talent for acting, and a gift for parody, and he was never in the slightest self-conscious when he was playing a part.

For instance there was Old Man Hopper, who was proprietor and headmaster at a local preparatory school attended by some of the younger McCormick fry. Mr. Hopper was a pillar of the local Ebenezer Chapel, and being virulently anti-Papist, he took a low view of the French, not for having disestablished religion, but for so largely remaining Catholic. All the boys in his school made jokes about it, and used to lead the old man on by some innocent question which, properly planted, would cause Mr. Hopper to break off his lessons and indict at length the nations which did not subscribe to the Protestant faith.

Archie, on the spur of the moment, put on one of Mr. McCormick's capes and a beret, assumed a false moustache, and, watched by the others from around the corner, went to knock on Old Man Hopper's door. When it was opened by Mr. Hopper, Archie, with a strong French accent and a confused grasp of English, applied for lodgings in the conviction, from which he refused to be shaken, that the sign advertising the school which said "Boarders taken" meant, and could mean, only one thing. Belaney did it perfectly, according to the witnesses, refusing to be put off by Mr. Hopper's protestations, and becoming more voluble and more incomprehensible the more his application was denied. Until Old Man Hopper was reported to have lost his temper, and before slamming the door in his face was heard to recommend to the Frenchman that he board the tripper ship at the pier without delay and return to his godless country.

But Mr. McCormick, who laughed heartily at the account that evening, said he did not doubt that Hopper had recognized Belaney immediately, and had only played up to him because he knew the children were watching. The old man was reported to enjoy a joke, and he had been dealing with boys all these years enough to know when his leg was being pulled. But the legend remained fixed with the Mc-Cormick children that Belaney had acted the part perfectly, and thirty-five years later when Grey Owl gave a lecture at the White Rock Pavilion in Hastings, and the packed theatre listened tensely as he spoke of the Indian people amongst whom his life had been spent, it was George McCormick's older sister, Mary, still living in Hastings in the 1930s, who coming out said to a friend, "That's Belaney, or I'll eat my hat."

I think Ada had hoped that he would grow out of his obsession with Indians; it reminded her, and her mother and sister, too much of George's failure to grapple with a profession while he dreamed of distant places.

Yet Ada could not help admiring the intense seriousness which Archie gave to the whole subject. He explained it all to her, illustrating his points with a tinted map he had prepared, showing the major linguistic divisions in Canada: the Algonkian in the east; the Iroquois in the south, bordering the St. Lawrence River and Lake Ontario; the Athabaskan in the north-west; and the Salishan and Wakashan on the Pacific coast.

He showed her where he had marked in the names of the tribes subsisting within these language groups; in eastern Canada, for example, the Algonkian group included the Montagnais, Napaki, Cree, Ojibwa, Algonquin, Têtes de Boules, Penobscot, Micmacs, and Wabanaki.

She was amazed at his knowledge of the detail. These names came rolling off his tongue without any hesitation. He was not interested in the romantic picture of the In-dians but in their mastery over nature, how they lived and survived in such a harsh climate, how they organized their lives, married, hunted, fished, trapped for furs, helped themselves to the bounty of nature but "farmed" the game so that the numbers of animals never grew less. They had to live by the furs they took, the game they killed for meat. The killing of game was regulated by each family in the hunting territory assigned to it by the common agreement of the band members. No one else could intrude there without the owner's permission.

She was amazed at all he had learnt. How on earth had

he acquired so much knowledge from books borrowed from the library and from the magazines to which he subscribed? But that was just like the boy. It was the same with animals. He knew everything about them, and the walls of his room were lined with delicate pen-and-ink sketches he had made of beetles, birds, and inhabitants of the forest undergrowth. He was a clever boy, with a fierce quality of concentration when he was interested in any subject. But what worried her was where this would lead. What point was there in being an authority on Red Indians? The alarming thing was that he was beginning to look like one and behave like one. He had even imitated the loping gait of the Indian.

Many years afterwards, Margaret McCormick, recollecting him in those years, said quite seriously that it could be a matter of speculation whether Grey Owl became Archie Belaney, or Archie Belaney became Grey Owl. It would be quite simple, she pointed out, for an intelligent Indian to copy exactly the characteristics of one so akin to himself in physique and temperament. How did the soul of an Indian find its way into a British boy?

But only a McCormick, broad-minded, generous-spirited, could speculate on that possibility. To the Belaney ladies no such considerations presented themselves. If he loved the open air so much, he should be a farmer. But when this was suggested to him as he began his last year at school, he was cold to the idea. He wanted to go to Canada and join the Indians, study their ways, and maybe write a book about them.

But how will you keep yourself, Archie? They all spoke at once, three women wailing at the prospect of a man not making a living.

He said that wasn't important. If he got there, he would make out.

It was the beginning of a year of argument, of tears, of appeals to his better nature. After all that Granny had done for him, how could he possibly be so cold-hearted as to contemplate leaving home and going so far away, when he might never see her again?

He set himself obstinately to break down their objections. He tried reason, persuasion, charm, hostility; and when these all failed he considered running away. But he had no money to get to Canada; he had spent all his pocket money on books, on stamps in writing away for information about the North, on feed for his menagerie, and on birthday presents and Christmas presents for his aunts and grandmother. His aunts inquired as to what other boys who were leaving school that year were going to do, and it happened that most of those he knew were going abroad, one to work in a bank in Montreal, another to farm on the Pembina River in Alberta. Still another was going out as a farming pupil to the Williams district in West Australia, and a fourth was going into the merchant marine. All were escaping from the constricting atmosphere of Hastings. But all, Ada pointed out, were going to learn something useful. Only Belaney wanted to go and live with the Indians. Be sensible, Archie dear, she pleaded.

Finally they came to a compromise. He would stay at home until he was seventeen, work in Hastings for a year so that he could continue to live at home, and put by what little money he could earn towards his eventual journey. Then, if he still wanted to go to Canada, the family would agree, provided he would become a farming pupil and learn to be a farmer while he was getting used to the country. If he would farm until he was twenty-one, only four years away, then he could do afterwards what he liked. But at least he would be a farmer, and if life with the Indians proved less attractive than he imagined, there was plenty of opportunity in Canada for farming work.

In the end he had to agree. What oppressed him most was the year he would have to spend in Hastings when he had finished school. He hated the prospect of office work. Ada secured him a job as a clerk with a firm of timber merchants named Cheale Bros. on the London Road. It was Archie's duty to check the timber coming in and going out, and planks of oak, ash, elm, beech, and pine, as well as fences and farm gates, coffin boards of oak and elm, and sawn fire-wood of oak, flowed in and out of the yard under his disinterested eye, and appeared and disappeared in the ledgers he had to keep.

He hated the monotony of the job. The only part that

gave him pleasure was collecting the accounts. For this purpose he had to walk all over town one or two afternoons a week. He loved the open air after the office's stifling fumes, compounded of coal smoke from the grate and tobacco smoke from his employer's pipe. The walk did not allow him to dawdle on cliff tops and forest paths. But it did allow him to daydream as he walked, and to fantasize the scene around him into rocky outcrops, coniferous forests, blue shining lakes, pine-needled paths, and the cold clear air of the Canadian northland. To come out of that illusory world into one of the narrow streets of the old town, knock on some door, pull the account-book from his pocket, and be faced by some elderly man hostile towards a collector, or whining with excuses for putting off the payment to the following week, was a painful shock which he found harder to bear as time went on, instead of getting accustomed to it.

Finally, according to Margaret McCormick, he relieved himself of his uncongenial job by letting down the chimney of his employer's office a small bag of gunpowder which, on meeting the fire in the grate, almost demolished the office, and certainly demolished the hateful job.

Sometimes on Saturday afternoons, while working at Cheale's, he would take the train up to the Crystal Palace to see the Empire display, and to pore over the bas-relief maps of Northern Ontario and Quebec. The remote Cobalt mining camp was much in the news, and the surrounding countryside was the subject of some elevated and highly coloured prose. He saw Cobalt, lost in this immensity of forest, Hudson Bay to the north. Like the slender fingers of a beautiful hand, the mighty rivers—the Mississagi, the Mattagami, the Abitibi, the Kapuskasing and the Harricanaw—flowed down from Hudson Bay, the sole means of communication in this green wilderness inhabited only by scattered Indian tribes and a few white traders and trappers. This was his goal. He fretted with impatience during this year of restraint.

He was seventeen in that summer of 1905, a tall, slender, handsome boy with a quick, radiant smile and a verbal felicity and humour which kept everybody around him happy. His aunts and his grandmother doted on him, although Ada was often sharp with him when he got above himself or charmed people too easily.

"It's false, Archie, don't you see? You make these people feel that you really care for them and are interested in them. And you don't. You couldn't possibly do so on such a short acquaintance. Then you forget them, and they are heartbroken, thinking you fickle in your affections. They don't see that you do this absentmindedly, whereas their minds are altogether on it. That's why it's false."

Remarks like this from Aunt Ada stung him. She was always trying to run his life. She couldn't possibly know what he felt. He wasn't at all the good boy she thought he was. He had got through the strains of pubescense fairly easily, helped by his music, which absorbed the fantasies that tease the imagination, and by the dominating dream of his life: to immerse himself in the Indian world and become one with them.

For this purpose he knew that he would have to be hardy. He trained himself rigorously to go without food or drink of any kind for a day, sometimes two at a stretch. Some nights he would sleep on the hard floor of his room, or creep out into the garden with a blanket, and sleep curled up under a tree until dawn arrived and kitchen blinds would be pulled up as early risers made morning tea. George McCormick confirmed that he never talked smut. He chastised his flesh, and thrust erotic images out of his imagination by a deliberate act of will, substituting for them fantasies of pulling a toboggan across a snowy landscape, walking across the ice of a lake in the moonlight, or packing a heavy load at a portage. Women were one day to be an overriding passion of his life, but that was to be when the rapturous dream faded momentarily as he discovered that visions when harnessed to everyday, practical life lose something of their brightness.

At seventeen, he was expected to have a sweetheart, and Aunt Ada, who had become part owner of a dog kennel with a Mrs. Holmes, hoped that he might be attracted by her partner's daughter, Connie. She was a pretty girl, two or three years younger than Archie, who meant to take up dramatic training when she finished school, and have a stage career. Archie was attracted by her, but a London actress did not fit in with his dreams of life in the wilds. They flirted, and he gave her a photograph of himself, and accepted one of her in exchange. Both photographs had been taken that summer by a Mr. Perry in Hastings. Archie appears keen-eyed, wondering at the mystery of life, a very vestal virgin; she a dreamy-eyed, bare-shouldered flower ready for plucking. These poses were wrought by Mr. Perry, who flattered himself on his artistry, and they probably truly represent the personality of each of the sitters at that time. We are all locked into our age, and 1905, like any other year, set its stamp upon all its artefacts, including those evolved under Mr. Perry's lights and settings.

When the year was up, there was another struggle. Ada would not hear of him going at the beginning of that terrible winter that blotted out Canada in ice and driving snow. It was finally agreed that he might go the following March. Toronto was selected as his destination. Perhaps some friend of the household, such as Dr. Ingles who had brought Archie through his near fatal attack of pneumonia and had become fond of the boy, wrote to a friend in Toronto who had been at medical school with him to inquire about the chances of Archie's becoming a farm pupil in Ontario. Perhaps the friend wrote back to say that there would be no difficulty at all in getting a job as a beginner on a farm in the spring, and when the boy arrived he would check the home to which he was going to make sure that it was all right.

He never spoke about these Hastings years afterwards to anyone, not even to Anahareo. What I have written here I learnt from his aunts and his mother and Mr. Overton, from the school magazine, from documents and stories that appeared in the press after his death from some of his surviving friends, and most of all through the genius for discovery of a remarkable researcher, Donald Smith. But I never had a word from Grey Owl. He told Anahareo of Ada, but Anahareo imagined someone in Mexico. Of the narrow life in an entirely female household in an English seaside town, Anahareo could have had no possible conception. He closed the door on all those years when the steamship *Canada* of the Dominion Line drew away from Liverpool docks on a March afternoon in 1906 and he waved goodbye to Aunt Ada, who had come to see him off.

I imagine the parting was a wrench for Ada, but to him it meant little. His mind was altogether fixed on what lay ahead. Ada left the dockside to return to her hotel. On board she had picked up in the writing-room a postcard of the vessel, and this she took from the shrine of relics she was showing me after his death. It was addressed to Carrie and posted the same afternoon; it was clearly postmarked March 30, 1906. It said: "Saw Archie off at 4 p.m. today. He is very happy and has already made friends with a man going to Toronto. Home tomorrow. Ada."

CHAPTER 4

THE ST. LAWRENCE was not open at that time of the year, so the *Canada* disembarked its passengers at Halifax, and the landing certificate in the immigration files in Ottawa shows that Archibald Belaney, giving his destination as Toronto and his occupation as "Farming", entered Canada by that port on April 6, 1906.

There is room for doubt whether he went straight to Toronto. No record of his life exists covering this time except a fictional account he later wrote, and even this has disappeared.

Thomas Raddall, a Canadian writer who has re-created Grey Owl's life in a book of unresolved mysteries,* believes

*Thomas Raddall, *Footsteps on Old Floors* (New York: Doubleday, 1968).

that when Archie landed from the ship at the old Deep Water Terminal in Halifax, he might have taken a walk to the Halifax Post Office, perhaps to mail a card to his aunts announcing his safe arrival, and in the streets about the Post Office found the "Green Market" which in those days was held twice a week in the vicinity of the Halifax Post Office. Micmac Indians used to come in to sell flowers and baskets, toys, bows and arrows, toy bark canoes, and similar handicrafts which they had made themselves, and Archie, fascinated by his first face-to-face contact with Indians, might have fallen in with these people, abandoned his plan to go on to Toronto, and gone off with them to the shacks and wigwams they lived in around the shore of Banook Lake, which was the beginning of a canoe route to the interior.

This interesting theory receives some support from the fact that Archie seemed in the years ahead to retain some association with the Indians of this region. In 1914, when he was on the run from justice, he disappeared from Northern Ontario, and when he reappeared in May 1915 to join the army, it was in Digby, Nova Scotia, where he told the medical officer examining him that he was camping by the Bear River, ten miles from Digby.

Even further support comes from the fact that when, for a second time, Archie had to leave Bisco in 1927 and began the long pilgrimage with Anahareo in search of new trapping grounds, the journey of nearly two thousand miles made a huge arc in this direction and came to a halt at Cabano, on the borders of Quebec and New Brunswick. It was here that he finally gave up trapping and began writing. It is significant that the reports of richer, unspoilt trapping grounds in this area came to him from a Micmac Indian who hailed from New Brunswick. There is a distinct possibility that this Micmac character, unique in that he is the only one in *Pilgrims of the Wild* who is not given his real name, never existed; and that what Grey Owl is giving us is a satirical sketch of himself, always dreaming of distant fields that are greener and lusher, and always ready to support his case with tall tales resting on no foundation that can be isolated and verified in the confusion created by the supporting detail.

Given the familiarity which he so often exhibited with the Maritimes and the Micmacs, Archie possibly did begin his Canadian life with the Indians there. But he could have spent not more than four months among them, not the two years which Thomas Raddall supposes.

Until this interesting supposition was put forward by Thomas Raddall, it had been assumed that Archie had gone to Toronto, and had worked in a large "dry goods store", probably Eaton's, for several months, until he could stand it no longer; whereupon he had made his way northward intending to find work around Cobalt, where silver had been discovered three years earlier. On the train he had heard the passengers talking about the fabulously rich hunting country in the Temagami Reserve where someone was said to be building a hotel on the shores of Lake Temagami. On a sudden impulse he got off the train at Temiskaming, about thirty miles south of Cobalt, and applied for work from a man he overheard talking on the station platform, Bill Guppy.

This alternate theory is based on the discovery after Grey Owl's death of a handwritten exercise book containing the beginning of an adventure novel about a young greenhorn, and his experiences, both humorous and harsh, in coming to terms with the North.

In the story Archie uses assumed names. The actual figures with whom he first came into contact are easily recognizable, now that we know more about his history in those years. Bill Guppy, Archie's first employer, appears as Jesse Hood. Michel Mathias, an Indian who worked for Guppy and who was later to appear in *Sajo and Her Beaver People* as Gitchie Mecquon, which in English means "Big Feather", and who was known to the white man as Quill, is here. This Michel was a cousin of Angele, the woman whom Archie later married. His bark canoe, also made much of in *Sajo*, is on display in the North American section of the Royal Ontario Museum in Toronto. Another character who appears in the lost manuscript is Both-Ends-of-the-Day, who was based on Old Misabe of the Bear Island band, whose tribal name this was. He was to teach the greenhorn how to read the book of nature. The part he

46

plays is fictional, of course, for at the time Archie joined the Bear Island band he would have been nearly one hundred, and he spoke very little English. But he must have represented to the boy the repository of all the ancient wisdom of the woods.

Too late now, I see in that unfinished story a barely disguised account of Archie's first year in the woods of Northern Ontario in 1906–7. At the time I saw the manuscript I did not know the truth about Grey Owl and Archie Belaney.

Archie had written it in 1917 while convalescing from his wounds in an English hospital, not knowing at the time whether he would eventually be sent back to France, or whether he would sufficiently recover to follow the traplines again.

His nurse had evidently attracted him very much, and he had fostered in her the illusion that he was an Indian; an Indian who had the itch to write about his far-off primitive country. He had written about seventy or eighty pages, and the nurse was showing a sympathetic interest in him and in his writing, when he married Constance Holmes, and never finished the book. When he returned to Canada he started to correspond with this nurse, but nothing ever came of this hospital flirtation.

Much later, in *Tales of an Empty Cabin*, Grey Owl wrote a story called "A Letter" about a returned Canadian Indian soldier, Ana-Quon-Ess, writing to a nurse about his delight at being back in the woods again.

Dear Miss Nurse,
Nearly four months now the Canada geese flew South and the snow is very deep. It is long time-since I wrot to you, but I have gone a long ways and folled some hard trails since that time. The little wee sorryful animals I tol you about sit around me tonight, and so they dont get tired and go away I write to you now. I guess they like to see me workin. I seen my old old trees and the rocks that I know and the forest that is to me what your house is to you, I have been in it agen and am going back there in three days more, till

Spring and the rivers run open agen and then I come out in canoe about last of April. I wisht youd ben here to see when I got back. The Injuns was camped and had their tents at the Head of the lake. I went up. They come out and looked at me and the chief took me by the hand and said How, and they all come one at a time and shake hans and say How. They ast me nothin about the War but said they would dance the Morning Wind dance, as I just came from East and that is the early morning wind on the lakes. Then they dance the next night the Neebiche, meanin the leaves that are blown and drift before the wind in the empty forest. . . .

The unfinished manuscript came momentarily into my hands in 1938 when the controversy over Grey Owl's Indian origins was at its height. It had been, since 1917, in the possession of Miss Helen Ryan who had undertaken to type it. She was an acquaintance of Connie Holmes, whom I did not then connect with Grey Owl.

I read the manuscript at a sitting that afternoon, while Miss Ryan and a representative of the newspaper which had bought the manuscript sat in the waiting-room. It was a cheap exercise book with ruled lines, about eighty pages of which were filled with handwriting which might have borne a faint resemblance to that of Grey Owl, but only if you were searching for a likeness. Many years afterwards, with more documents to compare, it was possible to see that in 1930, when he consciously and deliberately abandoned altogether the identity of Archie Belaney for that of Grey Owl, his handwriting as well as his name changed.

There was a resemblance of setting and style to "A Letter" but nothing was sufficiently close to prove that this manuscript was an early writing attempt by Grey Owl. All my instinct at that time to protect Grey Owl against the charge of being an Englishman rose to deny the validity of the manuscript. Besides, Grey Owl had been born in Mexico, and the author of the manuscript, by his own account, started out as a sales clerk in Toronto. I thought the manuscript had been unearthed to try to capitalize on

48

1. Archie Belaney at 13, Hastings, England.

2. Archie's mother, Mrs. Kitty Scott-Brown, at 30.

3. Archie's aunts, the Misses Belaney, Aunt Ada on the right, Aunt Carrie on the left.

4. Archie Belaney at 17.

5. An Ojibway band. Archie's first wife, Angele, is the figure third from left. Temagami Ned is the first person on the left.

6. Archie Belaney with some young friends in Biscotasing, 1913.

7. Archie Belaney in his Canadian army uniform at his aunts' house near Hastings, England, 1915.

8. Trapper's cabin in winter, snowshoes by the door. Photograph apparently taken by Grey Owl.

9. Archie Belaney (*right*) and Charlie Duval (*left*) on the fire-range near Bisco around 1920.

10. Ne-ganik-abo, one of the old-time Indians. He appears in *The Men of the Last Frontier*.

11. Alex Espaniel, Archie's best friend in Bisco, around 1920.

12. Archie (*centre*), a friend, and Jim Espaniel (*right*), preparing to perform a war dance on the Queen's birthday.

the similarity of names and that it was a coincidence, nothing more.

But what did come through, and should have told me that this was genuine Grey Owl, is the intense love the writer has for the land to which he has come. All that these rushing rivers meant, the giant rampikes, the high forests and hills rising like terraces back from the river valleys towards the height of land, the wide expanse under the huge bowl of sky of this great green earth, folding and falling and rising again like great sweeping green billows tumbling towards the Arctic, emerges plainly in this exercise book.

But I looked at this work as a publisher has to do at a manuscript offered for publication by an unknown writer. The story of the young man's struggles to be accepted by the hard-bitten guides seemed rather overdone, and anyhow it wasn't finished. I thought at the time that it was a mistake on the part of this unknown author to introduce the narrator as a department store clerk selling "gents' furnishings" across the counter, and dreaming of the day when he would be able to follow a trail and steer a canoe through the rapids as skilfully as the best of the Indians.

Now that patient research has shown that Archie Belaney and Grey Owl were the same man, I regret that summary judgement. Not that anything valuable was lost; the work was unfinished, and the story had all the blemishes of one written by someone not yet used to the technique of unfolding a narrative. But I should like to read it again, for what it demonstrates is not only the overpowering effect which the Canadian landscape can have on a sensitive mind, but the essence of what was, now we see it unfolding, the compelling force behind the whole of Grey Owl's contradictory career: the fear of being trapped by civilization, the constant urge to assimilate himself, like some chameleon, in the world of nature. Men were devious, animals were direct; cities were built of stone and men living in them had hearts of the same material. But nature was yielding and clean and fragrant. It opened its arms to those who loved it, and soothed away their cares. As the Indian in Grey Owl's letter wrote to the nurse when he was feeling sad:

I will lisen to the song of a bird for a little while. Now the curtain is pulled down across the sun and my heart is black. A singing bird comes and sings an says I do this an I do that an things are so with me and I will lisen an forget there is no sun, until the bird goes, then I will sit and think an smoke for hours an say to myself, thats good, I am ony an Injun and that bird sang for me. When the morning wind rises and the morning star hangs of the edge of the black swamp to the east, tomorrow, I will be on my snowshoe trail. Goodbye.

Ana-Quon-Ess.

On an afternoon late in August that year, four months after his arrival, Archie emerges onto the station platform at Temiskaming, a stop on the newly constructed and not yet completed Northern Ontario Railway, on the borders of Quebec and Ontario. Bill Guppy, a well-known local guide and colourful character, who was later to dictate his reminiscences,* recalls that he was approached by a young man who had just got off the train, and was asked for a job.

When Archie landed at Halifax, he had a trunkful of clothes and the equivalent in dollars of £5. "Now," he told Guppy, "I'm just about broke," and all that he possessed was carried in the rolled blankets slung across his shoulder and tied at his waist. Here is how he appeared to Guppy:

Facing me, towering over me, was a good-looking youngster, with sharp-cut features, darkish hair cut short and parted on the right side, a firm chin and a lively smile. I judged him to be about eighteen years old, or maybe a pretty husky seventeen. He was an inch or two over six feet in height, long and lithe, and was dressed in rough working clothes—heavy boots, corduroy trousers as worn by labouring men, leather belt, an old

*Hal Pink, *Bill Guppy; King of the Woodsmen* (London: Hutchinson, 1940).

50

jacket, a cotton shirt, a red handkerchief tied round his neck, and an old dented felt hat tilted sideways on his head.

The young man explains that he has come up with the silver rush, but that he's no prospector and would like to learn guiding. He likes the outdoor life, and he wants to get a start in something—"Anything", he says emphatically, "as long as it will take me into the woods".

A bargain is struck. Archie will work just for his grub during the coming winter, and in the spring Guppy will take him into the woods. Guppy is building his own camp on Lake Temagami for the tourists who are beginning to flock up to this hunting and fishing paradise, a virgin territory just opened up by the new railway.

The young man's accent was English, what Guppy and everybody else like him called Cockney, meaning the genuine thing, not the lah-de-dah English so offensive to the Canadian ear. He volunteered no information about himself, and none was demanded. In the North, a man's past is his own business. Guppy liked the cut of his jib, his ready smile, and his quick intelligence, and he thought he could make a good guide of him, so he took him and fed him and taught him from that moment on all that he would need to know to ensure his own survival in the bush, never asking him what part he hailed from, or how it was that he played so well the old piano that stood in the front room of the Guppy residence.

They came to call him the Professor, as a good-humoured tribute to such an unaccustomed skill, and he was taken into the family and made much of by Mrs. Guppy.

On Temagami Island in Lake Temagami, Dan O'Connor, who had settled there in the 1890s, was building a new hotel, to be called Temagami Lodge, and Bill Guppy and his brothers were aiming to get work there in the summer as guides to the rich sportsmen whom the new railroad was bringing into the district. Guppy also meant to build a small camp there himself, which could be the Guppy brothers' headquarters, where they could put up a guest or two wanting to do it on a cheaper scale. Archie, with his pleasant character and good looks, and his willingness to work for his board while he learnt something about the country, suited Guppy to a T. Guppy knew Lake Temagami, and was convinced that it was the most beautiful spot in the north country. The game was plentiful, the Indians were friendly, and he was all set to go. All winter he kept harping to Archie on the splendour of the lake, with its one thousand six hundred little islands dotted down the long, deep north-east and north-west arms of the lake, and the particular beauty of Bear Island, the headquarters of the Temagami band of Ojibways, just opposite that point on the shore where Temagami Lodge was building. Archie counted the days until the spring when they would move in there.

Guppy used the winter to teach him how to trap. He was continually surprised by Archie's store of knowledge about animals. He noticed that he was completely without fear of wild animals, and at every opportunity would approach them as closely as possible, "freeze" near them, watch their habits, listen, and later imitate their calls pretty well.

Guppy showed him steel traps, and the deadfalls and snares used mostly by the Indians, how they worked, the advantage of one over another in different conditions. Deadfalls were so contrived that when the animal tugged at the bait it displaced a stick, allowing a heavy log supported by the stick to fall, instantly killing the animal. Snares were made of wire, with a loop hanging from a bough over a "runway", the position of which might be revealed by tracks in the snow. The more the animal struggled, the tighter the noose was pulled, until it strangled the animal.

Guppy taught him much that he could not have learnt in St. Helen's Woods. How to snowshoe, and how to restring snowshoes when they were worn by the sharp ice; how to make his own axe-handles, how to load canoes and run the rapids, how to "carry" at a portage. It was a compressed course in woodsmanship, and Guppy never had a keener or a better pupil.

Besides Archie, Mr. Guppy had engaged for his Temagami enterprise an Indian woman as camp cook, and an old Indian from the Bear Island band, whose knowledge of the surrounding country and the best fishing spots on

Temagami and the neighbouring lakes would be necessary to increase their own range.

The main party from Temiskaming consisted of Bill Guppy and several of his brothers, together with Archie. They made a number of trips during the winter and early spring from Temiskaming to Temagami. The only supplies that could be taken in were those that could be carried on a toboggan pulled by a dog-team, but there was plenty of work to be done on the site before the snow cleared.

For the work in the woods they were joined by the old Indian. Except on the coldest days when the party huddled over a fire in Temagami, the work was interesting and exhilarating. The sweet, aromatic odour of pine and fir and balsam scented the cold, clean air. The sun, shining from a cloudless sky day after day, made the snow whiter and the trees seem a deeper green, and lent to the landscape an appearance of virgin purity.

Silence brooded over the sleeping lands, a heavy silence that was broken only by the sound of an axe or the shout of a man in Bill Guppy's party. Every now and then snow would fall from some overladen branch. There would be a singing sound as it brushed aside the fern-like lighter branches below it, a dull thud as it fell on the frozen ground, and then a whispering as a light shower of snow from other branches that had been disturbed by its fall fell after it.

The exhilarating air gave the party tremendous appetites. They ate bannock and moose meat and drank huge pots of steaming tea. After a day of work, most of which had to be performed on snowshoes, a day of lifting and dragging heavy burdens through the soft snow, they lay like tired dogs at night, sunk in heavy slumber. But it was healthy work. The party glowed with vitality. Excess energy and high spirits could not be entirely absorbed by the strenuous labour. They played practical jokes on one another and behaved like schoolboys when a moment's pause in any operation left them free to indulge their humour.

At night, sitting around the campfire, the older hands would tell stories of the trail, of heroes of the past whom they had known, of Indian fighters of an earlier day. When Guppy rising towards the end of the evening would stretch

53

and yawn, and with a "C'mon fellers, hit the hay" would start to beat the fire down, Archie would always try to spin out the session. He had an insatiable appetite for these things, and the men laughed about it, but were evidently fond of him, as Guppy's reminiscences show.

When it was too cold to handle an axe even with hands encased in woollen mitts and buffalo hide gloves, the old Indian and Archie would put on snowshoes and travel long miles through the surrounding country.

The purpose of these excursions was to teach Archie his way about the country so that when the spring came and the first tourists arrived, he could guide them on their trips.

They followed the courses of frozen rivers. Beneath them the ice was six or eight feet thick, and successive snow-storms had packed the snow deep on top of that, so that often only by the presence of trees could Archie tell where the river ended and the shore began. But the bays and inlets were easily decipherable. He learnt their names and their value as fishing grounds, the course the current took, and where submerged rocks were to be avoided. He studied the landmarks, relating them to the main camp so that after some weeks he could find his way from any point, and knew the exact distance he was from camp.

He learnt from his Indian companion many other things that were a by-product of these snowshoe trips: to inter-pret the tracks of animals and to judge the time since they had been made by the impression left on the snow; how to tell from the song of a bird or the cry of some little beast where life was hidden in this white wilderness that seemed so still and lifeless beneath its shroud. He learnt how to light a fire in the snow when the temperature was below zero and a howling wind sent a fine drift of snow racing along the surface, stinging the face and blinding the eyes the moment they looked up from the ground. He learnt how, when night fell suddenly upon them and a storm blotted out the landscape and the tracks that they had been following, so that it was dangerous to try to reach camp, to dig a bed for himself in the snow and burrow down without blankets or covering and without food to await the morning. Archie was learning the ways of the wilderness.

Archie and the old Indian went to Bear Island seventeen miles down the lake from Temagami. It was the head-quarters of a band of the Ojibway. A Hudson's Bay Company post was located on the island and formed a focal point for the band to sell their furs and buy their supplies.

A picture of what Bear Island camp was like at that time emerges from another essay in *Tales of an Empty Cabin*, "A Day in a Hidden Town". This describes a village in the Mississauga Forest Reserve, but there would have been little difference in the situations of the towns.

The day was clean and so cold that particles of frost danced and scintillated in the air. They set off at mid-morning, the old Indian in the lead breaking ground, Archie following. Where the river widened into a wide lake, almost circular, and hemmed in by precipitous hills covered with virgin pine, they turned towards an island that rose from the frozen surface in a small bay.

A water-hole cut in the ice was visible near the shore of the island, and from here a beaten trail wound up a low grade to a grove of immense red pines. Amongst these were the lodges and the tents of this "hidden town", pre-sided over at this time by Chief Standing White-Bear.

The village, unlike many Indian settlements, was a permanent one, for the country was still so plentifully supplied with game and fish that the search for new hunt-ing grounds, the motive power behind the Indian's age-old pilgrimage, was not here necessary. Their hunting grounds, carefully marked for families, and carefully hunted so that the game supply was maintained, lay on the mainland around the lake. The men could cross to the mainland, in the winter over the ice, in the summer by canoe, for their hunt; and in winter could lay profitable trap-lines not many miles from Bear Island.

They ate their dinner in one of the lodges on Bear Island, seated on balsam boughs, the temperature of the lodge heated to an almost unbearable degree by the small tin stove that roared in one corner, and by an open fire that crackled in another. Over the camp hung a mist of hoar frost, and every now and then could be heard the disturbing yapping of the huskies which were chained up a little distance from the camp. Inside the lodge in which they sat the odour of richly cooked moose steak and the pungent scent of well-boiled tea mingled in the heated atmosphere created by the two fires. Archie leaned back and listened while the Indian talked with the chief in swift Ojibway. Archie could catch a phrase or two, but not the general meaning of their conversation. He supposed that it had to do with hunting grounds and reports of game. Sleepily he leaned back and watched the Indian girls who had waited noiselessly and unobtrusively on them while they ate.

When they left the village and started back across the lake, darkness had fallen, but a splendid moon rode in a clear sky, and on the horizon the northern lights flickered and danced. It was almost as light as day.

The chief raised his hand to them in a farewell gesture, a small, still figure beneath the blackness of the pines. As they started on the trail home, the voices of the wolf-dogs rose one after another in a long-drawn-out sobbing wail, until they swelled into a chorus of unearthly animal cries.

On either bank of the river the trees rose in serried ridges until their tops seemed to brush the diamond-bright stars that shone brilliantly in the cold night, while behind them the northern lights wreathed fantastically against the horizon. The only sounds were the yapping and the maniac howls in the background, and the swish of their snow-shoes in the snow. Civilization, towns, the rustle and hurry of men toiling might have been another planet, so far did it seem from the still and frozen night that cupped in this savage silent world. One can imagine Archie's thoughts. What he had seen that afternoon was time and a people standing still. Not people abject, defeated, purposeless, even though they were doomed to extinction before the advancement of civilization. But a people proud and far-seeing, who knew that Nature and Man would last an equal time, and that it was undignified as well as unwise to take more of the fruits of the earth than one needed, or to ask more of Nature than she need yield to keep one alive. They were the wise people, they who lived on the pine-covered rock island and lived their lives naturally; if without hope for the future, without fear of it too.

56

All the summer of 1907 Archie worked as a canoeman and guide for Bill Guppy, and when, in the fall, the sportsmen had gone and Guppy and his brothers were returning to Temiskaming, he said he reckoned he would winter in Temagami. He had made friends among the Bear Island Indians and was beginning to learn their language, and he had made a special chum of Tommy Saville, who had been brought up in England in circumstances very similar to Archie's, and who had had the same passion to share the Indian way of life. When Archie met him, Saville had been living for seven years with the Ojibways near Gogama, north of Temagami, and had married an Indian girl of that band.

Guppy, ever-helpful, got him the appointment of mail carrier between Temiskaming and Temagami. This was a job which he was to take again for a few months at the end of 1908. At Christmas-time, when the trappers who made it their headquarters returned to town for fresh supplies, the few white families living in Temagami, and the younger Indian men and girls, all joined in a community celebration, and Archie's prowess with the piano made him a popular member. This was later reflected in the lost early manuscript where a dance on Christmas night is described. Particular attention in the narrative was paid to a Mr. Martie McGonigal, the pianist and self-appointed M.C. of the festivities. The scene was treated humorously, and there is no doubt whom Archie was parodying here—himself! For Mr. McGonigal's patter and asides as he auctioned the box lunches, with which the successful bidder got as his partner the girl who had made up the box, was in the accents of Grey Owl's particular brand of drawling humour which later was to make his lectures such a success.

When Guppy saw him again in the spring of 1908, he noticed how far he had adopted the Indian's ways. It was as though he had studied the Indian posture, a slight but perceptible forward inclination of the body, as though pressing against the headband that held the tumpline to which was attached the loaded toboggan, a way of walking as though wearing snowshoes, the knees lifting higher with each step. With his sunburnt and winter-wind-burnt face, with the high bridge to his nose, his long black hair untidy about his head, wearing moccasins instead of boots, and peppering his speech proudly with Ojibway phrases, he looked as much Indian as white man. Only the blue-grey eyes, the voice with its English drawl and its educated accent, showed his exotic origin.

Walking behind him on the trail, you could see that his clear eyes missed nothing: the print of a deer, the track of a marten, a tuft of white rabbit hair caught on a tree trunk, the teethmarks of a bear on a low-hung branch. He pointed these out casually, as one would remark on a sunset or clouds piled in the western sky. It was extraordinary that this boy was only nineteen, and had spent less than a year in the bush. Bill Guppy did not congratulate himself on his superior teaching abilities, but he does remark in his narrative, "He got the benefit of my hard-earned experience." Years later, when Grey Owl was hastening northward following certain hints dropped by the Hudson's Bay manager, who was also the Chief of Police, and was passing through the old hunting territory, burnt-out and ravaged now by the hordes of amateurs who took to the woods during the world boom in fur prices, he encountered in this desolation his old teacher, and paid him a tribute for all he had learned from him in the past:

> Our reunion was notable and all too short, with Bill Guppy, that king of all woodsmen, respected by all men, red and white, and whom the Indians called Pijeense—the Little Lynx. Time had changed him in no discernible way; he alluded to the subject of our last conversation, held fifteen years before. He still clung to his traditions and always would.

Archie was a born hunter, but he had a weakness as a killer: he allowed himself to feel. Guppy had been with him the day he killed his first beaver. It was winter, and they were crossing a frozen lake when they saw something moving on the ice, a small dark animal. Beavers stay in their houses below the ice all winter, Guppy explained, and this one, probably a young male, must have come up through a hole in the ice, strayed from its lodge, and got lost.

They manoeuvred it between them; it tried to escape past Archie. With a blow of his axe-head, Archie despatched it. "Got you!" he said, as he picked it up. Then his air of triumph faded.

"It seems such a pity to kill them—but, oh well, we've got to live."*

That feeling was never to leave him. In "A Letter", the Indian writes to the nurse: "I kill that lynx today and somehow I wisht I hadnt. His skin is only worth $10 and he didnt act cross, an the way he looked at me I cant get that out of my mind."

By chance, the Bear Island Ojibways were one of the several bands which were the subject of a survey conducted by Professor F. G. Speck in 1913 for an anthropological series being issued at that time by the Canadian government,† and it is possible to see them in their historical setting very much as Archie saw them five years earlier. Every member of the Bear Island band is listed, his totem is given, his territorial affiliation, his Wisana or animal visitant, his individual Indian name and the English translation of it, and often the reason for the nickname by which he was known.

From this it is possible to see that Angele Eguana belonged to the Nebenegwane family, one of the two most prominent families in the band from which the chief had traditionally been drawn; that her nickname was "Noonday woman"; and that in 1913 she was marked in the tribal roll as having married a white man, the only one of the band who had. Both her parents were dead when Archie met her, and she lived on Bear Island with an uncle and her grandmother. She was a young girl whose affections were not to be trifled with without retribution from an intricate but closely knit clan who would feel towards her as towards a sister or a daughter. This Archie was to discover when he overstepped the mark.

When we think of an Indian band, we have to think of a

*Pink, *Bill Guppy; King of the Woodsmen*, p. 118.
†*Family Hunting Territories and Social Life of Various Algonkian Bands of the Ottawa Valley*, No. 70 (Ottawa: Government Printing Bureau, 1915).

family organization much larger than a European one, where a father and a mother hold the positions of authority. We have to imagine a family organization based on territorial affiliations which are inherited, and which were then the sole means of supporting life.

As Professor Speck points out, modern European-American man engages in community activities as a hobby or interest; if he likes he can withdraw from them and live in solitude, provided he has the means to support himself. The Indian could not; his life was unalterably bound up with his community. He could not hunt without a territory, for all the male members of the band shared the right of hunting and fishing; the territory owned by the band was divided up into lots called nokiwaki, which means "hunting ground", the boundaries being determined by rivers, ridges, lakes, swamps, and clumps of cedar or pine. Hunting outside one's territory was punishable occasionally by death. One held one's right to this territory through paternal descent, but one could only operate it and live from it with the community's consent.

The Indian band system was thus very similar to the clan system in Scotland, where the chief of the clan once held paternal authority over what was in effect a large family, where the member could work his own land but only with the chief's consent.

In one other respect there is an interesting similarity between the Scottish clan system and the Indian totem system. As well as the family territorial groups, each member of the band owed allegiance to a clan group which was distinguished by an emblem called a totem. Just as Mac-Kenzies or Campbells or Mackintoshes or Frasers anywhere in the world may justly feel some sense of kinship with that clan and its chief, although generations might have passed since the paternal ancestor who bore that name left Scotland, so the Algonkians and many other Indian tribes felt themselves part of a group of people, members of which could be found in other tribes, who shared the totem and wore its emblem, and who would recognize in each other the common link of a distant paternal ancestor. The emblems were always animals: a loon, a caribou, a beaver, a kingfisher, even a pike or a rattlesnake; and there was always an historical reason for it, as there is for the bear or the deer or the lion in European family or regimental crests.

Angele belonged to the caribou clan.

In one other way she, like all other Algonkians, could be identified. Each individual had a Wisana, which means roughly an animal visitant, the term denoting some animal which, shortly after the birth of the child, comes near the wigwam, apparently to see the baby. This might be within a day or two of its birth, or it might not be until a year later. But until it comes, the child is nameless. It is born with a hunting territory affiliation, which is often associated with the name of an animal; it is born into a clan system and has its totem. But what it needs to go through life is the protective charm offered by some kindly disposed animal coming to bestow its interest when the baby is born. Angele's Wisana, her presiding animal, was the tomtit or chickadee. When it sang or hopped about near her, all promised well.

But she needed still a name by which others could call her, a name for common usage, and she had no Christian names from which one could be selected. This came when she began to be recognized as an individual. There was no naming ceremony; some aspect of her to the eyes of others, some characteristic, gave her the name which became hers as indubitably and irrevocably as though it had been bestowed at the font. For Angele it was Kiter.nakwa' ta Nau.kwigi jigo.kwe, which has really no precise meaning, and is described by Professor Speck as baby talk. Its generalized meaning is "Noonday woman", and if you can imagine a child of two or three learning to talk and repeating after its elders, parrot-wise, the Ojibway term for that, you would get a jumble of syllables which could be interpreted as that.

When Archie first came amongst them, the Temagami band had their clearly marked hunting territories radiating out from the lake, north, south, east, and west. All winter they lived on their territories, hunting game, not recklessly and extravagantly but as though they were farming it, allowing some portions to remain unhunted the way a farmer leaves fields to lie fallow and renew their strength.

In the spring the band came together on Bear Island for social reunion, using the island, and others on the lake which teemed with game, for food during the summer rest; hunting communally for this, instead of individually on their jealously preserved hunting territories. That lent a communal holiday air to the proceedings. Everyone was relaxed and happy. It was a time for courting and marriage. During this period, the catch was dried for winter use. Clothes were made, boats and snowshoes and toboggans repaired. Life was lazy, happy, beautiful. They lived in a paradise, and they knew it and were joyful with each other.

In 1907, the only way into this area was by water. The railroad being built northward had not yet penetrated the Temagami forest; it ran to the east of Lake Temiskaming. Not even the timber crews had started to fell the trees here. Dan O'Connor was building the Temagami Lodge, and the white population which made up the village of Temagami on the mainland consisted of a few white trappers, a forestry official, a Hudson's Bay trader, a church missionary, and a schoolteacher; an island of habitation in a billowing sea of trees broken everywhere by rivers and lakes.

There was no schooling for Indians, and Angele did not learn to read or write. But her imagination was not starved. There were myths and tales which had been handed down from generation to generation, nearly all about the animal world, and nearly all humorous in phrasing, each narrator adding his own touch which subsequent ones could take over to adorn their own telling. There are innumerable legends about Wisker-djak (meat bird—or whiskey jack) who likes to live with the Indians, and likes to tease them and make mischief among them. He was always a roamer, always hungry. He used to visit from one family of Indians to another. He was always looking for trouble and got it too, but in spite of all he was never killed. Indeed, no one ever wanted to kill him, even though he was causing so much mischief, because the people liked to have him around. He was a familiar sight to every Indian child, hopping about the clearing where the tepee stood, uttering his taunting cries, stealing everything he could get away with. All her life, Angele would have heard stories of Wisker-djak's pranks which had all taken place very long ago. What need of books when there was always someone to relate these myths, and others like them: of how Wisker-djak pursued the Beaver, or Wisker-djak killed the Bear (and got his own head trapped in the skull). Of how Wisker-djak invites the ducks to a dance, and how Wisker-djak fell in love.

Then there were the myths, sometimes inexplicable except to those nourished on them, which draw on the wisdom and experiences of one's ancestors. Sometimes the myths deal with animals, sometimes with the phenomena of nature. The Northern Lights, for instance, because of the seething sound heard in high latitudes, are attributed to the waves splashing against the rocky shores of the northern seas, causing a reflected glow in the sky; the rainbow is caused by the mist rising from great breakers or waterfalls over rocks; or the Milky Way, which the Indians called bines-imikan, or birds' path, is the means by which the birds follow their northward or southward course in their migrations, and sometimes it is the path which the spirits of the dead take in their migrating journey to the happy hunting ground.

All this Professor Speck observed, by coincidence studying the very band with which Archie was to become so closely connected. Angele had been born in the same year as Archie. Thanks to Professor Speck, we can picture her life growing up in the band. Of the two childhood's, Angele's was certainly the happier. She would never have known a moment of insecurity. Although she was an orphan, she was surrounded by relatives; in some way or another, she was related to everyone in the band. When in 1907 at the age of nineteen she went with some of the younger band to work during the summer in the pantry of Dan O'Connor's Temagami Lodge, she could speak nothing but Ojibway, and knew nothing about life except as it was lived in the closed circle of the band.

Some changes could have been noted in Archie. By September 1907, his hair had been uncut for over a year and was now tied at the nape of his neck by a strip of rabbit skin. His face and arms were darkened by the sun.

He was becoming more handsome as his face matured and grew thin, and his body broadened as his chest and shoulders expanded with the hard work in the open air.

He walked and talked now with more confidence than he had done. He had never known what it was to be shy, but his anxiety to learn and a desire to please in these new surroundings had made him appear a little diffident when he first arrived in the North. That was all gone now. He did not strut and he did not boast, but the things he did that were unusual and were talked about, such as his knife-throwing, and his inclination to take risks where other men hesitated, gave him the reputation of being a daredevil. What won people over most of all was the contrast between his gentlemanly manners and cultured voice, and his ability in the bush in spite of being a tenderfoot.

Practical jokes and verbal wit provided amusement in these sparsely inhabited areas where people had to spend so much time in solitude that when they came together there was a spontaneous eruption of horseplay. Archie delighted in this. Aunt Ada had oppressed his spirit too long, and in throwing her off he went too far towards the other extreme, and began building up a reputation for a picturesque profanity and a capacity to hold his drink. He also began to show for the first time an interest in the opposite sex.

At the end of the summer of 1907 he had told Bill Guppy that he would like to winter in Temagami instead of returning to Temiskaming. After a summer spent with rich tourists from the south, he was more than ever eager to identify himself with the Indians. Besides, he undoubtedly felt himself able to stand on his own feet now. After a winter and a summer of Bill Guppy's tuition, his characteristic desire to work alone asserted itself.

He had come to know some of the Bear Island Indians during the summer, and he wanted to penetrate their life, and perhaps share it. He did not confide this to Bill Guppy, and they parted on good terms, Guppy promising to be back again next spring.

It was in his capacity as mail carrier that he first met Angele. One afternoon in early winter Archie was making his way to the lumber camp, returning on snowshoes from Temiskaming, when a husky came rushing towards him, snarling. He bent down, his hands outstretched, and the dog suddenly turned from aggressive animal to fawning pet. He was still playing with it when an elderly Indian woman and a young, beautiful one came up together and called to the dog by name, "Wa-Goosh". Neither of them could speak much English, and Archie knew only a few words of Ojibway, none of which could be applied to the present situation. The dog quite plainly belonged to the woman, and they were evidently trying to thank him for having stopped it. By gestures and a few words they explained that the dog was pulling a sleigh on which there was a baby; somehow the dog had slipped the harness and run off. They had left the baby on the sleigh and must hurry back, but were indeed grateful to him for saving them running after the dog further. It is amazing how much can be conveyed by gesture, especially when one of the communicators is a young woman, both shy and bold at the same time, laughing at her own attempts to explain what has happened and at a young man's attempts to say something in return.

He walked on with them, and there in the sleigh was the baby fast asleep and untroubled under its bear rug covering. He accompanied them on to Temagami. They had come in from Bear Island to spend the winter, the young girl Angele, and her grandmother, Old Lady Cat; Angele to find work and to stay with her aunt, Mrs. Burroughs. Archie was invited to call at the week-end.

"Auntie" could speak English, and communication flowed between Archie and Angele under her strong guidance. He went often to this house during the winter, helped cut wood for them, and listened to Old Lady Cat's tales of the old days.

Old Lady Cat was known to everybody as "Grandmother" because she was one of the oldest women in the band. She had married from the Temiskaming band into the Temagami band, and Old Man Cat, her husband, was still flourishing. She had a fund of stories, recollections, folk tales, and superstitions; and once she had her pipe going and was settled down, and if she was in the mood, she could go on for hours. She knew more English than she at first revealed, and Archie's Ojibway improved rapidly in this company where he came to spend all his spare time. He became absorbed in the stories she told. Some of them were funny: "how the rabbit came to have so little fat", for instance, and "how the otter got its shining fur". But others were heavy with wisdom: how to take a freshly killed beaver's leg bone, with the muscle left on, and place it in the centre of a mound of ashes in front of an open fire. Then mark off in the ashes the direction of the wind, north, south, east, and west, and two additional directions, south-east and south-west for example, marking only six directions. The muscle would then be cut with a sharp knife, and the bone placed in the ashes. The leg bone would, after a little, as the heat affected it, move, and the direction in which the bone pointed would tell the hunter in which direction to move next to get the best game. Little beaver, friend of the Indian always, even in death!

At first what drew him so often to the house was Old Lady Cat's stories. In that dark living-room, where the fire burnt all winter, the smell of freshly cured skins, as well as of the pots bubbling on the stove and the old lady's tobacco, became familiar to him, and drew him back again and again. Of course he was attracted by the fresh, clean looks of Angele. They began to go off together for walks in the woods; he admired her strength and skill and knowledge of woodcraft, and she admired his handsomeness; he was so tall and lithe, and knew so much more than she did about those birds and animals amongst whom all her life had been spent.

She imagined what he would be like as a husband. There was surely no chance that he would even think of her as a wife. But she told Old Lady Cat what she was thinking, and "Grandmother" watched in that half-dark room. She then performed some private inquiries with a magic stone, a strand of hair, a good luck charm, and much muttering. But the answer was not clear. Hopeful, but not confirmatory.

CHAPTER 5

ARCHIE'S duties as mail carrier suited him temperamentally. He liked nothing better than to be alone, and to be able to keep his own time. He liked to travel in the early morning, and rest in the middle of the day, making camp, if he had to, just as dusk was falling. The distance between Temiskaming and Temagami in direct line was only fifty miles. In the summer, by water, it was nearer eighty, took five days, and involved many portages. In winter, when the ice came, it was easier to travel by snowshoe on the frozen rivers, and he took a more direct route southeast, crossing Rabbit Lake and avoiding the elevation all around him by staying in Ottertail Creek valley until he reached Lake Temiskaming. It was still an arduous journey which took three days of travel. With a day or two of rest at

67

each end, the journey occupied nearly a whole week. Then a week would follow in which he had nothing to do, and in these intervals he fell into the habit of going over to Bear Island.

During the summer when he was guiding, he had made friends with a lot of young Indians, and he found it pleasant when the "Indian summer" of the late autumn provided hot days, still evenings, and chilly mornings, to roll up in his blanket round a campfire after an evening spent talking with them. In the morning, he would be off before any of them was stirring.

When the snow came, the young men went out on the trap-lines, and the band at the village consisted only of the women and children and a few old men. These latter did a little hunting on the island, or on one of the neighbouring islands, or in the family hunting territories adjacent on the mainland.

This was how he came to know old Pete Misabi and Ned White Bear, and he went over with Angele to visit another aunt on Bear Island, Mrs. Petrant. There was a large family of Misabis in the band. The ancestor, a great-great-grand-father of the youngest member, was still alive in Archie's time, almost a centenarian in age. He was an Ojibway from the Georgian Bay area to the south-west, and had entered the band when he married the daughter of a former chief of the Temagami band. Ko-ke-ka, that bride, Old Lady Misabi as Professor Speck lists her, was also still alive. Misabi was nicknamed the "Giant" because of his great frame, and this tendency towards unusual height had persisted in his descendants. All the Misabis were tall, most of them the equal of Archie's six feet two. Ned, the other elder, whose nickname was "Both Ends of the Day", presumably on account of his liking for night travel, which Archie was to learn from him to appreciate, was a White Bear, one of the leading old families of the band. Frank White Bear, the second chief at this time, was his cousin. Ned White Bear spoke English, and was well known to the whites as Temagami Ned.

From these two ancients Archie was to learn a great deal. In all his books a character, an old Indian, Ne-ganik-abo, appears, who is both a repository of the wisdom of olden days in the forest and a teacher who imparts this wisdom to the young Grey Owl. Ne-ganik-abo, whose name means "Man That Stands Ahead" or "Stands First", could read the wilderness as we read a book, and as we are told in *The Adventures of Sajo* and in *The Men of the Last Frontier* Ne-ganik-abo is always described as "my mentor", and he is spoken of as Grey Owl's companion and teacher from his earliest days in the North. When Grey Owl sent me the manuscript of *Sajo* in March 1935 he told me that Ne-ganik-abo, who appears in *Sajo*, is the same old man referred to in *The Men of the Last Frontier*, and that the village where the events in *Sajo* occurred is that one, i.e. Temagami, "where I spent my own early days from about 15 years of age, and where I got most of my early training."*

Donald Smith, a young man working for a doctorate in history at the University of Toronto, makes the interesting suggestion that this fictional character is really a composite portrait of Old Misabi and an actual Ne-ganik-abo who lived on the Spanish River where Archie trapped after the war. This section of the country is one hundred miles away from Bear Island. Donald Smith suggests that the reason why Ne-ganik-abo was brought into the composite portrait was to avoid the identification with Ned White Bear and Misabi, for when he wrote these books, Grey Owl had abandoned his wife, Angele, but still had legal obligations to her which he was not fulfilling, and he did not want to give away his connection with the Bear Island band. This is an interesting supposition. But I think, borrowing from his idea of its being a composite portrait, it is more likely to be one of Old Misabi, who was too old to teach him but not too old to tell stories, and Ned White Bear, Temagami Ned, who, although elderly, was not too old to hunt and who could, and indeed did, perform the feats of endurance so graphically described by Archie in *The Men of the Last Frontier* and *Tales of an Empty Cabin*. By the time he was trapping on the Spanish River after the war, Archie had nothing to learn from anyone about his trade.

One other similarity I think favours my supposition. The name Ne-ganik-abo is not much different in sound from Nebenegwune. The family Nebenegwune, meaning "One Side

*A letter from Grey Owl to Lovat Dickson, March 17, 1935.

69

Wing", was the one to which Angele belonged. It is one of the leading families of the band, and the one with which Archie would have been most familiar. Many years later, when he was fleeing from justice at Bisco, he took for a short time the name of Mathias. The Mathiases were another large family of the Bear Island band, connected with the original Nebenegwune family. In all that he wrote about the Indians, one suspects, Archie rarely strayed outside his own experiences with the Bear Island band, and long after he had left them he used their names and their history for his tales.

His encounter with this band happened just as the security and isolation of their primitive, beautiful surroundings were beginning to be invaded by the slow encroachment of the tide of civilization from the south. This did not at first seem a threat. The white men offered employment, opened stores, brought in goods, and made life more lucrative and comfortable. But the arrival of the white man in mass threatened their hunting grounds, which were not protected by law, and loosened the cohesiveness of the band.

First had come the surveyors and the government men. Then, here and there, the white men discovered in the ancient rocks gold and silver and other metals. Dynamite shattered the rocks, shafts were sunk deep into the earth to claw out what they sought. Prospectors poured in on the new railway, and went off looking for claims. Over mine shafts houses and tents sprang up, and clearings were cut in the forest.

Then the timber-fellers came. Mills were erected, smokestacks poured smoke into the sky, and machinery shook the earth, and their refuse poisoned the streams and killed the fish.

All this happened outside the Temagami Forest Reserve. But already in the year of Archie's arrival survey crews were busy laying out a townsite in the little settlement of Temagami at the end of the north-east arm of the lake, and Orders-in-Council in Toronto were approving the lease of land for summer-resort purposes. Islands in the lake under five acres in extent were being offered at $125 for a twenty-one-year lease, and some bigger ones were being leased at $3 an acre. Dan O'Connor's lease of ten acres of island "1199", which became Temagami Island, acquired for the purpose of creating a large summer resort and outbuildings to cost the then fantastic sum of $20,000, was directly opposite Bear Island. Temagami Lodge was to give employment and wages to many of the younger Indians, for it was staffed almost entirely by them, and the customers who could afford the cost of guides and equipment to get them in there were good tippers. Archie's romantic dream of living with the Indians in isolation was shaken by the rumours of this paradise becoming a white man's holiday ground, and the Indians becoming servants in surroundings in which they were nature's masters. It made him despise what he had come from, and romanticize the more what he had come to.

What Old Misabi and Both Ends of the Day were telling him was of the glories of the past. These had not yet entirely faded. Old customs still held, old skills still prevailed amongst these people. These men's memories reached back into what had indeed been a golden age. In the lost manuscript shown to me in London, some excerpts from which came into the possession of Thomas Raddall, Archie described them both and the effect their teaching had on him:

> . . . Both-Ends-Of-The-Day, now old and grey and known to the whites as Ned, who talked of the old days when the Iroquois came up seventy years before [i.e. 1834] and made war, and how the Ojibway drove them out. Old Misabi, so old that he had hunted beaver on the Don River when Toronto was a muddy village where he sold his fur, and who followed a man's snowshoe tracks three months old in the dark, and was reputed to be able to draw 200 lbs. on a toboggan all day, over heavy snow, on a track unbroken save by his own passage ahead of the load. I could have listened to him for hours as he told me of feats of endurance and instances of skill, that made them famous in a land where force of necessity developed these powers to a remarkable degree. I stored all these stories in my mind, as patterns to work on; deeds perhaps that I might

never accomplish but goals towards which I would work.

Archie soaked himself in these things, catching them just as these old men were fading into dust. He began to take the Indian point of view and argue their case with his friends in Temiskaming and Temagami. Unconsciously he began to adopt their ways, especially their hunting tabus, and these he preserved all his life.

He noticed that different hunters had different tabus, and on questioning them, he found that these customs always related to some personal experience. For instance, one man, when he killed a beaver, would always cut a piece of the breast meat and leave it at that spot to preserve his power to kill beaver.

He noticed that hunters always placed the antlers of moose and caribou upon a trimmed tree stump, where they might be seen by passers-by, as evidence of the respect held by the slayer for his victim. To omit doing this would have been to weaken one's powers as a hunter.

The bear in particular was honoured. His skull was always painted with a black stripe from the tip of his nose to the base of his head, and another stripe at right angles to this across the crown; a black spot was placed in each quarter. Then a spruce tree would be trimmed of its bark, the skull would be tied to the trunk, and ribbon streamers tied to the top of the tree. Around the trunk broad red bands would be painted at intervals. Sometimes tobacco would be placed in the empty skull as a tribute to the animal, whom the Indians held in great respect. Grey Owl tells us:

> The bodies of beaver were laid in supposedly comfortable positions and the hands, feet and tail, severed for convenience in skinning, were laid beside or on the body. Whenever possible the body, with these appendages securely tied to it, was committed to the water through a hole laboriously cut in the ice. Those which were eaten had the knee caps, unusual adjuncts for an animal, removed and most religiously burnt.*

*Grey Owl, *Pilgrims of the Wild.*

72

And when asked why they did these things the reply was illuminating: "Ozaam tapskoche anicianibé, mahween—because they are so much like Indians."

It was a winter of metamorphosis: he was changing, and could feel himself changing, from a white man witnessing strange customs to a young man being initiated into ancient tribal rites and customs to which he was admitted as an heir. They no doubt liked his company; he was so eager to learn, so intense a listener to their tales. Old men suffer neglect, and it is painful. They responded to his interest by teaching him things that he could never had learnt from a white man, however skilled the white man might be as a woodsman. They taught him how to endure in the bush with nothing to eat but strips of dried moose-meat and tea made from the boiled leaves of Labrador sage, plucked from bushes on the trail. And to be satisfied with this, like the sage of Pelican Lake in *Tales of an Empty Cabin*, who found "in plain meat, tea, a little flour, a few dried herbs and a blanket the complete fulfillment of all his earthly needs".

They led him across unknown country in the dark in winter conditions that made movement of any kind often dangerous. They made fire with flint and steel, slept on a winter's night behind a sahaagan, a semi-circular canvas shelter, when sometimes a heavy snowfall forced them to make camp wherever they found themselves, and to do all this in the darkness—by the light of birch-bark flares—even when the snow was being driven by a howling gale.

He was fascinated by the images, finding them conjured up in a phrase that showed nature and man as co-existing in an ordered universe. "When the wind speaks to the leaves the Indian hears—and understands." He strained to hear what they plainly heard, to interpret signs and sounds, just as he had done in St. Helen's Woods as a boy.

There he had been listening to the piping of insects, the croaking of frogs. But here, there was a vast symphony, beneath a great bowl of sky: the smack of a beaver's tail on the water, just before he dives; the laughing owls' cackling whoops; the crackling sound of underbrush being broken by the mighty tread of a moose. He saw how if a man were to break a stick or shout or otherwise betray his presence, the whole forest would freeze, united in silence against the in-

73

truder. He saw that the Indians moved silently, and were themselves as much a part of nature as the animals they hunted. In all this these older men were pulling back "little by little, the magic invisible veil of mystery from across the face of the forest, that I might learn its uttermost secrets."

He was not only learning; he was absorbing the sacred mystery of these things.

In mid-summer 1908, Archie applied to Mr. Stevens, the storekeeper and a Justice of the Peace at Temagami, for a licence to marry Angele, giving his own age as twenty, and Angele's as eighteen. The licence was issued, but the wedding did not take place. Instead Archie suddenly disappeared. There is a story given by Miss Maud Leopold, who was the desk clerk at Temagami Lodge, that one day in 1908 she heard a great noise from the lake. She and others ran out of the hotel, to see Archie Belaney paddling fast in a canoe, with half a dozen Ojibway canoes in hot pursuit, in one of which sat Angele.

This story is given a certain credibility by Archie's own statement very soon afterwards to an employer, Bill Draper, for whom he was working on some claims on Animanipissing Lake. He told Draper that he had just got out of Angele's home on Bear Island when her family came at him with tomahawks. Archie also told Bill Draper that his mother was an Indian Apache woman, and that his father was a Scotsman, and that he had been born and reared in Mexico. This is the first recorded instance in which he used that story in the north country, expanding on the myth which he had given a brief airing in his schooldays in Hastings.

What turned the Indians of Bear Island against him remains a mystery. Or does it? Even without evidence from any witness, it is a reasonable assumption that Archie must have been attempting to anticipate pleasures that only marriage sanctified. But that it was the effective cause of postponing the marriage, and of his remaining out of sight for some time, there can be no doubt. For the next year there is no trace of him in the North.

But Hastings saw him in 1908, as the McCormicks remember. Behold the young adventurer, returned from far places, tanned by exposure, wearing moccasins and a wide-brimmed felt hat, as exotic in Hastings as the sombrero George had sported on the Parade while awaiting Archie's birth. He brought back a pair of moccasins as a present for his friend George McCormick.

The two friends got together immediately, but were not as comfortable with one another as they had once been. Something had come over Archie which honest George could not understand. Archie said that he had come home because his grandmother was ill, and he feared he might not see her again. He told George something of his experiences in Canada, but not everything. He wanted to get back to the Indians. Hastings gave him claustrophobia. He did not want to leave his grandmother while she was ill, but he said that another month of it here would kill him. George was not surprised when after three months he heard one day from Miss Ada that Archie had returned to Canada. He had gone without saying goodbye to the McCormicks. But they were understanding people, and they accepted as part of the mysteriousness they had always associated with him that he should come and go in this sudden fashion.

When he returned to Northern Ontario the trapping season had begun, and he was not seen around Temagami until late the following spring, 1909. Some account of an escapade in which he had been involved, which might have caused his death, reached Temagami, probably through one of the band who had been hunting with him in the lowbush area. He had made a bet with a white trapper that he could cross Algonquin Park and no ranger could catch him. This area is heavily stocked with wildlife, and all hunting and trapping is strictly forbidden there. No one is allowed into the Park carrying a gun. Archie had his slung across his back; he was unmistakably a trapper. His bet represented a double defiance. If caught by a ranger he would have a heavy fine to pay for carrying a gun and traps. It was the dead of winter, the temperature was well below zero. He would have to cross—at night to avoid detection—fifty miles of unknown country, wearing snowshoes. He said it could be done, and he started off.

It was essential for the success of his plan that no news

75

of it leak out, but a journey of this sort, undertaken in a spirit of bravado, could not remain secret. The Chief Ranger of Algonquin Park heard that a young woodsman was going to undertake this hazardous journey. The Chief Ranger was a man who admired the evidence of courage whenever he found it. He would have to arrest this young law-breaker, but he would do it fairly and give him a fifty-fifty chance to get out without getting into trouble. He, therefore, warned his men to look out for Archie, pick up his tracks and follow him, but not arrest him unless he set a trap or fired his gun.

Archie slipped across the Park boundary without being observed and covered a good bit of ground before one of the rangers picked up his trail. The ranger followed this without hurry, knowing that at some time Archie would have to make camp. Archie, pushing on ahead, turned now and then to gaze behind him, but no sign of any human figure could be seen. He was following the setting sun, keeping as steadily in line with it as he could and veering from it only when some natural obstacle prevented him from going ahead.

An attempt to shorten his route proved his undoing. Coming down the slope of a hill he saw before him the circular depression of a level surface which indicated a frozen lake. Dividing this surface from another just like it was a rough, uneven track which suggested that a narrow neck of high ground separated the parts of the lake. He made his way across this, but halfway over came the sound of an ominous crack, and immediately he knew that instead of dry land he had been traversing the none-too-stable roofs of a beaver colony which were now giving way under his weight. As these thoughts passed through his mind, Archie felt his feet sinking into the icy water below the huts. Grasping some of the stronger sticks, which were frozen into the ice at the side, he managed to pull himself out onto the level of the lake.

He had been foolish and he knew it. Getting wet in that temperature might bring to a tragic end not only this expedition, which he had so light-heartedly undertaken, but also his life. It was not possible to make camp here; the spot was too exposed and the smoke from his fire would attract the attention of half the Park rangers. Knowing that he was carrying his life in his hands he stumbled on, hoping that

76

every turn might reveal a hidden bivouac where he would feel safe to make camp. He pressed on for several miles in this way, but as time passed a dreadful certainty grew in his mind. His feet were frozen and the numbness was slowly creeping up his legs.

He walked on dazed and uncertain what to do. If he stopped, discovery would be sure; if he went on he would probably lose his feet, if not his life. Any risk was better than that, and he stopped there where he was and began to unstrap the snowshoes from his unfeeling feet. But as he stooped to pick up his axe he found he could no longer walk. He fell to his knees, gazing mutely at the snow, feeling lost and helpless in the growing dusk.

There, a little while later, the ranger found him. He took off Archie's moccasins and gave what first aid he could under the circumstances. Then, loading Archie onto his sleigh, he turned his dogs towards the Chief Ranger's cabin. As he was being carried across the threshold the Chief Ranger looked down at him and smiled.

"That was a bet we won, my boy," he said kindly.

For two weeks Archie remained at the rangers' headquarters, during which time he and the Chief Ranger became firm friends. The Chief Ranger was an expert on wildlife, and in Archie he found the perfect listener. For the fortnight that Archie was his guest, the Chief Ranger held forth joyfully on his favourite subject, and Archie listened eagerly. At the end of a fortnight, when his feet were healed sufficiently for him to leave, some of the rangers escorted him to the Park boundary.

Archie returned to Temagami and made his peace. By this time Tommy Saville was living on Bear Island with his Indian wife, and it is conceivable that he was instrumental in healing the breach.

The marriage plans were on again. Archie asked Tommy to be his best man. A young clergyman, holidaying at an adjoining island, was asked to officiate; and on August 23, 1910, at the Forest Rangers Hall on Bear Island, Archie and Angele were made man and wife. The hall was so crowded that Annie White Bear could not get in, and felt much aggrieved thereby, for she was one of the bride's oldest friends, and had come all the way from White Bear Lake for the event. After Grey Owl's death, when she was attesting before the Commissioner that this had really been a marriage and not a tribal ceremony, she said that she had been able to see, from the door of the hall, the table with a Bible lying on it, and pen and ink beside the Register.

After the wedding, which took place as the sun was setting, the customary wedding dance was held. But it was not one which was attended by all the main families of the band. Marriage, Indian-style, according to Professor Speck, was celebrated by no feast, dance, or ceremony. The man would simply build a wigwam and make a canoe and household utensils. The old folk would lead the girl to the new household, where the couple would live together. This marriage, solemnized by a Christian minister, is more likely to have been considered as a binding document on a white man, a slippery customer who had already tried to slip out of the bargain, than as an acknowledgement of the groom's religious convictions. The dance afterwards, Angele said in sworn evidence many years later, was held at what she calls a wigwam, which is the Ojibway word for house. Angele said it was called Turner's. It would likely have been a celebration open to all the younger Indians, with Angele's brother, a rather fierce-looking young Indian, and the kindly disposed Tommy Saville acting as hosts.

From this moment on, Archie was committed to the Indian way of life. He gave up guiding, and seems to have cut himself off as far as possible from the white man's world. His hair, cut for the visit to England, by the winter of 1910 had grown again to his shoulders. It was parted in the centre, and it was held out of his eyes by two strands of trolling line wound round his forehead. He never wore a hat, and from constant exposure to the sun his skin was burnt as brown as that of an Indian. Only in his blue-grey eyes, and the brownish tint to his black hair, was any difference to be seen between him and the Indians. He now spoke fairly fluent Ojibway; he wore moccasins made by Angele from skins he had trapped and cured himself. His deerskin pants and deerskin jacket had also been made by her. He was a picturesque figure, and several visitors to the North recorded their memories of him.

Cheerfulness and a lazy drawling humour had always been characteristic of his manner and speech, but something now subdued them when he came into contact with whites. Then he became morose, monosyllabic, and argumentative when contradicted. He toyed with his knife in moments of abstraction, and when angry, would spend long intervals throwing his knife at a tree trunk, a common enough trick in the woods. He began to get the reputation of being a bad hat, and seemed rather proud of it. And as though to support this view, he began to cultivate a picturesque profanity, which shocked some of the white visitors to the neighbourhood. That, no doubt, was his intention.

The young couple lived at first in a tent on the Bear Island Reserve. When the cold weather came, Archie went hunting with the band, and Angele moved into the house of her aunt, Mrs. Petrant.

Then in the late fall they went trapping in the Austin Bay district. At Christmas-time they were to return to town for the holiday, and to renew supplies. But Angele was pregnant, and they went back to Bear Island for the New Year celebrations. They had a merry few days there. Then Archie returned to the trap-lines in the Austin Bay area, leaving Angele at Bear Island for three months.

At the beginning of April the baby was stirring and the ice was breaking. Angele returned to Austin Bay and met Archie when he came in with his furs. In April a little girl was born and was christened Agnes Belaney. As soon as the child could travel they returned to Bear Island, living in a tent there throughout the summer.

In the fall of 1911, they were short of money, and Archie tried the unprecedented course of going to work at a mine on White Bear Lake, not far from Bear Island. It was the first and the last manual job he ever took. He stood it for about six weeks, and then, when the fall hunt started, he quit it and went off towards Lake Abitibi 150 miles due north, with a band of Indians, leaving Angele with the child.

One day in the spring of 1912, Archie reappeared in Temagami, walking along the Temiskaming and Northern Ontario railbed. Angele by this time had returned with her child from White Bear Lake, and was camping with a number of Indians on a little island near Bear Island. He tracked her down there, and seemed happy to see her. He told her that he had walked from Toronto: "Walk from there to come to see me. Walked himself. That is what he say anyway. I didn't see him walk. That is just what he told me. I believe him at the time." She spoke of him with pride after his death.

He was worn out and penniless. What had happened to his winter catch? She forbore to ask, and he did not explain. But she welcomed him back as her husband. He stayed three weeks or a month, saying nothing, remaining moody and dejected. Except that he seemed happy to be with her and the child. Occasionally he paddled up the north-east arm of the lake to the little village of Temagami. Sometimes, when he returned from Temagami, she noticed he had got letters from England. But he did not talk about them. She knew that he had come from England, and when they were courting he had sometimes told her about it. But it was impossible for her to imagine what it was like, and he had not talked of it again.

At the Temagami post office one day towards the end of May he was handed a letter from Aunt Ada. It was dated May 7, 1912, and it told him that his grandmother had died the evening before. He was hardly aware of a feeling of grief. Old people had to die, and she was very old. She had been married in the middle of the last century, and she had been a white-haired widow, dressed perpetually in black, ever since he could remember her.

What surprised him in the letter was Ada's sorrow. He was so used to her iron discipline that he could never believe that she had a heart. Every childish grief and sense of deprivation that he could recall had been attributable to her. She had always been sure of herself, and she had always been incapable of allowing anything for the weaknesses of others. He had never thought much about his father. But when Aunt Ada had made slighting references to him, and had hoped piously that Archie would not take after him, he had understood why his father had had to leave a home like that, dominated by this severe, starched-front old spinster.

Yet it was she who now wrote with sympathy and understanding of the long, sad life her mother had had. Her husband had died not many years after their marriage, and she had been left with the responsibility of bringing up three young children. Each of them had somehow failed her when they grew up, the girls by not marrying, and the son by spending all her inheritance, so that she died a relatively poor woman, and Carrie and Ada would now have to live in considerably reduced circumstances.

Ada said that Granny had hoped for so much from Archie. She had given him a home, paid for his education, and sent him out into the world. But Archie had hardly written since he left home the last time, and it had been particularly sad that no word had come to her during the last year of her illness. She had muttered his name quite clearly several times in the coma into which she had drifted two days before her death. Aunt Ada did not say that Archie had also been the name of her husband. That was Aunt Ada all over. She certainly made you feel your full burden of guilt. All the same she was cut up. He thought of those two old women, left now entirely alone, and hard up.

He had taken the letter down to the lake shore to read, and he sat on there, by his canoe, looking out over the water. He must, I suppose, have been recalling Highbury Villa, the way the furniture was set out in the drawing-room, the piano in the corner just by the French doors that led into the garden. The murmur of tea-time conversation, the scent of roses in the vases, white linen on the tea-tray, the tinkle of silver spoons against china. Orderly, neat, precise; narrow, stuffy, confined. All that he had gladly turned his back on for these pine-covered hills, the scent of spruce and the slapping sound of clear water, lapping now against the stern of his beached canoe. Gladly, gladly.

But the cleanliness pulled at his memory a little. And the conversation. It had not been clever, but it had been lively and stimulating. Sometimes it had ended in rows and storms and tears. But he had always been able to argue out with Ada any point which his mind was having difficulty in grasping. She had been stern and cold, but she had been a great teacher, and he wished that he could show her what he was now trying to write, word pictures of this northern country and its primitive people. He tore up everything that he did. None of it was good enough, and he had nobody but himself to tell him so.

Sometimes the lack of mental contact with anyone save the old men chanting their memories drove him almost mad. That was why he had to get away, and now after only a month back, he must leave again.

When he returned to Bear Island he did not tell Angele that his grandmother was dead. But he told her that he had a chance of work as a Fire Ranger in Biscotasing, a place in the Mississauga Forest Reserve about 120 miles to the west. He promised that he would return in the fall, and that meanwhile he would send her money. But he did not return until six years later when he came back wounded from the war, and when he returned he was a changed man.

CHAPTER

6

A RCHIE left no record of his thoughts, but that they
were along the line suggested in the close of the last
chapter is a fair guess. His grandmother had died
on May 6, 1912, and this was about the time of open water
when he left Abitibi and joined Angele at Temagami. He
would have had Ada's letter about a fortnight after his
grandmother's death. It was towards the end of May that he
left Temagami and went to Bisco where he joined the Forest
Service. In June, the various rangers would have been as-
sembling under the Chief Forest Ranger, Charles Duval, to
go out to the Mississauga Forest to take up their posts for
the summer.

I connect Grandmother's death with Archie's decision to
leave Temagami. He had been married to Angele for nearly

two years, but in that interval had spent no more time with her than part of the fall following their marriage, and the summer of 1911. He was continuously leaving; no sooner back than he was off again. Angele's words are there to confirm what we know was a Belaney characteristic, a domestic claustrophobia, a feeling that he must break out or die. "He liked to go travel in the Indian way," said Angele to the Commissioner who was hearing her petition for support from his estate. " 'I will come back again sometime,' he said." And she was content to wait. It was the Indian way.

His aunts knew nothing of his Indian marriage and his child. Aunt Ada thought of him as a Forest Ranger, overseeing the Indians in their reserves, guarding the great forests against fire, the animals against slaughter, exploring unmapped territory in this huge northern wilderness, as vast and mysterious to her as the rain forests of South America. Aunt Ada gathered all this from his letters, and so great was her pride in him that she showed some of them to the Headmaster of the Grammar School. In the autumn 1912 number of *The Hastonian*, reporting the "doings and whereabouts of Old Hastonians", the editor, a trifle inexactly, but following the text of the letters which had been shown to him, affirmed that

> A. S. Belaney has for the past eight years held a position as "forest ranger" in the service of the Hudson Bay Company of Canada. His duties are to keep the streams clear, look out for forest fires, prevent poaching, and to keep the Indians in their own "reserves". A thorough knowledge of the Indian dialect secured him this appointment. His story (which we hope to secure for some future number of the "Hastonian") is as full of sensations as the most highly coloured cowboy drama ever shown in a "film".

And indeed, extracts from A. S. Belaney's diary appearing in *The Hastonian* the following summer term certainly depicted an exciting existence. This was Archie's first appearance in print. One needs to make allowances for the relentlessly humorous style characteristic of school magazines. What is most revealing is the unexpected white man's superior attitude. This was certainly not a true reflection of his feelings. But already he was trying to be a writer, and he did not yet dare to contravene the conventions firmly established by his early romantic reading.

I had intended to come home this fall, but three other fellows persuaded me that the happy hunting grounds had descended and located in the country North of the Abitibi Lake, and it seemed like throwing away good money not to go, so here we are.

We had quite an interesting time with these Abitibi Indians when we first came up here. We crossed Abitibi Lake and then went up the Circle River and allowed we'd locate up there, which we did.

We were all fixed up and our traps out in the best hunting country we could find, when Mr Indian appears on the starboard bow, and remarks that white men are "some" spurious, and that our appearance on the scene is both obnoxious and unnecessary. Fortunately, I can murder the beautiful flowing gutturals and meat-axe noises made by the red brother, and was able to converse with our new-found friend. He was evil-looking, with long yellow teeth set far apart, bow-legs and a long mat of hair. He claimed to be the chief, and of course I translated, and the rest of the fellows endeavoured to look impressed. He had with him about fifteen gentlemen full of whisky and good manners. They carried their nerve right with them, but no soap apparently. They all wore shirts outside their trousers, some had moose-hide leggings, and all had moccasins. Some had Stetson hats, one had a Panama, some had no hats at all. They had a very quick, piercing look in their eyes, and seemed about half civilized. The chief spoke very fast for about half-an-hour. Sometimes when I missed a chapter or two I had to ask him to back up a little and repeat. He stood up, waving his arms and gesticulating wildly, one moment drawing things upon the floor with his fingers, the next stretching up on tip-toe.

When he had finished, I felt I was a lowdown, miserable, no-good white man, who had robbed the poor unsophisticated Ajibway gentleman before me of his hereditary hunting grounds. I wished that the earth would swallow me up, and I shrank beneath the glare of this haughty and magnificent chief.

But unfortunately I am a man of sin and the haughty chief looked about as magnificent as two cents in a collection plate. I invited them to "git", and they got.

That night, overcome with a desire to kill time, one of them tried to pry off our only pane of glass with his knife. Gejik, who was keeping watch behind a brush pile, put a bullet through the glass. At the same time we threw out our own pail of rabbit and partridge soup, scaring the visitors and allowing the soup to scatter hither and thither with reckless abandon on the floor.

Of course that started the circus; our friends began to make barking and yelping noises in which the dogs joined, and we began to wonder if there would be four guides less at Temagami next summer.

We were in no position to make terms, being over 150 miles away from Lake Abitibi in a straight line, and we didn't know exactly how far by canoe. The chief extended a polite invitation to separate ourselves from the vicinity. We didn't see the point at first, so he went out and stole a lot of our traps and sprung others and we saw at once that he'd steal our fur and traps right along and we'd have the worst kind of trouble, so we pulled stakes and went back over the two mile portage. In our hurry (believe me it was necessary) we ran rapids we would not otherwise have run. I got stuck crossways on one rapid and came near upsetting and got some of my stuff wet. Another fellow upset and lost a good deal of stuff, and I tell you it looked tough seeing the poor fellow holding on to his canoe in that rushing ice-cold water. I was at the top making preparations to run, but he was right in the only place that could be run, and if I struck him with my canoe I'd kill him. So I got my canoe over the portage and with the help of another fellow rescued most of his stuff. We lit a big fire, dried him out and camped.

We wanted to get to Abitibi Lake before the river froze, and it was a race. The new ice was making all the time faster than we could go, our canoes were cut and torn by the ice, and we were kneeling in ice-cold water, soaking wet, with a cold freezing wind blowing. After we had broken ice enough to run a cold storage plant we reached Abitibi Lake and found it was frozen for half-a-mile out from the shore.

The ice was not strong enough to walk on but too strong to be broken. I never felt so miserable or as near real despair, as I did then, and the others were the same, for if we couldn't land we stood a good chance of freezing to death. We found a route to the shore where the rushes and reeds had kept the water from freezing very hard, and after twisting and winding about for an hour-and-a-half we eventually reached the shore. We could hardly stand but we said nothing. We cut some wood and built a big fire and thawed out and ate lots. After that we were as merry as ever.

We finished fixing up camp yesterday and started today setting traps. I found one track and tried to walk on the new ice on the creek. I finished up at the bottom of the creek, and finding the water cold, continued observations from the shore. This was more tedious, the bush being very dirty but safer. We saw some mink and fox tracks, lots of rabbits, and large quantities of partridges. Expect to go and see the nearest traps tomorrow, before dinner. We are on nobody's hunting ground here, and it'll be a very big Indian that shifts me.

This is the most silent country on the face of the

globe, silent as death except for the booming of the ice on the big lake.

There were some moments when he yearned for the companionship of his own kind, moments when he was sickened by the mangled bodies, the fur matted with blood, which had to be taken out of traps, when the intense cold or the burning heat and the flies in summer could not be endured, when he longed for the endless struggle to slacken enough to dream.

This thing of hunting and living in the bush generally is not what it is in books [he confides to his brother-Hastonians]. It looks very picturesque and romantic to wear moccasins, run rapids, and shoot deer and moose, but it is not near as interesting as it seems, to be eaten up day and night by black ants, flies and mosquitos, to get soaked up with rain, and burnt up with heat. To draw your own toboggan on snow-shoes, and to sleep out in 60 or 70 degrees below zero.

A man that makes his living in the bush earns it. I am telling you all this because I have heard that the life of hunters, Indian and woodsmen generally, is an indolent life, spent mostly in smoking, gambling, fighting and eating. This is not true at all, and although I won't do any work when I can possibly get out of it, I have failed so far to do so.

The vast area of lonely land between James Bay and Lake Huron is criss-crossed with waterways which thread through rocky outcrops and escarpments that can rise as high as 1800 feet. It is possible to travel across this area from north-east to south-west by canoe for a distance of 650 miles. The Abitibi and the Mattagami flow northward into James Bay, the Spanish River southward into Lake Huron. At Gogama the height of land is reached, where the rivers divide, and a portage of five miles from Dividing Lake to the Spanish River watershed marks the northward from the southward slope of the land. Northwards Canada flattens out eventually into the black swamps and reeking muskeg of the sub-arctic regions on the shores of the great inland sea formed by Hudson Bay and its appendage, James Bay. Southwards it subsides from this flow of rock, washed by swift-running rivers, and dense with stands of pine and spruce, to placid waves of grass and bushland that penetrate down to the ravines which open into the Great Lakes.

In their restless seeking for new hunting grounds, Archie with his Indian companions had covered a good deal of this country. Not only then, but forever, they were on the move. After the war, in the summer of 1919, when he was a Forest Ranger, he and his Indian companion, Alphonse Tessier, travelled 3200 miles of distance by canoe and portage in five months, covering their allotted area six times in the course of the summer. In those early years before the war, he and his companions at different times had worked westward from Lake Temagami, guiding fishermen and hunters down through Manitou Lake to Wanapitei Lake, a distance of 70 miles, and then northward up the Wanapitei River, feeling their way along a maze of waterways which had been traversed two hundred years before in the westering probe for furs. Westwards lay the Spanish River, and the mighty Mississagi, and Biscotasing. Bill Draper, a mining prospector who was developing some properties near Bisco, came upon Archie, whom he had known previously in Temagami, in Bisco that summer of 1911.

Along this watery route Archie might also have run into Charlie Duval, the Chief Forest Ranger for the Mississauga Forest area, and learnt then that if he came back next year there would be employment for him. For there he is, "A. Blaney", recorded on the payroll of the Department of Lands, Forests and Reserves for the year 1912 as a Ranger on the Mississauga Reserve, earning the sum of $225, and listed with him are eighteen other men, the prototypes of the characters who were to appear in the chapter called "Rivermen" in *Tales of an Empty Cabin*. When he introduces them in that book, they are at Bisco in 1920, assembling to go down the Mississagi on the morrow. These were to be his heroes, these

> happy, careless voyageurs, gay caballeros of the
> White Water who whooped and laughed and

shouted their way down or up unmapped rivers,
and thought their day would last for ever . . .

whose threnody he is singing in this marvellous imaginative
recapture of that year of 1912.

How I loved them, with their trousers baggy at the
knees from long hours, and days, and months of
kneeling—no, not in prayer, but in a canoe. . . .
How I loved them for their sharp-barbed, gritty
humour, their unparalleled skill in profanity, their
easy-going generosity.

White man, red-skin and half-breed, they belonged
to that fraternity of freemen of the earth whose
creed it is that all men are born equal, and that it
is up to a man to stay that way. For in this society
the manner of a man's speech, where he comes
from, his religion, or even his name are matters of
small moment and are nobody's business but his
own.

He dwells lovingly on each man's quality and eccentri-
cities. "All the characters are real in this line-up," he writes,
"and well-known to me, though two or three names have
been altered." There is Gus, whose handshake makes strong
men wince; Zepherin, huge, and a kind of human cyclone,
who "has a fog-horn voice, and a smile that would, if
measured, cover about a quarter of an acre." Don't shake
hands with him, Archie advises us, just bow from the waist.
You'll recover quicker. And Baldy, undersized, who is convinced that the world is made for big men, and who, to
prove that he is as good as any of them, carries outsize
loads on every portage. Zepherin says of Baldy that he talks
good English for a small man; and Zepherin laments that
Baldy has never been the same since the mouse kicked him.
Then there is Nikolas, who has the reputation of never
speaking unless he has something to say; and Matogense,
the Indian, who has not yet broken the threads that bind
him to his primeval past, and who is reputed once to have
put out a forest fire by incantation, and whose wife made

90

their eldest daughter swallow a fish, so she could "swim good".

And above all, there is "Charlie Dougal" who was C. A. Duval, the Chief Ranger of the Mississauga Reserve,

> a go-getter and a devil for speed, burning holes in the scenery with fiery invective as he drives his brigade with speed and more speed, for miles and more miles a day. (We like to be driven that way; everybody is out to beat last year's record.) . . . he eats his meals walking up and down, claiming that rest only softened a man and lowered his efficiency, gaining the apt title of Quick-Lunch Dougal.

He is seeing it all with an eye that takes in this unity of man with his natural environment. In these rough, sometimes drunken, often fighting men bound together in companionship, sharing dangers and hardships and high moments of hilarity, he finds his heroes, and at the same time the spring that releases his power as a writer. He was as yet years away from putting them and their background into books. But the attachment had begun which was to govern his whole life hereafter. It was not to the Indians alone, or the wilderness alone, or to the animals alone. But to man and animal and nature as blended parts of the wilderness, to the beaver as little brother of the Indians; to the men, Indian and white, who draw their sustenance from the bountiful breast of nature without injuring it. He himself is proud to be a part of it. Unconscious as yet of what he is doing, he is recording these things in his memory, a slender young man of twenty-four burnt dark brown with six years of exposure to the elements, his long, dark hair held out of his eyes by two strands of trolling wire.

"We thought he was a white man with a streak of Indian in him," says J. W. Cooper who was in that party. "He was a great showman, showing off with all kinds of Indian stunts, and was an adept at throwing knives. He was in his glory when reciting original poetry, and after giving one of these pieces he would say: 'That's by Bill Shakespeare, Tennyson, Browning, etc.,' and laugh. He seemed a remarkable, likeable man who, even in those days, wanted to hide his past. The other men put him down as a McGill man, and the rumour was that he belonged to a prominent Montreal family, but nobody appeared to know. He seemed to have Indian characteristics about some work, but when it came to a canoe trip, he excelled."*

Cooper's partner on this particular patrol in the Mississauga Reserve was Maurice Kingsford, who remembers his first sight of Archie in 1912. Archie had just returned from his winter trapping on the Abitibi which had taken him as far north as Moosonee, situated in the great archipelago formed by the Abitibi and the Moose rivers where they run into James Bay, and young Kingsford, who was talking to Mr. Duval when Archie came up, noticed that his face was as "black as pitch". When Mr. Duval remarked on this, Archie said there were so many mosquitos at Moosonee, where he had just come from, and such a hot sun, that his skin had been burnt "as black as the arse of a tea-kettle". At which, not being used to such vigorously expressed metaphors, young Kingsford had burst out laughing. "Whereupon," he recorded, "Belaney turned his very solemn visage upon me, and I realized that he was evidently a man to be treated with kid gloves."

He was at the height of his vitality and strength, and he gloried in it the way a young male animal does. What he admired in these Rivermen he endeavoured to emulate. In the same spirit he had tried to sink himself in the Indian way of life, and had succeeded well enough so that in outward appearance he seemed now to others to have at least a streak of the Indian in him. From them he had learnt his skills. He was as good a woodsman as any of those in Duval's brigade, and there is plenty of evidence that Indians and white men alike respected his ability as a canoeman. Jimmy Espaniel tells us that. Often, says Jimmy, they made journeys of fifty and sixty miles a day, carrying at least a two-hundred-pound pack, sometimes more, and the canoe on top of that, over portages that might be two or three miles long. This was after the war when his powers of endurance were diminished by his wounded foot and his damaged lung. We were men in those days, says Jimmy

*Letter to the *Globe & Mail*, Toronto, April 25, 1938.

Espaniel, not in self-admiration, but stating a statistical fact which should be borne in mind. "He was a good paddler, a good canoeman, and I used to like paddling with him. He had lots of power. . . . He always was paddling in the stern. Once in a while he'd try the bow but he didn't like it."

Their admiration was mutual, for Archie recorded of Jimmy Espaniel that he had an unconquerable singleness of purpose which took him far in a day. "He'll get there, or be found dead on the way," Grey Owl says firmly.

He had never been happier in his life. The Rivermen became to him what the McCormicks, with their laughter-filled home, had been in far-off, half-forgotten Hastings days. In their company he could relax into humour or soar into poetry without any self-consciousness. The mighty Mississagi River, cutting its way through two hundred miles of forest, exacting tribute from countless small streams, flowered in his imagination as some mighty oriental chieftain whose path of conquest was to be traced through the four thousand square miles of territory through which the river tumbled and flowed, untamed, defiant and relentless, "arrogantly imposing its name on all the surrounding country."

When the fall came, and he was paid off in Bisco, he could not bear to leave all this and return to Temagami. He decided to stay and trap out of Bisco, and he put up to begin with in Mrs. Legace's hotel.

Mrs. Legace (pronounced locally Legacy) was a character, and her clients, all single gentlemen of robust habits and strenuous voice, gave the establishment quite a distinct reputation. Bisco's proper name was, and still is, Biscotasing, but nobody called it that. It had once been an active trading post, and it was still one of the main centres of the fur trade in Northern Ontario. The Canadian Pacific transcontinental railway ran through it, and a sawmill and timber yards had settled in the area as being adjacent to the great forests and to the railway. About half the population of the town was Indian. The men of the town were trappers and fur buyers, logging men, and railroad men, with their assorted wives and children.

In Archie's time these lived in some thirty or so houses which were perched among the rocks above Biscotasing

Bay. The Hudson's Bay post was the centre of the town's life, and the Hudson's Bay factor was the leading citizen and authority: Mr. Woodsworth by name. Except on Sundays, when Mr. Woodsworth adorned rather than dominated the scene. For, in addition to the houses, there were two churches in Bisco, "a short rifle-shot apart", as Grey Owl puts it. Divine service at one or the other, Catholic or Protestant, occurred when one of the divines from up or down the line could spare time from his labours among a score or so of similar little settlements to put in an appearance. Then the occasion became social as well as ecclesiastical, acknowledged sinners coming with the virtuous to share the service and hear the latest news of the Northern Ontario neighbourhood.

As for visitors to town, there weren't many; the aforesaid clergy, itinerant fur buyers, sellers of insurance policies, and the like, put up at Mrs. Legace's. Her establishment, a large square-timbered two-storey house, containing nine bedrooms and painted a slate colour, was really a boarding-house, not an hotel. But as it was the only place in town for a stranger to eat, and as Mrs. Legace took overnight lodgers, as well as permanent ones, it liked to think of itself as something rather grander. The privy was in the yard. In the dining-room two long tables, each seating fourteen diners, sufficed for the general run of the clientele. But a small table for four was always set, ready for superior customers such as visiting clergymen or salesmen, or any well-dressed stranger who happened along. Privacy was something you said goodbye to for the duration of your stay. But the food was good, the company lively, and Mrs. Legace's tolerance broad and deep. Archie was happy there for some weeks while he was collecting stores for the winter trapping.

But he could not keep away from the company of Indians. The contrast between Mrs. Legace's all-white boarding-house and their humble shacks, teetering on the edge of the water, struck him with bitter force, feeding that acerbic strain in him which always nourished itself on such contrasts. He saw as slights and indignities things that were not intended as such; for instance, being unable to take them into Mrs. Legace's and share a drink. The power of words in him, bursting for expression, was like the surge of blood to a man's head in a fit of temper. He had not yet learned how to say what he wanted to say, and the resulting frustration led to purposeless quarrels, and to gestures that were lost on the Bisco crowd. The Indians were at this stage profiting economically from contact with the white man. But Archie saw them as oppressed and kept trying to arouse them to protest.

He began to speak Ojibway, affecting not to understand English, to Harry Woodsworth's annoyance, who knew what a game this was. He spoke of his father's exploits in Mexico and of his Apache mother. Bisco was incredulous, for he spoke much better English than any of them. He still some-times played the piano at Mrs. Legace's, conjuring out of that battered instrument elixirs of sound that made the company still and quiet. You did not learn that in an Indian encampment in Mexico. Nor how to quote Bill Shakespeare, and Tennyson, and the rest.

Mr. Woodsworth liked to think of himself as one of the most respected citizens of Bisco. Your credit at his store, established in a momentary glance from his keen eyes, set your standing in the community. I suppose that Mr. Woodsworth was not consciously aware of his power to make or break a man locally. But he had that power, and he did not take to Archie. Hudson's Bay factors don't get their local chieftainships by accident. They have to have character themselves, as well as ability to keep the local population under control. For in remote places, as Bisco then was, they act not only as fur buyers and retail merchants, but as bankers, moral censors, and social leaders, in the absence of anyone better fitted to take on these jobs.

Mr. Woodsworth did not like white men playing Indian seriously. He did not have the slightest comprehension of what drove Archie to it, and would not have had, even if it had been explained to him by Dr. Freud himself.

Archie trapped out of Bisco for two winters, and worked with the Forestry Department from there in the summer, avoiding Temagami and his family. At first he meant to go back, but the temptation to stay in Bisco was strong. He liked the company of this little town, the trappers, white and Indian, the fur buyers, the young bloods, Indian and white, who skipped from job to job, timbermen one season, guides and packers the next. They formed an admiring audience for his tall tales, of which he was building up a splendid repertoire. He liked their appreciative laughter, their awed silence when he was profane in his original and shocking way; they liked his knife-throwing and expert rifle shooting. He was a born actor, and he needed an audience as a flower needs the sun.

"He never mingled with older people, but always mixed with the younger men who looked upon him as a sort of God," said Mr. Woodsworth, who in time was to come to regard Archie as the scourge of Bisco. "He was always practising with a knife and gun. He became quite an expert in throwing a knife and also an excellent shot with a rifle. He would practise by the hour throwing knives into a log wall at the side of a house, whether it was his own home or not as long as the wall was wood. He was never much at home but spent practically all of his time amongst the Indians both at Bisco and in the woods. All at once he seemed to change and he became more or less of a renegade getting himself into more trouble and mischief than a young boy."

In his second winter season trapping out of Bisco, Archie took into the woods with him as a trapping partner a young Indian girl named Marie Girard. When he came out at open water in the spring of 1914 she was pregnant.

He was in Bisco for only a week or ten days, and then he was off on another job. The Ontario Forestry Department had taken into the Mississauga Reserve an additional four townships on the Goulais River, and Bill Draper was being sent by Charlie Duval into these townships to clear out any prospectors who might be there. Draper was allowed to select his own staff for this journey, and he chose Archie as his assistant. Within a week of that time they were off.

In his younger days Bill Draper had been light-heavyweight boxing champion of the Royal Navy. He had prospected in Africa and smuggled ivory out of the Belgian Congo, before emigrating to Canada at the turn of the century. He was ten or fifteen years older than Archie, and he thought he knew how to manage this obstreperous young man. Between them as the years went on a strong affection grew, and they had some lively parties together when they met. Bill Draper could outdrink Archie, and out-tell his tall tales with even more amazing exploits taken from actual life; while on the trail Bill Draper's back was just as strong, his skill with a paddle just as high, as the professed master of these arts, Archie, who loved to impress his young audience in Bisco.

They were to be away all that summer of 1914 in very remote country where they would have to cut their own portages and blaze their own trails, and they might easily go for weeks at a time without seeing another soul. Such toil and such isolation shared by two men is a test of character.

They went down the Mississagi River and then up the Aubinadong River to its headwaters, and here they had the luck to locate an old Indian trail that led across to the headwaters of the Goulais River. They were working down the Goulais River on September 12 when they met coming up it two timber cutters who hailed them and told them that Canada, along with the whole British Empire, was at war with Germany and Austria.

For an ex-Navy man this news was what the sound of a bugle is to a war-horse. Dropping all thoughts of any remaining prospectors who might still need to be cleared, Bill Draper ordered about-ship. From a lumber-camp near by they managed to buy a two weeks' supply of grub, and they then paddled hard for Bisco. The return journey took two weeks; they arrived back in the town on the last day of September 1914.

Archie proceeded to celebrate their return and the outbreak of war by some rifle-shooting exploits and knife-throwing at human targets that put some of the older citizens in fear of their lives. Nagging at him was the worry about Marie Girard. She knew that he was married, but he could be forced to support the child. Archie seemed to have had not the slightest feeling for the girl herself. But other people did have. They all knew that Marie Girard had been with him in the woods all the past winter, helping him to trap. A certain bias against Archie began to build up, and this only seemed to make his behaviour more outrageous. There were one or two arguments, and Archie pulled his knife and threatened, and that gave Mr. Woodsworth his opportunity. He wired Inspector Jordan at Chapleau to come down and arrest this troublesome fellow. Warned of this, Archie told his loyal following that he would never be taken alive. There was only one way to come from Chapleau just up the line, and that was by train or speeder, a small platform mounted on railway wheels propelled by an internal combustion engine. He had time for a final gesture. With his rifle slung on his shoulder and his pack on his back he marched up the hill past all the houses which lined the little street, past Mr. Woodsworth's office, up to where the two churches stood a hundred yards or so apart. There he unslung his rifle and took a shot at each belfry in turn, making each bell ping. Then, shouldering his pack and slinging his rifle once again, he gave the call of the hoot-owl, repeated it thrice, and disappeared into the bush.

When Inspector Jordan arrived, no trace of him could be found, though they beat the neighbourhood pretty thoroughly. Mr. Woodsworth decided to keep the warrant which Inspector Jordan had brought down with him. He put it in his safe for another day which he was sure would be coming.

And then the fall colours blazed, and after the wind had taken the leaves the snow came and shut off the little town from the outside world, except for a few minutes each day when the transcontinental roared through it, setting off a rattling echo as the train ran between the rocks and leaving the ensuing silence deeper than before. From Archie Belaney came no word. He had disappeared as if into thin air.

In the winter of 1914–15, Marie Girard bore a son. Soon after the birth she developed consumption, and in a few weeks' time was dead. The little boy was taken over by Mrs. Alec Langevin and raised with her own children, until he was old enough to be sent to the Indian School at Chapleau. Of the father, no word was heard until June of 1915, when Private Belaney wrote to his friend Bill Draper, from Digby, Nova Scotia, where he reported himself to be waiting with his unit for a transport to go overseas. To Bill, his "father confessor", he sent some money from his army pay, asking him to pass it on to Marie Girard.

CHAPTER 7

IGBY, NOVA SCOTIA, was more than a thousand miles away from Bisco. Why had he gone so far? The warrant he was evading was not for such a serious crime, and he could have escaped it just as well by crossing over the Quebec border one hundred miles away. And if he wanted to evade arrest by joining the army, he could have done that anywhere in Ontario, seventy-five miles away in Sudbury, for instance. But nothing is too fanciful in dealing with Archie.

Thomas Raddall believes that he spent the winter shacked up with the Micmac Indians on the Bear River which enters the Bay of Fundy near Digby, and that at the end of the winter he joined the army at the nearest recruiting post, which was Digby. Raddall believes that Archie had known that village in his first few months wandering in Nova Scotia when he came to Canada in 1906, and that, escaping from Bisco, he had made his way there by rail, canoe, and foot, looking for the protection that this spot alone could give him.* Someone down in this part of the world evidently stood in a special relationship to him, and drew him like a magnet, for when he did join at Digby he gave as his next-of-kin a name which could be either John McVail or George McNeil, giving as an address one near Saint John, just across the Bay of Fundy from Digby. Had George Belaney not after all died in Mexico, as had been reported? Did he live on here in Saint John under a different name? When Grey Owl said that his father was a Scotsman named George MacNeill, had he all the time been telling the truth? Was he living with the Micmac Indians, and had Archie spent the winter lying low with him here, just where he had possibly spent the first few months of the summer of 1906 when he had landed in Canada?

These are tempting theories, but there is no firm evidence for them. Archie Belaney was a mysterious man, as his father had been before him. No one reported seeing him during this period. Yet his appearance was unmistakable, and he had done nothing to disguise it, for when he enlisted on May 6, 1915, he was the same tall, long-haired, dark-skinned, hawk-faced handsome man who had stood on the hillside that evening at Bisco eight months before, hooting defiance at authorities in the little town which had tried to constrain him.

He was not likely to be happy in the army, where authority orders one's life day and night. Within twenty-four hours, his long hair had been shaved off, and he had been put into army boots. With the other recruits, he was given hours of foot drill to sharp, reiterated commands. His comrades thought he was part Indian. He said nothing about himself. Watching him throwing his knife at a target whenever they were at rest, and shooting with his revolver at tins thrown into the air, they thought he was a bit wild, and treated him with respect.

A month after he joined the army he was shipped in a draft to England, and two months later was transferred to

*Footsteps on Old Floors, pp. 106–7.

the 13th Montreal Battalion, now known as the Black Watch, and sent to the trenches.

I can well believe that Archie Belaney was an unreliable and irregular soldier. Everything in his character and temperament must have revolted against what he now had to submit to: the trenches running with water, the mud, the discipline, the confinement. He was not a coward, nor was he flamboyantly brave, but when he could act in defiance of authority, he showed the reckless courage that was typical of him. Once, near Messines, an abandoned and heavily shelled farmhouse stood in no-man's land between the lines. To be seen moving in that devastated landscape brought instant death. But Archie crawled out, made his way to the shelled farmhouse, and came back with a sack of vegetables and a bottle of wine. No one on either side had spotted him during the hour and a half he had been away.

Noting such exploits, his platoon commander thought that, given the right conditions, he could make a very valuable soldier. He noticed his strange reticence, and the fact that he held himself aloof from his comrades, and he noticed the passion he had for field-craft. Even in the midst of this devastation, when it was dangerous to appear silhouetted against the sky, or to pause in passage from one place to another, Belaney would ignore commands to keep moving and watch an animal or a bird, or would trace in the ruined ground the passage of a scurrying field-mouse. Lieutenant MacFarlane told Thomas Raddall* that Belaney had infinite patience and the gift of absolute immobility for long periods, and as he was a good shot with a rifle, MacFarlane made him a sniper-observer.

This gave Archie what he preferred, isolation from the others, for snipers were nearly always stationed in the communication trenches so that, if spotted, the resulting fire would be away from their own troops. It also absolved him from the direct and constant supervision of an officer or a sergeant. There, in the Messines area, he watched the slow advance of a watery Flanders spring over the flat, sodden landscape. For everybody it was hell, but for a man of Archie's temperament it was nearly intolerable.

In January 1916 he sustained a bullet wound in the wrist,

*Footsteps on Old Floors, p. 111.

but this was treated in a field hospital where he was kept for a week and then sent back into action. On April 24 that same year, he was struck by a bullet which damaged the bones at the base of the toes of his right foot. He was sent back to England where an operation was performed to amputate the fourth toe of the right foot to save the foot from being permanently maimed.

He must have been happy to be finished with the war, at least temporarily, but everybody who saw him at this time records how unhappy he looked. His wound had been reported in *The Hastonian*, and as he was at the Canadian Convalescent Hospital at Bromley, not too far away, there were a number of visitors from Hastings.

Amongst those who came was Connie Holmes, whose mother was a friend of Aunt Ada. In the ten years he had been away she had changed into an attractive young woman and was attending a drama school in London. She too found him altogether changed from the schoolboy she had known. "He had all the glamour of a wounded soldier then. Lines of pain had given character to his dark handsome face. . . . We fell violently in love."*

For over a year, Archie was moved from hospital to hospital in England, and in due course, when he was moved to a hospital in Hastings, they were married at the beautiful Church in the Wood at Hollington, on the edge of Hastings.

I don't quite know how this marriage was engineered. But I suspect that Ada and her friend Mrs. Holmes helped to bring it about. Perhaps Archie was moaning about never being able to tramp the woods again, and Ada hoped that the romantic dream of Canada might be over and that on discharge he would settle down in England, and once again there would be a Belaney man in the house.

It was a foolish risk for him to have taken. He must have known that his marriage to Angele stood in law, and that he was now committing bigamy. And right under Aunt Ada's nose! On the other hand he had not seen Angele for four years and had heard nothing from her in that time. She would have been able to find out from the Indian Agent that he had joined the army, and the Agent would have been able

The London Daily Express, April 21, 1938.

102

to advise her that she was legally entitled to his separation pay allowances for herself and Agnes. She had made no such claims. Perhaps he thought that by now she had forgotten him and taken up with some other man. Perhaps he really believed what he once or twice later was reported to have said, that the man who had performed that ceremony had not been an ordained minister but a student for the ministry, as yet unlicensed for the work. He had told his aunts nothing about this marriage, curiously repeating in this his father's action with his first marriage. He was always a secretive man, and so Connie found him to be once the marriage had taken place.

"Then I began to find him strange, secretive—almost sinister. He wore his black hair as long as army regulations would allow, and was teaching himself to speak Red Indian dialects; he practised them frequently on me."

The marriage was not a success. Nor were the further operations on his foot. At the end of the summer he was examined by a medical board, and three doctors signed a form on which his injury was said to be incurable and his foot permanently deformed. It was decided to return him to Canada for further therapy and eventual discharge. He was given a 20 per cent disability pension, and on September 19, 1917, he sailed from Liverpool to Canada.

He went alone. Connie Belaney did not relish the prospect of life in a cabin in the bush with this sinister man. She must have felt only relief at the prospect of parting with him. Two-thirds of his army pay was assigned to her as his wife, and it was only when this stopped with his discharge in Toronto on November 30, 1917, that the question of divorce came up.

The passage back to Canada was slow and uneasy. I remember it, for by chance I was travelling in the same convoy. We seemed to slide sideways to Canada, plunging into crevasses and climbing cliffs on the mountainous seas. There were perhaps a dozen ships in the convoy. The ships were roughly arranged in several quadrilaterals, extending over several miles of tossing ocean, and two destroyers whipped in and out of the pack every hour of the day like collie dogs herding in straying sheep. After darkness, the little ships slipped apart, for safety in navigation, drawing

103

in again towards each other as the murky dawn coloured the dark ocean with light spilled from the sky. All night, although not a light was showing, the reverberation of so many propellers must have echoed in the watery caverns of the ocean, where the submarines lurked.

It was September 1917. The submarine attacks were at their height, and once during the passage, as morning dawned, word spread among the passengers that one of our ships had gone down during the night.

To Archie, impatiently awaiting the sight of the Canadian land mass, each day was torture. For most of the voyage the sea was rough, and his foot was too painful to deal with the rolling deck. There was nowhere to sit in the open well between the decks except on top of the hatches. He knew none of the men he was with. They were nearly all wounded men, wearing hospital blues, and they came from all parts of Canada.

He was in a black mood and did not want contact with anyone. The parting with his aunts in Hastings and his wife in Bayswater must have left him in a sardonic state of mind. What he hated was to be constrained. Domestic ties were like shackles round the ankles of a prisoner. No doubt he contrasted Angele's acceptance of his departure with Ada's and Connie's tearful farewells. He knew that he was a disappointment to his aunts, and that his wife not only did not love him but was frightened of him. None of his own dreams looked like coming true. He wanted to be a writer but nothing that he wrote came alive. If it was funny, as it often was, for he had an inborn gift for telling an anecdote, it seemed inane and imitative. If it was serious he got bogged down with the argument. The terrible barrier that a writer has to break through if he is to give a sense of reality to what he writes and hold the reader's interest bruised him as time after time he hurled himself against it. He thought with the unquenchable hope of the genuine writer that when he got back to the woods again, he would be able to write. He forgot that he was carrying with him into that longed-for place the burdens of mind and conscience, the weaknesses of flesh and resolution, and the strains on his temperament that made him on the *Llandovery Castle*, pitching its way westward towards Canada, such a difficult fellow. Partly to ex-

104

cuse himself to his comrades for his unfriendly attitude, he emphasized the Indian traits in his character; the actor making up his face for the part he was to play, his mind already assuming the disguise.

As the ship neared Belle Isle, and the great Canadian hills loomed dimly out of the morning mist, the men all crowded the rails. They were in the Gulf of St. Lawrence, and as though these waters were out of the war zone, the sea, no less rough than it had been, had a quieter sound as the waves washed against the ship. Large sea-birds manifested themselves, and the unforgettable scent of land wafted the pungent smell of brine away to where it belonged, out there in the surging wastes.

When the sun banished the sea mists it revealed a sky as blue as only a northern sky can be in September. The long arm of the land slowly extended and began to encircle the ship. As the ship and the shore came to meet each other the crimson and gold of the trees covering the whole land like a tapestry reminded him of the northern woods. It was just at this time of the year, before the freeze-up, that the trapping parties would be setting out for their grounds. It was a time when a man was happiest, leaving his domestic ties behind, loaded up with supplies to see him through the winter, moving all day along the rivers between banks and over portages to a cabin where he was king. He could hardly wait to get there.

But although he soon got his discharge in Toronto, the Pensions Board insisted on therapy, and he knew that he could not tackle the woods on his own with his foot in this state. He was kept in Toronto most of the winter, attending hospital as an outpatient, but he was allowed leaves, and when the first one came at the end of October, he was torn between a desire to go to Bisco and see his old friends, or to Temagami and see Angele. He decided to do both by stopping off at Lindsay and getting Angele to meet him there. He said to himself that this was so that he could give her some money and some clothes for herself and Agnes. But he must have been afraid that she might find out about his English marriage. How to explain to anyone, much less to someone as simple and true as Angele, what had driven him to it. It was possible to be drawn at the same time by two contrasting emotions, a nostalgia for English life, the stronger for its contrast with Flanders, and the genuine attraction native society had for him. But the quality of the rapture had been sure enough. He was to return to it again and again. He wrote now to the Chief Fire Ranger at Temagami, asking him to tell Angele that he was going to Bisco to see Lloyd Acheson, the Chief Ranger there, and asking her to meet him in Lindsay.

However it was contrived, the meeting lasted four days, and it lit again in Angele's mind her inexpungeable love for this unsatisfactory husband. Years afterwards she recalled it with feeling. In her halting Ojibway tongue, translated by the Court reporter, she recalled:

> He said 'I come from the war,' and his foot here is sick when I seen him. I sleep with him that night. I think four days he stay, I don't know really. I can't say. Happy. I just think I got married that day. Feel that way anyway. I love that man and I love him still.*

She did not see him again for eight years, and with the fortitude of her race, she put up with it. She knew that he was having trouble with some woman in England. In her Ojibway and broken English, she explained that he did not want to stay with her. "He was afraid of another person. He did not like to stay with me again, stay at home."

"Why didn't he want to stay with you?" asked the Special Examiner at North Bay.

"Why?" Angele replied. "Because he is supposed to have got a wife over there."

"Do you know when he got the wife over there?" persisted the Special Examiner.

Angele: "I cannot say. He got trouble from England woman. That is all I can say."

"Well, he go to the Front, that is all," she says at another point. "He different man when he come back. He want to

*Examination for Discovery of Mrs. Angle [sic] Belaney before Mr. A. B. Girard, Special Examiner and Counsel, at the Court House, North Bay, Ontario, June 12, 1939. This was preliminary to the trial in the King's Bench Division "In Re Belaney ('Grey Owl') Estate, Belaney v. Yvonne Perrier and Shirley Dawn" on November 25, 1939.

travel all the time." She had noticed that in him before he went to the war, when he was still living with her in Temagami. "He liked to go and travel in the Indian way," she explained proudly.

During the four days they were together in Lindsay another child was conceived. Robert Bernard Belaney, or Benny as he came to be called, was born on July 11, 1918. This visit to Lindsay must have been before his discharge if the child was his. Pressed to give the date when this meeting took place, Angele says, "Well, the leaves were like this [the hearing was on October 6, 1939], just Fall. Just fish spawning. Late in the Fall. Late, late in the Fall. I see spawning fish all the time. I wish I could speak English good."

But he was anxious to go to Bisco again. "He wanted so bad to go. I said if you want to go there, well. He went away. He took the train."

He gave her money for Agnes's support, a fur coat for herself, and warm clothes for both herself and Agnes. But he went. Bisco was not to be resisted.

CHAPTER

8

A RCHIE's longing to get back to Biscotasing was intense, but he must have felt an undercurrent of trepidation as to how he would be received. He had left there in 1914 only one jump ahead of Inspector Jordan. He knew that he would be counted responsible for Marie Girard's sad end. Everyone knew that he was the father of her child. He had sent a little money through Bill Draper, but he had not written to her himself, nor done anything about the child. Alec Langevin and his wife had taken the little boy and had brought him up with their family. He would be nearly three now, and Archie would surely be expected to acknowledge him as his son and pay for his upbringing.

It would have been easy to dodge these troublesome reminders of the past by settling somewhere else. But that was out of the question. There was only one Bisco, and one group of familiar faces. These spelt home to him. The citizens might curse and revile him, and try to run him out of town, but their faces would never close up into those narrow, pale, unfeeling masks he had renewed acquaintance with in this last year on the streets of Hastings.

In his imagination the little town, set between its two rocky points, was perpetually bathed in sunshine. Everyone knew everybody else; they even knew the identity of strangers, where they came from and when they were leaving. There was only one street to be remembered. It wasn't a street but a track, and it wound up from the lake to behind the depot. On it stood the Hudson's Bay store, presided over by the magisterial Harry Woodsworth. A little farther up the street was the combined pool hall and confectionery store run by the genial Bill Orange, who was "Father Confessor" to anybody in trouble, advancing loans and dispensing, instead of moral advice, practical suggestions on how to handle fixes that now and then wound themselves around anyone who liked a bit of fun but forgot to weigh the consequences.

He saw them all in his mind's eye: Ed and Mrs. Sawyer, "long-time residents" as the Chapleau paper always referred to them in its news from Biscotasing. And Mrs. Legace and her boarding-house collection of eccentrics, trappers, and prospectors in from the woods to get fresh supplies, or anxious for a social break after too much solitude in the woods.

He knew them, he knew them all! From the Reverend who came down by train from some other railroad stop in his extensive parish and put up at Mrs. Legace's, enduring the particular hell of Saturday night in a small town's meeting-place before donning his surplice and greeting his parishioners at the church door next morning, to the lumbermen who were making good wages in the forests around Bisco, and the Indians and Métis who lived by fishing and trapping. From the leading ladies of the town, who took themselves very seriously, to the Indian and white girls who took nothing seriously, and kept the town on its toes. The little town rocked, it vibrated with life.

109

It was not like a small town in Southern Ontario separated only by hydro poles and featureless country from a similar settlement ten miles away. Bisco was isolated, hemmed in by the forest, barricaded by its rock and its rushing rivers against the defiling touch of man. He longed to get back there, as he had longed years before to get to Canada and live amongst the Indians. He wanted to fill his scarred lungs with the cold, fresh, balsam-scented northern air, and he wanted to feel paths softened with decayed pine needles beneath his injured foot instead of the granite-hard pavement beneath those hateful army boots. He felt so weak that he did not know if he would ever be able to follow a trap-line again. He had not knelt in a canoe for over two years, or lifted one over his head at a portage. He had to make the attempt again, but it could only be made in familiar waters and along trails he had known for years.

He was running away from furies he had aroused, from a wife left in England, from Angele still in Temagami and probably now pregnant once again, from his aunts who would soon learn of his Indian marriage when the divorce came up, from the memory of grey, rain-swept muddy fields, smashed buildings and equipment, and the stink of death. From all these things Bisco was a haven, and the disapproval that might be expressed by its citizens was something that he knew he could eventually dissolve by the exercise of a little charm. It had worked before; it would do so again. After all, the population when he left had numbered only eighty-odd. It was a small, it was a beautiful world, and he would live there on any terms.

He had not reckoned with the changes that three years of war-time conditions would bring even to little Bisco. It had been a lumber-town as well as a headquarters for trappers and the fur trade, and the headquarters for a railway gang. To the collection of buildings had been added in his absence a section house and a building to house the railway gang, while the lumbering company had put up an additional store for its employees. The number of trappers had thinned, for most of them, being young, were away at the war. But the population must have jumped from about eighty to well over two hundred and fifty. There was still only one street, but now it was occupied, not to say desecrated, by strangers leaning up against buildings as though they belonged there, and committing the unspeakable offence of wondering where the hell you'd come from.

Archie was not long in being identified, and he saw them eyeing him with curiosity as local inhabitants filled them in with his past exploits. He reacted to their stares in his characteristic way, dramatizing himself as the tough hombre, born in Mexico of mixed parentage, quick with the knife, a dangerous man.

As Bill Draper said, "He always wanted people to think of him as being ignorant and without education." This wasn't humility, it was inverted pride. The wild streak in him, said Bill Draper, was not inherited but got from a queer piece in him that said, Be a wild man, be an Indian. Disguise the fact that you have had a good education and can read music. Pretend that you are playing by ear. If it is difficult to disguise that you are soft-spoken, lard your language with obscenities, and announce that you believe in neither God, devil, nor man.

This was not at all the right attitude for the penitent, and what may have impressed the young strangers in town left Harry Woodsworth, the Hudson's Bay factor, cold. Archie paid an early call on Mr. Woodsworth to express his regret for all that lay in the past, and his intention to lead an honest and upright life from then on. Mr. Woodsworth took from his safe the warrant for Archie's arrest which had been there since his exploits in September 1914. But he did not serve it. It lay on the desk, a warning signal, while Mr. Woodsworth read him off a lecture which Archie received with bowed head, the very picture of remorse, except for a gleam in the eye which must have been there, for he was soon up to his old tricks again.

These were to be trying years for him. He was not really the local bad man who mindlessly got drunk and got himself and others into trouble. He was a man clutching a romantic dream which he refused to give up, while he shivered with the gusts of cold reality blowing against him. Mr. Woodsworth and others thought that he preferred the company of Indians because he had no backbone to compete with his own kind. The Hudson's Bay factor was to complain when Archie started trapping again that he was a poor trapper, that such fur as he got was often unprime, and acquired only because he had a good trapping partner. Woodsworth had no conception of the self-disgust with which, after all these years, Archie still lifted the mangled bodies from his traps and then skinned them ferociously and quickly because the action went against something instinctive in him which could not and never would be suppressed.

He began civilian life again by joining the Fire Service. Lloyd Acheson, the Chief Fire Ranger at Chapleau, took him on, and appointed him his Deputy on the lower Mississagi River. The job gave him a chance to travel the old trails again, and to test his endurance as a canoe-man. Travelling by himself on his patrols, he found himself stiff and awkward and out of condition to start with, but within a few weeks he had become again the first-class canoe-man he had been before the war. It was May and the weather was at its best, the country seductive and beautiful and teeming with life. Once again, after a long separation, he felt the physical thrill as it drew him into its lonely beauty.

But the loneliness was broken every now and then by the obscene clatter of technology, cannibalizing the forest. Just before the war the federal government had set up a Commission for the Conservation of Natural Resources, the aim of which was to bring together federal and provincial ministers whose departments controlled these natural resources, and representatives of those industrial firms which were coming in to the North. The purpose of the Commission was to ensure that the resources were not too rapidly depleted or unprofitably farmed. The forests were but one out of the ten or so resources which engaged the attention of special sub-committees. Decades ahead of its time, this Commission nevertheless did marvellous work for the few years that it was in existence, until the outbreak of the war put a stop to it.

What Archie saw as he journeyed through the country to the west of Bisco on his return were the scars, deep, imbedded, permanent, which now marked the face of the wilderness. The scene is graphically described in the opening chapter of *Pilgrims of the Wild*.

112

What had been a Garden of Eden when he first came to Bisco in 1912 looked, only six years later, as though a drunken party had taken place. He saw that this was entirely due to the entrance of the white man and his technology into the domain of the Indians who had taken from the land only what they had need of to sustain life. With the Commission out of action for several years, forestry was conducted wherever access to the railway was possible, with the result that the debris from the sawmills and the log booms polluted the rivers. Not only that but the brush fires the loggers started sometimes got out of control and were hastily abandoned by those who had started them. Prospectors, ranging freely over the land, frequently started small fires to expose the rocks or make them more accessible. When he and Bill Draper had travelled through this country in the summer of 1914, they had had to blaze their own trails and cut out their own portages. They had travelled then for days, sometimes weeks, without meeting a living soul. Now, barely five years later, he met men every day. It was said that the population of the area had doubled since before the war. Nearly all the newcomers were engaged in the timber trade. Part of his job, if they were cutting timber, was to make sure that they had valid licences. He felt like a policeman on a beat asking for identity papers, plainly showing that he did not approve of what they were doing before ascertaining whether they were doing it legitimately or not. They took quick offence at his attitude. Tempers flared. There were one or two dangerous brushes when guns were drawn and Archie pulled his knife.

But the moments passed, and he went on, a tragic actor on a desolate scene; an old frontiersman now, making a last stand against the onrush of what they called civilization. He could not object to others sharing the beauty and the bounty of nature that the wilderness offered. But not to tear the heart out of it, mock its silence with their explosions, burn its woods, slaughter the animals, poison the fish, and seduce the Indians from their ancient ways, their traditional dress, and their bark dwellings, leaving them to wander around like third-rate citizens in cheap, shapeless store suits.

Everything tried his temper. His wounded foot slowed him down on the portages, and as he carried loads up in-

113

clines his breath laboured through lungs damaged by the whiffs of mustard gas he had had in France. He had lost a lot of weight and was now as thin as a rail. There was still plenty of fish in the clear streams; here and there he saw beaver houses, heard the slap of their tails as they dived at his approach. They seemed more fearful than they had been. He called to them, "Mah-wee, Mah-wee," but silence followed his calls, which, like everything else, did not seem as good as they had been. He felt the dampness on the ground at night, something he had been quite unaware of five years before. He brooded by himself, and when he came back to Bisco for fresh supplies he was edgy and quarrelsome.

He took to buying a bottle of whiskey blanc from the local bootlegger, who had his own still and sold his product at fifty cents a bottle. It was fiery stuff, but it was good for lifting the clouds of depression for a little while. But when the clouds returned they came back even blacker and more menacing. Then a flaming row would happen, someone in authority would say he was going down to the depot to get Joe Bolton, the agent and telegraphist, to wire to Chapleau to send down the police; and Archie would get out of town, calling from the water as his canoe pulled away with the thrusts of his paddle the derisive, the defiant hoot of the owl. And Bisco would breathe freely again, noting gratefully that increasing distance between him and them was diminishing the resonance of the calls. He acted tough and they began to believe what he had told them about his Indian birth in Mexico, and how his father had been shot there in a gun-battle, and that he had made his way back to avenge him. Tall tales had always been part of the backwoods entertainment. But a tall tale would be nothing if it was not given half-credence, even while it was scoffed at. He frequently, to the great discomfort of the senior citizens in the community, gave demonstrations of his prowess with a revolver or his knife; anyone as good as that might have shot up a whole town. Even in this exotic if small society he began to be regarded as someone out of the ordinary; and like an actor who has had a thin scattering of applause he threw himself resolutely into the part he was creating.

It was probably during the summer of 1921, when he was fire-ranging on the lower Mississagi, that a lawyer from

Sudbury came to Bisco, representing Connie Belaney, who demanded a divorce on the grounds that he had abandoned her in 1917 and had not supported her since. She did not pursue the claim that he had been already married when he went through a marriage ceremony with her. The desertion issue was quite clear.

The lawyer, J. J. O'Connor of Sudbury, took the train to Bisco. He probably expected some trouble from Belaney, of whom Mrs. Belaney may have given him a very lurid description. The guide who escorted him to the ranger's cabin, a few miles west of Bisco, may also have supplemented this account.

But on the evening of their arrival, Archie was playing another part, that of the reasonable man whose calm meditations are disturbed by the fussy demands of an egoist. The surprised Mr. O'Connor related: "At that time Belaney was deputy fire-ranger, and the most blasphemous kick-in-the-pants go-to-hell individual I ever came across. He took notice of the papers in his study, and was so undisturbed that he had me as his supper guest in the ranger's cabin." Where, no doubt, he turned the conversation to serious topics such as how valid was the assumption, so calmly taken for granted by the white race, that their culture was necessarily "higher" than an aboriginal one. If so, his irony would have been so light that the lawyer would not have been sure whether it was all a joke or meant seriously.

But this was only an evening's mood. He was more often quarrelsome than blithe. He had this wonderful sense of humour which made listeners roll on the ground or slap their thighs and roar with laughter when he chose to exercise it. At other times he would be moody and dangerous. Sometimes he mixed the two moods, and then he could be outrageously funny and at the same time very obstructive.

They had little to amuse them other than what their own invention provided, and it was the custom in Bisco to wait, as though for a "revelation", for something to happen to liven up the evening.

Ted Cusson, who trapped with Archie the following year, when asked how an evening in Bisco might be spent, recollected the successive simplicities from which a riotous evening could be brewed.

Well, we would meet the train, then wander over to the store, have a little chat with one another there. Then someone would invite you over to where there was a barrel of moonshine. This sort of made it a little parleyvous round there. And sometimes we would decide to go and look at the fishnets, or if it was early in the spring, go and look at some of the traps. Then someone would suggest that we do a little bit of hell-raising or something. . . .

The something was usually a practical joke, like cutting a corner post under the dance-hall so that the people would come running out thinking an earthquake had happened.

Or Bill Draper would decide that he would tap a gallon jug of whiskey blanc that he had put by for a rainy day in Ernie Pellerin's tool chest as there were no private places if you lodged where Bill did, at Mrs. Legace's. I imagine everybody was in a pretty advanced state of inebriety when Bill recalled the gallon lying at Ernie's and asked Archie to go and fetch it for him. It was a hot, breathless evening in high summer, so Bill, to get a laugh, called out as he left the room: "Better put on your snowshoes," and an even bigger laugh still when he added, "And take your axe in case Ernie's out and he has locked his front door."

So Archie set off, but went first along the passage to his own room to get his snowshoes. These he gravely put on, and the next thing the convivial party in Bill's room heard was a thunderous crash as Archie glissaded down the stairs, and Mrs. Legace's screams as she came out of her room and saw him land, waving his axe. The party in Draper's room lay low. Either Archie would get the gallon or Ernie would be out, and that was that. They only hoped, if he did get it, he would not drop it on the way back. "Crazy Indian," said Draper, and they all laughed. You never knew with that guy. Half an hour later there was a tremendous racket, as Archie returned with the gallon jar intact and, still wearing his snowshoes, mounted the outside steps and made his way into the hall and up the stairs.

"You got it, then?" they cried, and the bung was drawn and the party was proceeded with.

But the next morning Bill Draper was aroused early by an

indignant Ernie Pellerin. Ernie had got back late the night before to find his front door shattered and his tool box cut to splinters. Neighbours had told him that the damage had been done by Belaney, who had appeared on snowshoes and, getting no answer, Ernie being away fishing, had cut down the door with his axe and broken open the tool box to get at the jug of whiskey. Archie had explained to shocked neighbours that the whiskey belonged to Bill Draper, who had ordered him to come and fetch it and to take his axe in case Ernie was out.

Draper promised Ernie that Belaney would make restitution, and he lost no time in going over to Archie's place and getting him up out of bed. Draper's language was anything but restrained, and Archie maddened him by playing the part of a reasonable man who had been intent only on doing what his friend had asked him to do. "Did I get it?" he asked anxiously, as though an inadequately performed task was what Bill was beefing about. "That's good! Then, let's have a drink."

But the humour of the situation was now lost on Draper. He used strong-arm methods, "waltzed" Archie over to Ernie's house, made him survey the damage he had wrought, asked Ernie what it would cost to repair it, and insisted on Archie there and then producing the forty dollars, which was the sum Ernie named.

Legends of his wild actions still circulate in the neighbourhood. One wonders if they haven't been a little added to because of his subsequent fame. The stories that persist are all connected with his nerve—he feared neither God nor man, and his demonstrations of stout atheism greatly impressed this little community of simple folk as being vastly daring. God had such powers of retaliation that it was well to stay on the right side of Him. But Belaney treated Him so off-handedly, with such awful familiarity, that even being in Belaney's neighbourhood when he was in this mood was felt to be dangerous.

And yet they could not help laughing admiringly, for he was a smart fellow, and often seemed to get the better of his Great Opponent. Tipped out of his canoe in Hogs Trough Rapids on the Mississagi because one of the canoemen had got his paddle caught under a rock, Belaney lost no time when he staggered ashore in portaging his canoe all the way back to the head of the rapids. Then he shook his fist at the heavens and yelled, "Now, damn you, see if you can tip me again!" before kneeling in the canoe and pushing off. He came flying down through the leaping waters to where the rest of the brigade waited below.

At another time, in the Five Swells rapids on the same river, he had on board a divinity student, who thought it expedient to bend his head and say a prayer as he surveyed the dangerous course the canoe was to take. When he had said his Amen, he looked up and saw Belaney glaring at him. "Do not pray to your Lord as I am your Jesus while you are in my canoe," said Archie.

He would have known that stories of these exploits would spread everywhere, thrilling some hearers, outraging others. The born actor would have been unhappy without his audience. But these were not just flamboyant gestures; they expressed anger and frustration at the way everything was going to hell with this fine country and nobody was doing anything about it. It was the familiar rage of the romantic at the steady, obliterating, purposeful advance of the "realists", who were taking over the earth and putting it on a business basis. Everything had to be made to pay—the forests burned and cut, the rocks blasted, the animals slaughtered, the Indians employed on jobs, the land enslaved—in order that civilization might triumph.

He stood out a David against this Goliath, defying it in every way he could. God was on the side of these people, therefore God must be defied, and the defiance must be seen and heard in order that others might be emboldened to act likewise. Much of the reputation he got for being a wild man, a totally disruptive and unreliable fellow, came from these gestures, which hardened into myth, when they had grown and swelled by constant repetition.

If Archie had been a weak, vain character he would soon have become an out-and-out drunk—there were plenty of them in the North—and descended step by step into apathy and sloth. But he had this vision of a perfect world which was being fatally blemished by people in authority. He did not know the cure for it—yet. But he was against Authority. He struck out blindly. Even the King on one occasion earned his abuse.

Bill Draper tells the story of going to church one Sunday morning with Billy Miller, a clerk in the Hudson's Bay store, and his wife when they met Archie, wearing his old soldier's coat, hands thrust deep into his pockets, looking for something to liven up the day. When he learnt where they were going, the familiar gleam must have come into his eyes. He asked if he might accompany them. What Christians, themselves all washed and dressed up for the occasion, could have refused their poor brother his humble plea? The church was packed, and the minister was in great form. After a particularly uplifting sermon which was listened to with interest, for it contained up-to-date news of parishes and personalities up and down the railway line, the congregation got down on their knees for a round of prayers, the minister declaring that first they would pray for the King and the Royal Family. Immediately Archie, who had been sitting slouched in the pew while the others knelt, got to his feet and shouted, "To hell with the King," and sat down again. Bill Draper seized his arm and told him to shut up, but Archie wore that simple, earnest expression he had worn when he set out to get Bill Draper's gallon of whiskey from Ernie Pellerin's locker. He answered Bill's fierce whisper with a nudge, and speaking in an ordinary conversational tone which could be heard by half the congregation, he said, "That's telling them, eh Bill?"

The minister, temporarily baffled, had stopped praying and was looking towards the congregation, while those near the pew in which Archie sat were whispering vehemently and shaking their heads disapprovingly at Archie.

"Who wants to pray," inquired Archie of Bill in the same clear conversational tones, "for that so-and-so when it is us poor beggars who need prayers?"

He walked away calmly after the service, nodding and smiling at everyone and appearing quite unconscious of the black looks being cast towards him. The next day he was on the station platform while they were waiting for the east-bound when he saw the minister, who was there to catch the train, talking to Bill Draper. Draper was apologizing for the infamous conduct of the man who had come into church with him when the infamous one himself strolled up, a good-natured smile on his face.

"Why, hello, Parson," Archie said. "I hope Bill and I didn't upset you yesterday. It was just one of our jokes. You've got half an hour before the train is due. Won't you come up to our room and have a drink with us, so that we can let bygones be bygones?"

"He always brought me into it as though I had been part of his doings," complained Bill. And quite often Bill was indeed part of the doings, for Bill had this streak in him, too—he loved excitement, and often got carried away. He just wasn't smart enough for Belaney, whose public displays of bad behaviour had in them, as I say, this deep protest against authority which in one form or another governed all their lives.

Archie had good grounds for his belief that things were going to hell. Trapping in the few years after the war had become very different from what it had been in the days when he first came to the North. Then there had been recognized trapping grounds, known to everybody and honoured by everybody. No animal was overtrapped, each trapper being careful to cultivate his ground so that he could be sure of a steady supply.

But the high fur prices obtainable after the war, and the accessibility of the best trapping grounds to the new railway, had brought into the North an entirely new breed of get-rich-quick operators, who honoured no unwritten laws and were out to make as much money as they could, as quickly as they possibly could. They had no feeling for the country, and none for the animals they were after, killing pregnant female animals instead of releasing them, dynamiting beaver houses, and destroying the young before their fur was prime. They quarrelled with each other, unlike the trappers of the older days, who were as brothers to one another. For a ten-dollar licence anybody could be let loose in the woods, with traps and guns and with but one thought in mind, to make a killing and get out.

All this was hateful to Archie, who had been inducted into trapping by honest Bill Guppy and the Bear Island Indians.

Archie had fallen away a little from the strict ceremonial of the hunt taught him by the old men of Bear Island. But he still thought of animals, as he had done from childhood, as living, sensitive things, with as much right to existence as man, and it maddened him that there should now be this indiscriminate slaughter. His response was to move farther and farther out from the places of settlement like Bisco, and some of the younger professional trappers who also resented the lawless grab that was disfiguring the land near the railway followed him there. Amongst those who joined him was young Ted Cusson, who had begun trapping after the war. He became Archie's partner for one winter, following him up to Abitibi and even as far east as Doucet in Quebec.

Ted Cusson no longer traps. He lives in retirement now near North Bay. He remembers well the old days when he and Archie worked together. Their trapping ground was about 120 miles from Bisco. It took two weeks or more to reach, as everything making up a winter's supply, as well as their traps, had to be packed in on their backs over portages, including the canoe. Leaving Bisco around the middle of September when there were good cool days and lots of sun, they could be pretty sure of making the trip without getting their stuff wet. They would pass through some beautiful lakes, through hills that at that time of the year were ablaze with colour. There were fish in plenty; they just took what they needed. The woods were full of moose; there were birds and rabbits with which to vary the diet. They made flapjacks, sat around the fire at night talking and smoking, then rolled in their blankets to sleep in the deep, fresh silence of the northern woods.

These journeys to the trapping grounds would become a golden memory of easeful days and calm nights. But once they were there the hard work started, and they were bone-weary when they returned to their cabin at night. Where their trap-lines ran there was a new growth of poplar and aspen and small birch; ideal country for beaver to establish themselves in. Farther down the river—they were on the Obinet, a tributary of the Mississagi—there were white pine and red pine and spruce, and here they could trap for fisher and marten and lynx.

A week or so before Christmas they would make their

way back over the ice to Bisco to replenish their supplies and have a bit of fun. They would stay until after New Year, and then return over the ice-bound rivers and continue trapping until May.

Those were memorable days, when they were young and strong and time seemed everlasting. Archie was living in the past. Away from Bisco and the frictions that got him into trouble, he became more and more like an Indian, less and less like a white man. There was good reason for this; the Indian was much closer to nature, and his ways were best when man was alone in a world populated mainly by animals. Archie and Ted did not communicate by shouting to one another but by using a call that would not disturb other animals. It was the call of the hoot owl, a sound which carried well from a distance. This was to become Archie's signal, the one always associated with him afterwards, plaguing the memories of elderly and respectable citizens of Bisco hearing it at night flung from the hill on the other side of the lake, where the winter traveller, dragging his loaded toboggan after him, Indian-fashion, would emerge from the bush to the open expanse of the frozen lake and would pause there to send this haunting cry shivering over the ice. They would know that the trouble-maker was back, and their peace was to be threatened for as long as he remained in town.

But even their distant trapping grounds were now being invaded and poached by the new men who, having damaged the fur-bearing districts nearer Bisco, were now forced out to more distant fields. Archie's anger grew, and became more dangerous. Where he had once threatened with a knife, he now carried a gun. But nothing could stop them coming. As fur prices mounted their methods became more ruthless. The beaver houses lay deserted and fallen in, and side by side with the invaders now came the lumbermen, cutting out the finest trees, leaving behind stumps that stood there, mute and mutilated, for years afterwards until a fire came along to burn over the whole area. And often when the tree had been felled, if it was found not right on the butt, it was not dragged out or removed but allowed to lie there, with

122

the trees it had crushed in falling, a sacrifice to the greed of the industry.

The lumbering companies swept like locusts over the land. To get their big machines in they had to cut portages. The old ones, where they existed, were laid out like a cow trail, taking advantage of every lower grade to ease the burden of the man carrying the load. But the lumber companies cut straight through the forest, a path sixteen to twenty feet wide. Through this great opening beat the hot summer sun, and the canoe brigade found themselves exposed to heat and flies, and cursed Mr. J. R. Booth, the lumber king, back there in Ottawa.

Then the slash that remained behind when this great swath had been cut became tinder dry. Months after the timber crew had passed on to other fields a forest fire would kindle from these great heaps of dried sticks. Hundreds of animals would be burned alive; those that survived would move out, until finally the fisher and the marten had almost disappeared from the forest areas.

In the summers he returned to guiding, for he knew the country now like the back of his hand. Temagami made a better headquarters for that than Bisco, and in 1925 he headed there for the summer season. It meant that he had to renew his contact with Angele and his children, but as he was out guiding for most of the time he saw but little of them.

Angele remembered the month of his return to Bear Island. It was July, the month of flowers, as the Indians call it, and he remained until September. She was to see him only once again after this summer, on his way back from seeing Anahareo. But fourteen years later, after his death, she was to recall this final parting.

> He wasn't bad friends with me when he left me. No bad friends. He shook hands with me good. He says, 'I will come back again. Don't worry what you do. I go away. I will come back some time. I like travel.'

She had made him a new leather outfit, and she and their daughter Agnes, now fourteen years old, went to the station to see him off. He was taking the train to the North. He did not tell them where he was going, and Angele suppressed any curiosity she may have had. She knew that she was pregnant again, but she did not tell him of this either.

Agnes had never seen her father before he turned up this summer. She had been mightily pleased to find herself possessed of a father, and Archie, who was always especially gentle with children, soon made friends with her. She had only been to school a little, and believed that she could neither read nor write. But she had learnt a little from the contact. Partly as a game, partly with a sense of responsibility aroused in him by the sight of a Belaney so abysmally ignorant, he taught her the letters that made up her name, and how to combine them so that everyone would know that they meant Agnes Belaney. She practised for hours, for week after week, until with fearful effort and fierce concentration and, in the end, a sense of joy such as a creative artist feels, there on the paper was her name made by her. Time after time she wrote it down. It was the most exciting thing that had happened in her young life.

He had been guiding out from Wabikon Camp during these months, a large island close to Bear Island, where a lodge had been put up and tourists were crowding in. Something had happened there during this summer which he did not tell Angele about. He had met a young girl, Gertrude Bernard, whose dark, slender beauty and graceful ways he could not forget. For the first time in his life he felt himself to be in love. All his other affairs, his marriages even, with Angele and Constance, as well as his many passing indulgences, had been sexually prompted. But he persuaded himself that this was different. She was an Indian girl, but an emancipated one. She was educated. She had an ease of manner that startled him. She was an Iroquois from the Ottawa Valley, and she was up for the summer working at Wabikon Lodge. She was nineteen—dark, slender, and as beautiful and as lithe as a panther. She was sitting reading on the dock one afternoon when he swept in with a swift stroke of his paddle, jumped out, and pulled his canoe up on the shore. His approach had been so silent that she was startled. She lowered her book, took him in, then began reading again while he watched her. She assumed that he was an Indian. He wore deerskin trousers, hitched up and supported by a highly coloured Hudson's Bay belt, and a worn buckskin vest. His long black hair hung to his shoulders. His face was dark and very handsome. She looked again, just to check this fact, and found him staring at her quite unabashedly.

They did not exchange words until much later, and when they did they began on a teasing note in which she felt herself at a disadvantage, for he seemed so much a man of the world, and he kept setting traps for her into which she would innocently fall, while he laughed uproariously. Although he had signed on as a guide, he did not live in the staff quarters at the side of the hotel. Sometimes he camped down near the shore; at other times he disappeared overnight or was away for several days guiding parties through the chain of lakes that linked up with Lake Temagami. But at the dances he sometimes played the piano, and afterwards they would walk together along the trails that followed the shore, as other couples did, and they talked. He did not tell her much about himself, except that he was half-Indian and had always lived in the woods. He knew England because he had been over there in the war, and he told her something about that, and about looking up his old relatives on his father's side. He told her he was a trapper, and guided in the summer to make a grubstake. She told him about her family who lived in Mattawa, and it seemed strange to him that she, who was descended from Iroquois chiefs, had never been in the bush, while he had hardly ever lived in a town. He had put out of his mind altogether that distant childhood in Hastings. He wrote home no more. He had almost come to believe himself in the story of his mother and father living in Mexico, and of his birth there in an Indian encampment.

Before they had known one another for more than a week or two a telegram came for Pony, as she was familiarly called, to tell her that her little niece had died and asking her to return home. Archie was out on a four-day trip when the wire arrived, and she had to leave without saying good-bye to him. At home in Mattawa she found her father disconsolate, and when he begged her not to leave him, she wrote to the manager at Wabikon to say that she would not be returning.

Then she told her father about this man she had met, and asked if she might write and suggest that he visit them when the season closed at Wabikon. There had been no talk of marriage, but Pony was in love, and she was pretty sure that Archie was in love with her. As she said with that engaging frankness that was always to be a part of her charm, she thought she was irresistible, and that he only needed a slight push to start rolling in the required direction. Her father agreed that she might write. The very next day, before Archie could possibly have received the letter, to her intense surprise she saw him enter their front gate, stand there for a minute with his back to the front door as though hesitating, then square his shoulders as though a decision had been reached and come marching up to the front door.

There were exclamations, followed by explanations. No, he hadn't had her letter. He had made up his mind to visit her and had written to tell her he was coming. But the train being in the station when he got there to mail the letter, he just came, bringing the letter with him.

This was his teasing way of talking, which she had not yet learnt covered his feelings when they were aroused. But as they talked it came out that he was in trouble. All he would say at first was that he had slugged the station agent at Bisco a couple of times, that the police had been sent for, and that a warrant had been sworn out for his arrest. The row had occurred because the agent, Joe Bolton, had given to another guide a telegram that was intended for Archie. The wire, which he had been expecting to arrive, asked the agent to reserve a guide for a wealthy sportsman who was coming up for the fall hunt.

But pasting a telegraphist doesn't usually involve a warrant for arrest, and then it came out that this was not the first time he had been in trouble in Bisco. He made a fine tale of the first brush he had had with the law. There had been an attempted rape of a little girl, who had identified her assailant, a local man. Archie had taken his knives, gone after the man, cornered him, and then proceeded to frighten the life out of him by standing him against the door and

126

throwing knife after knife at him, framing him in. Unfortunately, the man had moved his arm after being told to keep still, and that knife had drawn blood. Terrified, the man had gone to the police at Chapleau and laid information against Archie; a warrant charging Archie with attempted murder had been taken out, and Archie had had to take to the bush. He had waited there several days until the police had gone, and had then come back. He learnt that the police, failing to find him, had tempered justice with expediency. The warrant had been left with Mr. Woodsworth; it was in the safe at the Hudson's Bay store. It would not be withdrawn, nor would it be served as long as he was of good behaviour. But if he got into trouble again and caused an uproar, then bang! Mr. Woodsworth was authorized to serve the warrant on him, and he would be up on the attempted murder charge. Now he was in trouble again for pasting Joe Bolton, the C.P.R. agent, and there was that warrant sitting there in the safe, with old Woodsworth ready to nail it on him. Did she see why he had seized the opportunity to pay her a visit? Archie forbore to mention that Mr. Woodsworth had been nursing this warrant in his safe since 1914.

Pony thought he was terrific. It had all begun through taking the law into his own hands and punishing a rapist. She was in raptures over this hero who looked like a film actor but had the stern sense of justice of a man of integrity. Her father came in, and he and Archie took to each other immediately. After supper they sat there reminiscing about the old days and exchanging stories of Indian heroes of old. She left them absorbed in their mutual memories of the past.

CHAPTER 9

ANAHAREO, as Gertrude came to be called, had been born in the year in which Archie had come to Canada. When she met him at Wabikon Camp, he was thirty-six and she was nineteen. Her home was a frame house beside a stand of pine, just outside Mattawa, where she lived with her father and some younger brothers and sisters.

Anahareo's mother had died when she was four. On her mother's death, she and a younger brother had been put to live with an aunt. As she grew up, friction developed between the aunt and the niece, and after a few years Anahareo begged her father to let her come home and manage his house for him. Her father had finally agreed, but had got his mother, then an old lady aged ninety, to come and live with them.

Anahareo never says much about her father. He appears in the beginning of *Devil in Deerskins*, in which we have a glimpse of her family playing host to Grey Owl; he seems an amiable man who had no idea of how to manage his daughter. One wonders about him, and about the dead mother, who produced this unusual girl. For if the setting is domesticated, Mr. Bernard's history is not. He was a Mohawk of the Iroquois Confederacy, a descendant of one of the tribes who had fought during the American War of Independence with the British under their Chief, Joseph Brant and had later settled in Upper Canada. According to Grey Owl, Anahareo's grandfather was one of the original Mohawk rivermen who had helped to make history along the Ottawa River, and who had been enlisted as boatmen for the Red River Expedition of 1870 and the Nile Expedition in 1883–4. Anahareo's father had been one of the rivermen in the days of the great square timber-rafts.

But now at sixty he was an elderly widower, working as a builder. He emerges in *Devil in Deerskins* somehow rather lost-looking, a little confused by the barely explained presence of this striking-looking young man his daughter has met up at Temagami, who has descended on them now with all the seriousness of one about to propose marrying his little girl. The young man is plainly an Indian, but Mr. Bernard is puzzled by his blue eyes, and by something strange in his accent. But when Grey Owl calmly explains that his father was a Scotsman and his mother an Apache, Mr. Bernard says that while he is Iroquois, his own great-grandmother had been Scots. Her name was Mary Robinson, and she had been captured by the Iroquois when she was small. In the Revolutionary War, the Christianized Iroquois constantly raided the Americans and brought captives back with them. These, especially children, often showed no desire to return to their homes after they had lived with the Indians for a few years, and so it had been with Mary Robinson. She had married a Mohawk, and had become Anahareo's great-great-grandmother. Old Granny of ninety, who came to live with them, was a granddaughter of Mary Robinson and Naharrenou, a chief of the Mohawks, who was thus Anahareo's great-great-grandfather, and from him she derived her name Anahareo. She thus came of a proud race, and something of this was visible in her appearance and manner.

But she was also an ambitious girl, with hopes at this time of higher education than she had been able to receive at the local school. She thought education would enable her to escape from her narrow life in Mattawa. She was beautiful, far more beautiful than she herself realized. For what struck anyone about her immediately was something that was not reflected in her mirror. She could see only her face, and sometimes her figure. But she could not see the lithesome grace with which she moved. Her skin was tawny-coloured, her eyes dark and lustrous, her hair a shining black. She had the beauty of a healthy young animal, but what she desired to have was the beauty of the models she saw in magazine advertisements.

She had been brought up on the outskirts of a small town, living rather poorly, but pridefully. She describes in *Devil in Deerskins* her simple home. One sees it in one's mind's eye, remembering Grey Owl pushing back the little gate and walking up the path to the front door. It was different from the hidden town on Bear Island where nearly twenty years before he had seen Angele. Yet Mattawa in other respects was not much different, say, from Bisco, a half-and-half place now, where industry and commerce had almost blotted out the marks of the great Indian tribes who had once settled there.

There must have been something of Mary Robinson in Anahareo's character, for she was to prove not at all the romantic dreamer who at the moment thrilled to the tales her father and Archie exchanged that evening, but a woman of purpose. She thought she had fallen in love with this handsome stranger, and she assumed that he had fallen in love with her, or why had he come all that way to see her before he had received her letter inviting him?

To give the men a chance to talk she had left them after dinner that evening, and had gone over to the house of a friend where she often stayed the night. She came back in the morning, expecting that Archie would have been approved by her father, and that that day or the next, or some time on his visit, he would be asking her to accompany him on this journey into new trapping country which he had told them about last night over the dinner table. Instead she found him strapping up his pack to leave.

130

He offered no explanation. His face was set and stiff as though he was offended. Yet she was sure that he loved her. She saw him jump the freight as the train was coming slowly out of Mattawa station, a typically Archie-like gesture, if only she had known it. All he said was, "I'll hop on here—to avoid the crowd, you know."

Nearly every day after that for the next few weeks she received letters from him, long passionate love-letters that told her how much he wanted her, but made no practical suggestions for getting her. Then silence fell, silence absolute. She thought of him out on his trap-lines. She did not see in her imagination the twisted bodies caught in the traps, but only the tall figure in the parka hood bending down over something on the ground. She saw him in his cabin with the stove roaring away, while he sat at the table and wrote her that long letter that could come any day now and break this unbearable silence.

But five months passed without a word. She fell deeper and deeper into the fantasy of love, like someone drifting into sleep. Then one day, in February, not a letter but a telegram came. It was sent from Forsyth, several hundred miles to the north-east in Quebec. It was signed "Archie". The message was brief and appealing: "Please come up for a day or more Reply Yes".

She walked seven miles to where her father was working, and got his permission to make a week's visit. Then she got into the train, and began the long journey into the wilderness.

Archie was also having his fantasies, and they were a good deal more painful and regretful. He knew that he could not marry her. Bigamy might be conveniently forgotten when four thousand miles and centuries of polite English life separated one bride from the other. He knew by this time how susceptible he was to women, and how the passionate and delightful absorption he was now feeling would fade swiftly when the woman became a burden or a tie.

He knew that he suffered from domestic claustrophobia. He blamed Aunt Ada for that. This girl was expecting marriage. He couldn't offer it. He could not make love to her, and then abandon her under the excuse of getting away to his trap-lines. She was an Indian, the descendant of Iroquois chiefs, in his mind the epitome in grace and beauty of Hiawatha's Minnehaha. She was the ideal companion for whom he had been seeking all his life, and now that he had found her his past mistakes rose up to shut her off from him.

He could neither have her nor keep away. When he went to visit her, it had not been to seek her father's approval but to be with her, to be reassured that she was as desirable as he had dreamed. When he left her he was asserting his strength of will. He could never have her, so he went away without speaking. But then he could not stop thinking of her, and the letters poured from him, and in these he let down his guard and told her everything that a passionate lover might be expected to say.

But he twisted and turned even there, backtracking from his own ardour, passionate one moment, mocking himself the next; telling her about his daily life, the animals he had seen, how deep or firm the snow was, how the sky looked as you came out of the woods at the top of a rise, and the clear-washed blue of the northern sky, unbroken by any cloud, hung before you, enclosing this silent world. Cunning man that he was, he laid his bait skilfully, familiarizing her with the things that he loved so that she might begin to want to know them for herself.

When he left Bisco and began his long trek north, he had first made a detour by way of Temagami to see Angele. Angele says that he asked her to come with him. If he did, then it might have been because he thought her presence would insulate him against the over-powering desire for Anahareo which was driving him towards a step he might bitterly regret. Angele could not leave her children, and he did not want them. She let him go, as she had so often let him go before. I think he must have been relieved.

At Forsyth he sent his last letter to Anahareo and dis-appeared with his two fellow-trappers into the bush. This was when silence had fallen. The snow came. They had built their shacks, got their traps ready, assessed the prospects of the ground. These were not much better than they had been at Bark Lake, but they were full of hope at the begin-ning of a new season. Archie found a spot that he liked. He wanted to build a cabin of his own there, on the line of their trapping territory but several miles from where the others were. He chose the position, not only for its natural beauty, but because it offered protection from the prevailing winds. The site was beside a basin-shaped lake which was at the head of an open-water route and a hunting-ground of some hundreds of square miles. It was forty miles from Forsyth. A trail broken years before wound through the trees, now running along the shore of the lake, now diving into a valley, and being seldom used, it was not an easy path to follow. This was part of the charm of the setting to him, its accessibility to anyone who knew how to reach it, its complete privacy from trails more commonly used. He was a queer one, thought his partners. They knew about Anahareo and what she meant to him, and good-naturedly they helped him put up the cabin, although he would not admit he was inviting her to share it with him. He always had to have his own landing-places, apart from where other men landed. They helped him cut the logs and chink them. They were all happy, working in the beautiful last heat of the Indian summer, the smell of the woods strong about them while the vigorous winter was poised to strike.

He went through the winter without weakening in his resolve. Then in February he had to go to Forsyth for some supplies. Before he went he took a burnt stick, and inscribed on the log over the doorway, PONY HALL. He spent six days in town, twice as long as he had planned. It was on the first day that he sent the telegram to her, and on the second that he had her answer; and it was on the evening of the fourth day that out of the train at night stumbled this small figure whom he had summoned up out of his dreams, as Aladdin had obtained his desires by rubbing the lamp.

Both Grey Owl and Anahareo have given accounts of their lives together. Grey Owl's in *Pilgrims of the Wild* is the most revealing, even though it is shaded with that deception which had now become second nature to him; that he was a Métis of the woods, the child of an Apache woman and a Scots father, and that Anahareo came up there to marry him.

> The affair was quite wanting in the vicissitudes and
> the harrowing but stirring episodes that are said to
> usually beset the path of high romance. The course

of true love ran exasperatingly smooth; I sent the lady a railroad ticket, she came up on the pullman and we were married, precisely according to plan.

The complications started afterwards, Grey Owl goes on. And he reveals what these were in a very acute piece of self-analysis. The lady was not used to the bush; he had been so long a part of the bush that it was she who seemed to him to be the intruder, demanding his attention when it was fastened on more serious things like preparing the traps, and then bewailing his absence all day as though a man could stop his work and just idle. She had firm standards of conduct, believed in polite conversation, thought it was a mark of respect to others to dress as well or as neatly as possible. He had adopted the rather flamboyant style of dress offered by the Hudson's Bay posts: highly coloured shirts and neckerchiefs, ornate belts, long fringes on vests or leather jackets, intricate bead designs wherever they could be applied. Canoe and snowshoes and traps were cared for lovingly, being continually polished or wiped. But the same care was not lavished on the human face or body. Disordered clothes, long unbrushed hair, careless speech made deliberately ungrammatical, were signs of a man's vitality and independence of spirit. But they did not go over with the lady. And soon he realized that this one was unlike any girl he had ever had to deal with. Before he had always longed for freedom, and obtained it by trick or discretion, almost as soon as he had got himself entangled. But this one was not to be shaken off. In Anahareo, Grey Owl had got a woman of character. He was to be reminded sometimes of the way Aunt Ada had dominated his life.

In *Devil in Deerskins* Anahareo is intent on telling how she, an Indian but unused to the bush, survived the harsh rigours of the life into which she was suddenly plunged. Her account is more romantic: She is not the natural-born writer that Grey Owl was, and though one feels that she is being totally honest the superficially racy style succeeds almost in disguising what a tough little creature she really was. Listen to Grey Owl:

I speedily discovered that I was married to no

butterfly, in spite of her modernistic ideas, and found that my companion could swing an axe as well as she could a lip-stick, and was able to put up a tent in good shape, make quick fire, and could rig a tump-line and get a load across in good time, even if she did have to sit down and powder her nose at the other end of the portage.

Yet he is a bit shocked by her adaptability, even by the outfit she has brought with her: breeches, top-boots, men's woollen shirts. She would have fitted better into his romantic conception if she had appeared in the voluminous plaid skirt and head shawl still worn by Indian women in the North, although their men had taken to European suits.

But these workmanlike clothes disguised the purest innocence about what bush life was really like, and long before the forty-mile snowshoe journey from Forsyth was over, she was longing for rest. They had stayed at Forsyth for a couple of days before starting in, so that she could meet his friends, rest up from the journey, and practise some snowshoeing. They had fun in the evenings, but during the day he was the stern taskmaster, making her walk in Indian file, and carry a load so that she could toughen up. He told her that all wilderness trails which are cut through trees are cut to the width of a man carrying a canoe, so that there is not room for two to walk abreast. He told her that in the bush man and woman share alike, that each must carry the same load and put up with the same hardships, and that there could be no place on the trail for a weakling.

Already, when they start out for Forsyth, Pony feels that she has failed, for the pack she is carrying cannot weigh more than ninety pounds, while the huge, shapeless mass he carries on his shoulders which is bound by a tump-line to his forehead must weigh several hundred pounds.

They arrive at the campsite after dark has fallen, and she has to sleep the first night in a tent with snow walls. Boy, is this going to be tough, she thinks. But there are only two days left of the week's absence her father has granted. The next morning Archie reappears, bright and early, to show her Pony Hall, which was there all the time, but has been kept for a surprise. He has to leave her that day, he tells her, to visit his trap-lines, and he comes home at night, happy to find the new cabin warm and lit, supper ready, and this beautiful girl waiting to receive him. When she starts to get sleepy, he leaves her and sleeps in the snow tent.

One can see them falling in love with one another in these romantic surroundings. As lovers do, they told each other stories of their pasts, Anahareo of her great-great-grandfather after whom she was named, of the aunt who had brought her up after her mother's death, and of her homelife in Mattawa. Archie told her of being brought up by his grandmother and his two aunts, and of how Aunt Ada had so taken over his young life and smothered it with her care and officiousness that in desperation he had once tried to murder her. Even after this long time he had only to think of her and the oppressions of his childhood rose up to darken his mind, often to make him resort to sudden acts of violence such as shooting off his rifle into the ground, or stumbling out of his cabin into the darkness, cursing her aloud.

Yet Anahareo told me later that he could also be very funny about Ada, mimicking the shrill accents of a scold while he parodied a lecture on the virtues of cleanliness and godliness, and the shortcomings of little boys. She never left him alone. Admonishments in the form of printed texts had adorned the walls of his room. DO NOT FORGET TO CLEAN YOUR TEETH was placed over the washstand. HAVE YOU SAID YOUR PRAYERS? inquired a framed one on the back of the door. Others asked whether he had brushed his suit, or urged him to make an inspection of his nails.

He could not have disguised the fact that Aunt Ada and Carrie and Grandmother Belaney had lived in England, and that his early years had been spent there and not in Mexico. But he insisted on his half-Indian parentage, saying little about his mother and father. It was not until after his death that Anahareo, who was to come to know him better than anyone else, was finally convinced that he had no Indian blood at all.

He told her about his early experiences in Canada, beginning at Bear Lake. Then he told her about Angele—the truth this time—and that he had married her. He went on to tell her about going overseas in the war, and about marrying Connie Holmes. He even told her about Marie Girard, and

136

her little boy, and about Angele's children. He was making a clean breast of everything, except his parentage.

There is no question but that he was very much in love with her, and he now knew that she was in love with him. But the circumstances here were different from any that had prevailed before. Pony was the dominant character. She wanted this man. But she wanted him body and soul, not just on second-rate terms. His confession was a defence, put in because although passion drove him strongly, he felt his freedom threatened. The old waves of domestic claustrophobia arose inducing a kind of nausea. He had to escape, yet he could not escape from this slim young figure with the straight back, and the head held high, and those brown eyes which drew him on while every instinct warned him against the trap into which he was walking.

In the end it was she who had to temporize. The next day was to be the last of the week's visit, and it was to be spent snowshoeing the long trail into Forsyth. When he came over from his tent in the morning to get her, she said that she had decided to stay another week. At the end of that time, she said she would wait until Easter, but must be out by then so that she could go to make her confession. No doubt by that time much talking had been done, but these two strong wills still battled against each other. She would not stay permanently, nor would she go. She hung irresolute, which was both maddening and exciting to Archie. She interrupted his work, hating to be left alone, but horrified, when she accompanied him, by the sight of the animals that were caught in the traps being given the death-blow. She chattered when he would be silent, became melancholy when he brooded over maps or passed an hour in the evening cleaning his traps or mending his snowshoes. Yet when he wanted companionship, how gay and enchanting she was. He was continually conscious of her Indian-ness, and it made him feel proud that he, who was an adopted Indian, should be showing her the Indian way of life.

When they came out at Easter-time they found a little pile of letters, five of them, which had been held at the store for her. They were all from her father, and had been written over the two months that she had now been away from home. The last one was an ultimatum: either return with this man as your husband, or do not return at all.

Poor father. We all pity the innocence of our fathers.

She went to Senneterre, fifty miles to the east, to make her confession. The priest heard her out; then he asked if she did not have something to add. On her denying this, he asked: "Are you not the girl who is living in the woods near here with a trapper?" A fierce argument ensued in which she protested that she had done nothing wrong. It ended in her stumbling from the confession box without absolution.

Poor Anahareo. We are driven to our desires, fanned by the intolerable suspicions of others who do not realize how we have fought against surrender.

So in the end they were back in Pony Hall, but not before a chance encounter had given them the absolution they needed. While they were still in Forsyth, Archie was approached by two Indians who had known him during the winter before Pony came. They were from the Lac Simon band. Two of their number had been arrested and were in jail at Amos under charge of setting fire to a trapper's shack, flattening the stove pipes, dumping the trapper's winter provisions in the snow, and pouring coal oil over a bag of traps, a heinous offence in itself since it is difficult to eradicate the smell which frightens off game approaching the trap. The Indians' defence was that the trapper was using strychnine as bait for wolves and foxes, and that this had poisoned their huskies. It was the old war between the Indians and the invading trappers, described so amusingly by Archie in his article in *The Hastonian*. But the Indians had destroyed property and put a man's life at risk in the winter by destroying his shelter, and a stiff jail sentence seemed the certain outcome. The Indians wanted Archie to come and speak for them.

So instead of returning to Pony Hall, they went first to Amos, east of Senneterre. There Grey Owl, as a half-breed trapper himself, who knew this country well and had had dealings with the Indians of this band, spoke so eloquently as a witness for the defence against the risk of using strychnine in a country where the huskies are let loose to follow

138

along the shore while the Indians travel in their canoes, wherever that is possible, that the two men were given comparatively light sentences of thirty days. Chief Papati of the Lac Simon band was so grateful for Grey Owl's intervention that he insisted that Archie and Pony should accompany him home to join the feast celebrating his golden wedding before returning to Forsyth.

The account Anahareo gives of the old Chief, a Christian and a deeply religious man, who conducts the marriage and burial services among his band, is a persuasive one. At this moment she and Grey Owl are facing the prospect of separation for the summer, for now that the trapping season is over—it has been a poor one financially; he has spent too much time on his love-affair—he must go fire-ranging to make his winter stake. She cannot return home on her father's terms. She decides to go prospecting in the Rouyn district; the search for precious metals, always unsuccessful, is to become an abiding passion in Anahareo's life—but she is sad at parting from her lover, and Chief Papati finds her in tears. In his speech at the feast, looking over at Archie he says to the band

> Just now my friend spoke to me, and he told me that if he and Anahareo can have our blessing and love, it will make their lives together more happy.
> They are good, and everyone of us loves them. Now, together, we will pray to God and ask him to keep the black clouds of sickness and sorrow from their trail and make their hearts and their souls shine with truth and happiness while they are living, and afterwards, in the Other World.*

Then Chief Papati reached out and joined Archie's hand in hers, while all the Indians bowed their heads in prayer. It was in this way, Anahareo says, that they came to be married.

For two years, from February 1926 until the late spring of 1928, they led this troubled existence. Each of them had to yield a little to the other in the process. Their battles were fought out of sight, and their happy hours passed with no

*Anahareo, *Devil in Deerskins* (Toronto: New Press, 1972).

one to see them but the animals which shared this remote spot with them. Grey Owl was solitary by nature; contact with his fellow-men always got him into trouble. He loved the silence of the woods, and the communication with the living creatures of the forest. It was his business to hunt them, but not ruthlessly to exterminate them, and he paid those that he was forced to kill the respect due to an honoured foe.

For Anahareo it was much harder. To begin with, she was younger, gayer, naturally gregarious. She was at the beginning of her adult life and it was not working out as she had dreamed it would. Her break with her family must have been painful for her. She had no one in whom she could confide except this man who in such a short while had come to absorb her life, but who could turn often and disregard her altogether as though she were a complete stranger.

Then she was living rough. The frame house outside Mattawa had not been the acme of comfort, but it wasn't like this, filled with a man and his possessions, his traps and snowshoes and paddles and wet clothes. The smell of moccasins and wet leather jackets hung heavy in the air, and outside, wherever one looked, was only the endless forest stretching away to the Arctic, and the white canopy of snow that deadened all sound.

The adjustment to each other's presence was often painful. Grey Owl, engrossed by his work, was inclined to talk of nothing else. In the evenings he laid out trails and pored over maps or, absorbed in plans for the next day, whistled softly to himself as he worked over his snowshoes, or tested the springs on traps, seemingly quite unaware of the deepening silence of the figure opposite him, and the look of sadness settling on her beautiful face. He brushed aside with a scornful laugh her suggestion that she should accompany him on his patrols. If he had known the idiom he would have called her "little woman" and would have said that her place was in the home. He meant that when he said, "Trapping is the thing we have to live by. It's not a picnic and it's never fun. I can't watch a trap and watch you too. And if I didn't watch you, you'd fall through the ice and take me with you, or land us in some jam that would mean the death of one or both of us."

Anahareo was silent, but not being of the stuff of which "little women" are made, was only the more fiercely determined to share Grey Owl's life instead of becoming a mere appurtenance to it like his snowshoes, his canoe, or his maps. So one morning she watched him through the cabin window and waited until at the top of the farthest knoll he turned to wave goodbye. She knew where he was going: to a sheltered bay that lay eight miles from the cabin. It was early in March. There had been a fresh and heavy fall of snow, covering the hills and valleys around the cabin with a soft, white, and immensely fine blanket, dear to the imagination of designers of Christmas cards, but an abhorrent hell for those who have to travel by snowshoes. For her first essay at independence, Anahareo could not have chosen more unsatisfactory weather conditions.

She was not yet an expert on snowshoes like Grey Owl, who for twenty years had lived on them for five or six months in the year, and besides she had not his height and immense stride. She forgot that it was because he had reduced his pace to suit hers that she had had no difficulty in keeping up with him on the few short excursions they had made together since she came. When she was three miles from the cabin on this winter morning, although she had hurried so that perspiration streamed from her, she still had not caught up to him, and she was beginning to think her plan condemned to failure when suddenly, at a turn in the trail, she saw him a quarter of a mile ahead of her, kneeling over a trap he had evidently set at that point.

She came up behind him as quietly as she could, and succeeded in getting within twenty-five yards of him before he straightened up and turned and saw her. The look of utter surprise on his face struck her as comical, but she did not dare to smile, so apprehensive was she of the outcome of her plan.

The outcome lacked a little of that dramatic air she had both hoped for and dreaded. His greeting of her was gruff. Now you are here you had better stay, was all that he said in effect. He told her not to keep too close to him, and when he paused, to pause also, and above all to keep silent. When they went onto the ice of the lake she was to take special care to keep at least twenty yards from him, for the weight of both of them on a spot where underneath a swift current might be running might land them both in the freezing water.

The day proceeded silently, the traps were managed with ruthless efficiency. When once or twice a badly wounded animal had to be put to death she watched with her hand at her mouth and with frightened eyes at the look that came over his face as he raised his axe to give the death-stroke. She could not recognize in features so distorted the face of the man who could be passionate or indifferent with her, but never as ruthless as this.

It was a day that she never forgot, a day which, though he did not realize it, marked the great turning point in their lives. Not even the ridiculous anticlimax could restore the old even temper of their relationship. On their way home in the afternoon they crossed the ice of a small bay to cut a mile or two off the trail. A little way out from the shore, Grey Owl paused and tapped the ice with the iron-shod staff he always carried. Then he stood and seemed to listen for a minute or two. Cold, and anxious to be home, Anahareo crept nearer until she was within twenty feet, instead of that many yards, of him. Suddenly there was a crack as though a pistol had gone off, and she felt herself sway as though she stood on a small raft that bobbed in the wash of a passing vessel. Then, to her utter consternation she sank swiftly through a hole in the ice and came to rest when the water reached her waist. It was so intensely cold that the shock took her breath away. She could only utter a frightened gasp as the breath left her body.

Again the situation was wanting in drama. An heroic rescue to the sound of endearments from her partner was evidently not to be her reward. Grey Owl stood with arms folded, and on his face the look of the sergeant-major who sees a recruit drop a rifle on parade. Then, saying nothing, he dropped full-length on the ice and, distributing his weight equally on his toes, his hands, and his chest, crawled slowly forward until Anahareo could grasp his staff. Under his instructions she broke more of the ice around her, her teeth chattering and her body almost numb with the cold. Then, again on his instructions, she reached the other end of the staff, and, letting her weight fall slowly forward in the water and keeping herself as still as possible, she clung to the end of the staff and felt herself slowly pulled out.

When she was safe on firm ice again, Grey Owl told her to fasten on her snowshoes and move as quickly as she could back home, no matter how breathless or tired she felt. She started off, thinking to herself how ridiculous she must look, not knowing how pathetic a little figure she seemed to Grey Owl as chattering with the cold she started to run in the direction of the cabin.

Before she had gone half a mile her clothes were frozen stiff. Where her breeches clung to her knees she could feel the skin being chafed off. Round her waist and on her hips, where the breeches fitted tightly, she could feel, at every step, a sharp pain as though a knife cut her flesh. She was sobbing when she reached the cabin. The fire had gone out, and it was as cold inside as it had been out in the open. Shaking with the cold, exhausted with a run of over two miles, she unlaced her heavy boots and pulled them off, drew her heavy woollen shirt over her head, and slowly finished the excruciating task of pulling off her breeches. Then, small, frightened, and full of shame she crept between the blankets on the bunk. There half an hour later Grey Owl found her. He drew back the blankets, and with gentle hands dressed the cuts and abrasions on her body.

A situation as tense as this could end only in complete disruption, or by one party to the dispute giving in to the other. Both Anahareo and Grey Owl were intelligent enough to realize this, but inside, each had a devil of pride which made the second alternative impossible. Yet disruption, meaning separation, was something that neither of them could bear to envisage. Their love was passionate, and in these weeks alone in the bush together had taken deep root. A compromise was temporarily reached when Grey Owl consented to take Anahareo with him on the trail each time he went out, and when he promised at the same time that the trail should end at the cabin door. Inside, conversation about his work should be taboo. Neither at meal times, nor when they spent the evening by the fire should the talk be all of traps and plans for killing. Archie, whose conversation had been only of these things for twenty years, wondered what they would talk about, and to the first evening under this new regime he brought a glum, but dutiful, face which made Pony laugh aloud.

He suddenly realized that he had not heard her laugh for a long time, and it brought a feeling of contrition to his heart. That evening, and many that followed it, were happy ones, the happiest he had spent in his solitary life. In them was laid the foundation of that lasting love they had for each other, which was to stand so much stress and strain in the twelve years that lay ahead.

He had been a solitary trapper, and it was a new experience to feel himself being watched at his work. It emphasized certain aspects of trapping which he himself had always hated, certain horrible moments such as those in which a wounded beast had to be put to death, which, with the ruthlessness that sprang from the pity he felt, he always made as savagely brief as possible.

He knew now that behind him, at such moments, Pony would be standing, and often his own feelings, stirred enough at what he had to do, were the more harrowed when the dying gasp of some poor creature was not loud enough to drown the moan of a human voice behind him. An awareness of all this made his hand less sure, and once or twice the wounded animal slipped from his grasp and crawled away from him moaning with pain, and he had to lunge after it to retrieve it for the death it was trying to escape.

Once a wounded lynx squirmed from his hand, but instead of trying to escape, it made its way towards Anahareo, staring at her in dumb hopeless appeal for mercy from the axe that was close behind it. When the axe fell, as it then did swiftly, Grey Owl looked not at the dead body at his feet, but up at the eyes of the woman with him; and read there the same stricken misery, the same utter terror, he had seen so often in the dumb eyes of condemned animals during the past twenty years.

Things he had barely noticed before now stood as mute witnesses of the suffering his presence in these woods inflicted on animal life. When they came upon a trap and saw the body of an animal caught in it, frozen in the shape of the last contortion it had made to retain its spark of life; when traps set for fur-bearing animals revealed, when they came

144

13. Anahareo at Wabikon Camp on Lake Temagami in 1924, the summer she met Grey Owl.

(*top left*) 14. Archie before a cabin at the Marquis River, Abitibi, Quebec, around 1927.

(*lower left*) 15. Archie and Anahareo holding McGinnis and McGinty, near Doucet, Quebec, around 1927.

(*below*) 16. Grey Owl and a beaver, probably at Riding Mountain National Park, 1931.

(*below*) 17. Grey Owl holding Jelly Roll at Métis, Quebec, 1929.

(*left*) 18. Dave White Stone, an Algonkin Indian from Ontario who lived with Archie and Anahareo at Birch Lake.

19. Grey Owl, 1931.

20. "Beaver Lodge" on Lake Ajawaan.

21. Grey Owl
feeding a beaver
kitten, probably
at Prince Albert
National Park.

22. Inside "Beaver
Lodge", Grey
Owl's cabin on
Lake Ajawaan,
Prince Albert
National Park in
Saskatchewan,
1936.

23. Grey Owl talking to his daughter Dawn in Saskatchewan, around 1927.

(*above*) 24. Grey Owl on snowshoes at Lake Ajawaan, mid-1930s.

(*right*) 25. Grey Owl canoeing near "Beaver Lodge", 1936.

(*left*) 26. Anahareo canoeing with daughter Dawn at Prince Albert National Park, around 1936.

(*below*) 27. Anahareo at 25. Some years after the photograph was taken, it was sent to the Misses Belaney by Archie, who had inscribed on the back : "This is my wife Gertie, an Iroquois chief's daughter. 31 years old. Tall, slim & very strong. A woman of great courage & a true partner. Well-educated, talks perfect English; everybody likes her."

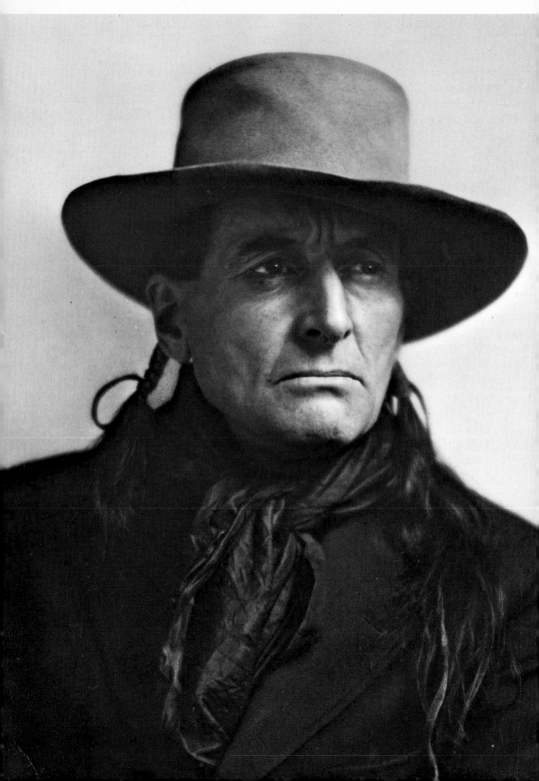

28. Grey Owl, portrait by Karsh. (*Copyright by Karsh of Ottawa*)

to them, the mute, icy bodies of harmless little squirrels and
birds, caught there accidentally; and most of all when they
came to a trap and found not the dead body of an animal but
its paw, chewed off so that its owner might be set free;
when these things happened as they did nearly every day, he
was reminded of the sum of suffering he had brought to
these creatures over the years, and he thought that Anahareo
must feel like Dante being escorted through the circles of
Hell.

Conversation could not avoid this topic, and walking
homewards at night, Grey Owl, feeling the silent challenge in
the depressed figure at his side, would try to justify trapping
as a means of making a livelihood. Expertly done, it brought
very little suffering in its train. The sights she had seen were
distressing, but when she became used to the life she would
not notice them; and when she had seen an amateur, or
get-rich-quick, trapper at his work she would realize how
little suffering in comparison the trained trapper inflicted.

But the sum of the whole thing was that this was the only
way he had of making a living. Without fur they would
starve. Unless she wanted to leave him she must join him,
and learn, as he had had to learn, to withstand the shocks
that went along with the trade. He was right. Pony was a
sensible woman; she adjusted to the life to which she was
now committed, becoming in the process so adept that she
was able to take her turn at breaking trail through heavy
falls of new snow, and handle traps by herself, effecting with
an axe-handle the deadly blow that extinguished the life of
some struggling beast. But she did not try to make herself
hard; she kept herself continually conscious of the anguish,
and with gentle hands that showed compassion laid the dead
beast down. Grey Owl noticed this, and it made him think of
what he was doing, for he too had felt this when Bill Guppy
had first taken him out on the trap lines.

Neither of them now spoke of these things. He saw that
she was trying to be a helpmate to him, and he could see
what the effort cost her. It spurred him on to make an effort
himself in the things that he knew she wanted. He left his
job outside the cabin, and neither of them talked of their
bloody occupation once they were inside it. He helped her to
decorate the cabin and make it homelike, and while she

sewed at night he told her the old legends of the Ojibways that he had learnt in his first years on Bear Island and from the Espaniels in Bisco. And because he had this gift of telling a story, and such a wonderful sense of humour, there were no longer silent evenings but evenings gay with laughter and tense with the suspense of mysteries of the forest and ancient legends that had been handed down from generation to generation of the people of the wilderness.

"We were very happy at last," says Grey Owl, remembering those years when they lived in almost complete isolation, seeing only the occasional passing Indian or trapper on his way somewhere else, or the few families at Forsyth.

Pony found him an enchanting companion to be with. Information about animals poured from him. She had never heard anyone talk of them except as something inferior. He spoke of them as a proud and distinct species of life. He told her that all wild animals have a love of amusement; that a bear will climb a tree for the express purpose of sliding down it, then climb back up and slide down again just for the kick he gets out of it. He told her about bears that will climb a snow bank and then coast down it on their behinds, uttering short sharp barks of pleasure, and do this for hours at a time.

He told her that eagles, loons, beavers, and others mate for life, and that an otter when tamed will follow a man like a dog. That eagles, hawks, crows, and gulls make a practice of flying into the wind during a gale, then, turning, allow themselves to be swept before it for great distances. He said that muskrats are unwelcome guests in a beaver lodge, for they do not have clean habits like the beaver, and besides they nibble away constantly at the beaver's supply of winter feed. The otter, on the other hand, is quite a welcome visitor because he gets rid of the muskrats.

Then he told her that not all animals have the same capacity for suffering, some reacting to inhibitions and instincts rather than being prompted by reason. He told her about a moose who stood guard over the dead body of another young bull; the attachment of a friend. She could see him there, a solitary mourner, his great head of horns not bent to feed but looking mournfully at his dead friend.

146

Grey Owl made the animal world come alive for her, making her notice things she had never noticed before, a spider joy-riding on a chip, a gossamer cable thrown out ahead of him into the wind providing the means of loco-motion. Once when they were in the canoe, a swimming squirrel, driven off its course, climbed on to his paddle, scampered up to the gunwale, ran along and sat on the load in the stern, chattering volubly until they reached the next portage. He showed her that another living world of char-acters—clowns, artisans, the mean-spirited along with the nobly generous—existed alongside the human one, their thread of life rooted in nature as ours is. She felt as though she had had a film removed from her eyes, and that she now saw clearly where before she had peered through a mist, or even not bothered to look. She knew that she was going through some unusual experience, and that kept her own tempestuous nature from breaking out too often.

These experiences happened to her in the months of May and early June, after their return from Amos. And then it was time for him to leave for his fire-ranging job. She could not come with him. That was flat. Wives were forbidden to join husbands. He had to live in men's quarters, and climb a 106-foot ladder to sit all day with binoculars in the look-out tower, sweeping the land below for the betraying wisps of smoke. Pony went off on her prospecting trip to Rouyn. They were to meet again in the fall at Forsyth, get together their winter supplies, and head for their winter hunting territory.

But Rouyn didn't work out, and the reason that it didn't has something to do with our story. These two lived in poverty. They began the trapping season with a debt owed to the store-keeper for a winter's supply of food and clothes. The furs they brought in in the spring washed out their debt, and enabled them to have a little over for a brief space of leisure, usually taken at the beginning of summer and perhaps just before the end. To live, Grey Owl had to have a summer job, guiding or fire-ranging.

It was Pony's romantic dream that by staking a claim which would assay well, they might find a quick route to fortune. It is every prospector's dream. Only one in ten thousand makes it. She went off to Rouyn, where copper and gold had been struck a few years before. But she was handicapped by having a pet wolf pup in a crate, in addition to her other baggage. Soon she was out of money and nearly out of hope. Besides love was nagging at her; she missed her man's presence. Soon she was back besieging the Chief Forest Ranger's office and insisting on joining her man. Somehow she prevailed, although it was against the rules. They camped out all summer. In their spare time Archie tanned hides, and from them Pony made mitts, moccasins, leggings, and a leather shirt. During this time, in wonderful summer weather, when all nature was busy and alive, working out its complicated peculiarities under the summer sun, he told her more of its secrets, and she became as responsive to it as he was.

When the summer job was finished, they had enough money in hand to grubstake them, and the North was beckoning them to their winter work. After much poring over maps, Archie decided that this winter, the winter of 1927-8, they would go into the Jumping Caribou country. He told Pony: "We'll just keep going until freeze-up forces us to build."

I think—no, I know, from what he wrote afterwards—that he had hopes of finding a territory not yet spoiled by the insistent, inobstructible advance of eager fur buyers, and greedy trappers and lumbermen. They were like termites teeming over one another, pushing hard against the North, fouling the country they passed over, leaving in their train jagged stumps of timber cut, burnt-out patches of forest, a land denuded of wild life. Especially of beaver, the most sought-after, the most valuable of all furs.

Even as they went into Lake Attik, from which the Attik River flowed, the signs of profit-seekers were to be seen in the absence of beaver. Once, not many years ago, the traveller off the beaten track would have seen on every hand the mark of their industry, in felled trees and in dams obscurely raised, or heard, in the sound of the slap of their tails on water, the presence of these animals who were blended into Canadian history, and as much a part of the landscape imaginatively as the poplars beside the lake, the pine forest climbing over rocky hills, the thunder of cataracts, and the smell of balsam and crushed pine needles: the whole intricate orchestration of the Canadian woods.

And now it was silent as the grave. The landscape was dead of sound, or the sound when it came was delayed, muted, and distant, as though the animal making it was hesitant and doubtful. His ear caught the inquiet, unhappy note. It was bush telegraph, signalling to him that the Frontier was on its way, calling him to join it if he wanted to be saved.

They travelled by canoe, north-westward from the transcontinental line. The temperature was dropping below freezing at night, and ice particles clung to the reeds at the edge of Attik Lake. In a stand of jack pine they put up their winter cabin; it took a matter of days only. From this centre he would set out his traps in a radius pointing towards the North Pole.

It was a queer season. A sense of doom hung over everything. "Although we did not realise it," wrote Grey Owl afterwards, "the day of the trapper was almost done. The handwriting was on the wall, but although it had been painstakingly inscribed there by ourselves, none of us were able to read it."

He thought at first that the catch was poor because the ground they were working, he discovered from some Indians who passed through, had been trapped over by a noted hunter who had evidently cleaned it out the previous winter. But this did not explain the lack of almost any animal life. The wilderness seemed to have been abandoned by its animal residents; it was as though there had been an exodus *en masse*.

By long hours on the trail, and resetting his traps quickly, he managed to collect a fair burden, although nothing like his catch in previous winters. Meanwhile world prices of fur had started to fall, and were dropping every week or so. As though serviced by the most efficient telegraph service in the world, word of falling prices reached from Amsterdam and London and Montreal even to the Arctic Circle. When Archie and Anahareo came out to the post in the spring their diminished sleigh-load of furs made only six hundred dollars, hardly enough to clear their debt at the store, much less set them up for a summer's journeying to the next and more remote trapping ground which might be found unspoilt.

There was nothing for it but to go back into the bush for a late spring hunt. There are reasons why beaver are not hunted at this time of the year. The fur is not in good condition; the female is usually pregnant, and in destroying her the trapper is destroying the young unborn. But it is a time when beaver are easier to trap. A restlessness seizes the male. He gets a wanderlust, and often strays far from his lodge, and with that retreat cut off, leaves himself more open to predators, human as well as animal.

Anahareo had given up trapping just before the season closed. She had come upon a lynx in a trap she had set some ten days before. The weather had not been cold enough to put him out of his misery. He had gnawed at his trapped paw until the bones were bare of flesh. Then hunger had driven him. Dragging the trap to the limit of the chain, he had stripped the bark off every tree; and in the end he had kept himself alive by eating snow. He looked at her, when she came, as a rescuer, not as the one who would extinguish the spark of life he had been desperately trying to preserve. She would have let him go, but he was in too poor condition. He could barely crawl. Quickly she dispatched him. But this was the end. She made up her mind that she would never set another trap.

"For me now," Anahareo wrote, "the time dragged. Was this to be my way of life?" The thought was unbearable. But so was the alternative—to leave Archie.

When he had made his catch, he went the rounds, collecting his traps. She came with him, glad that the killing season was over. At a small lake he lifted a beaver trap, only to find that the chain had been cut, evidently by the beaver who had been caught in it, who had then sunk with the stone to the bottom of the lake where it would have drowned. It would certainly have been a female, who would have been near the lodge nursing her young while the male wandered away.

The trap had gone, and with it the beaver; a wasteful occupation altogether. They were about to leave when two

150

small heads appeared above the surface. Kitten beaver are unable to remain under water for any length of time, and bursting lungs had driven them to the surface when they had been unable to find their mother in the house.

Archie raised his gun to shoot them, then lowered it again, and said to Anahareo:

"There are your kittens."

"Let us save them," begged Anahareo, and then in a lower voice, "It is up to us, after what we've done."

And truly, what had been done here looked now to be an act of brutal savagery. And with some confused thought of giving back what I had taken, some dim idea of atonement, I answered, "Yes; we have to. Let's take them home." It seemed the only fitting thing to do.*

Anahareo lifted them from the pond and put them inside her shirt, and there they stayed without sound or movement.

*Pilgrims of the Wild.

CHAPTER **10**

WHEN at Anahareo's urgings Archie allowed her to pick up these two beaver kittens out of the water, instead of despatching them with his gun and selling the small furs for what they were worth, he was approaching his fortieth birthday. The rescue was a momentary impulse to please her. All the same, he had no intention of keeping these kittens, and he told her so. He could sell them alive to the storekeeper in Doucet for ten dollars apiece when they came out again. His melancholy mood when they had taken in their winter catch to Doucet a few weeks before had made Anahareo suggest that he should get on the train and go and consult the doctor at Senneterre. But the trouble was with his spirit, not his body. Depressing reports of falling fur prices, coinciding with the evidence of the ground emptying everywhere of game, particularly of beaver, combined to make him feel that the North was finished.

He saw, himself nearing forty, and no better than a vagrant moving aimlessly across the face of a disfigured land. The hunters and the hunted were being driven together towards the rim of the world. The bones of the buffalo herds had whitened on the prairies for years. Now deserted beaver houses and broken dams littered the lakes and waterways of the North. Even the Indian villages were being deserted. Many Indians now lived in cheap frame houses instead of in teepees in the hidden towns in the woods. They wore store clothes instead of the deerskin jackets and fringed trousers of a few years before. Some of them even sported outboard motors on their canoes, and fished with rod and reel. The death rate among them was high, for they were eating food to which their systems were not accustomed, and living in ill-made houses heated by stove-pipes to blistering temperatures, instead of in teepees, draught-proof from the banked snow which shut out the wind, and warmed to an even temperature by their own body-heat. The Indian, the buffalo, and the beaver, the aboriginal inhabitants of this continent, were being wiped out by civilization.

Bones everywhere, death and dying, mutilation and mourning. The world was becoming a graveyard. All his life had been directed by a dream, and now the clouds of fantasy which had sustained him for so long were being dispersed. He had never wanted for money before. And he had always used up what he had earned. When he needed more he had only to help himself from bountiful nature.

But in this spring of 1928 he realized for the first time that the trapper's day was over. Ever since he had left Bisco three years before in the search for new hunting grounds he had been aware that wildlife was diminishing, but he had not felt the financial effect because the steadily increasing prices paid for furs made up for the smaller catch. A good season's trapping had always netted him fifteen hundred to two thousand dollars. This last season, however, had brought him only six hundred dollars, barely enough to pay his bill at the store for the last winter, with nothing in hand for the summer.

153

It was not in Pony's nature to brood about the future. Nor was it in Archie's. But they had to eat, and that had meant making this late spring hunt. Pony was happier than she had ever been with these kittens for pets. But for Archie at first they were living symbols of how far he had sunk in his desperate efforts to survive.

While he was out on his trap-lines, she remained around the camp all day with the kittens, and soon the three were fast friends. With only the slightest hesitation, they had accepted her in place of their missing mother. She fed them with the man's help. But hers was the hand that held their small heads steady as the stick with the food on it was passed into their inner mouths, and she it was who kept filling the tub with life-giving water. She played with them by the hour, and was there to pick them up and allow them to snuggle against her breast in those terrifying moments when they woke up after a sleep and whimpered for re-assurance that all was as it had been before sheer weariness had tumbled them into unconsciousness.

Archie, when he returned in the evening, saw this, and felt himself an outsider, regarded furtively and calculatingly by the two kittens as though being weighed up as friend or enemy. It amused him, who had always been able to gain the confidence and affection of any animal, that it was he who should now be regarded as the intruder. He held back from making any advances, knowing that eventually the kittens would have to be sold; and perversely, as always happens with animals and children, his resistance to their charms aroused their curiosity, and they made little tentative approaches themselves towards him.

One of the kittens was a male, the other a female. The male kitten was the more venturesome, and it was he who, belly flat to the ground and as elongated as he could make himself, sniffed warily at Grey Owl's moccasins, then put out a small hand, so like a human hand, and clutching at the fringes on Archie's trousers, raised himself to his full height and peered at the man.

Archie sat on at the table writing. Sometimes now he was not out all day. A few weeks after they had captured the kittens, an elderly Algonquin named Dave White Stone had happened to pass their camp. Dave had known Anahareo's father, and so had stopped to eat and chat. He had slept that night rolled up in his blanket outside their cabin beside the fire. The following morning, with the casualness of his kind, he had thrown in his store of supplies and elected to remain with them for the time being as Archie's partner. As Dave now checked the traps every day, Archie could remain at the table writing. The urge to write down what he felt about the North pressed upon him. He had a lot to say, and he was taking endless pains to make it interesting.

He had begun during the past winter to correspond with his mother who, after some years of silence and of feeling hurt by his neglect, was driven to seek his advice when the son of her second marriage, Leonard Scott-Brown, applied to become a clerk in the Hudson's Bay Company. Leonard joined the Hudson's Bay Company in London on June 16, 1928, and was sent out to Moose Factory on August 14, where he was to remain until his resignation in March 1930.

Eight hundred miles of bush and rock separated Moose Factory from Doucet, and it is unlikely that the half-brothers ever met in Canada. It was a coincidence that Leonard should have come into the fur trade just as Archie was to vow to give up trapping beaver. Archie did not tell his mother about this vow, partly because he had never confided in her, and partly because it occurred to him to use her for another purpose.

Now that he was busy writing, he wanted to find an outlet for his work. He thought of English magazines. He could not send manuscripts from the bush back and forth across the Atlantic. He needed a reliable agent. Aunt Ada, whose judgement he respected, would be too critical of his work. Mrs. Scott-Brown, voluminous correspondent that he knew she could be if given half a chance, was just the ticket. He sent her "The Falls of Silence", as soon as he was satisfied with it. It was an article of about three thousand words, an account of a trapper's life in Northern Ontario, and its chief interest, which the title he gave it perfectly reflects, is the loneliness and the beauty of the northern woods, which it perfectly conveys. The tone is nostalgic, even elegiac, and the magazine *Country Life*, to which Mrs. Scott-Brown sent it, caught that note when they published the article nearly a year later. It appeared in the issue of March 2, 1929, the

155

author's name being given as "H. Scott-Brown". In the following week's issue a letter from Mrs. Scott-Brown appeared, pointing out that the article was not by her, but by her son, Archibald Stansfeld Belaney. The editor appended an apologetic note to her letter published in the correspondence column, explaining that hers was the only name that appeared on the typescript.

This was odd, for by the time the article appeared, Archie had introduced himself by letter to the editor and quite a correspondence had ensued. The correspondence had in fact begun nearly a year before the article was published when Archie wrote to the editor saying that he understood from Mrs. Scott-Brown that they desired some photographs to illustrate it. He enclosed a batch, and from those that were reproduced with the article we can see what the cabin at Lake Attik looked like.

"The Falls of Silence", his first published work if we except his contribution in 1914 to *The Hastonian*, is written as though by a white man. The Indians are spoken of as part of the scene. But there is no attempt on the part of the author to identify himself with them. The style has none of the colloquialisms and grammatical misuses he was later to cultivate in order to give a sense of reality to his claims to be a half-breed struggling with a strange language. For the moment, and only for the moment, he writes as what he was, an educated white man who has a passionate love for nature; the sort of writer, in fact, whose work readers of *Country Life* were accustomed to read every week.

The article leaves no doubt about his feeling for the Canadian wilderness. This is not a pose but a passionate sense of identification. It is the land, more than the animals or the description of the trapper's life, which he wants the reader to appreciate,

> a land of shadows and hidden trails, lost rivers and unknown lakes, a region of soft-footed creatures going their noiseless ways over the carpet of moss, and there is silence, intense, absolute and all-embracing. It is as though one walked on the bottom of a mighty ocean of silence, listening, waiting for some sound which must eventually break it.

156

A curious echo, this, of the one serious note struck in his humorous article in *The Hastonian* sixteen years before. "This is the most silent country on the face of the globe, silent as death except for the booming of the ice on the big lake." "The Falls of Silence" is a descriptive piece, carrying no particular message except the melancholy one that the day of the free trapper is passing.

> The real trapper (by which I mean the one who spends his days in the Strong Woods country or farther north, not the part-time trapper out after a quick fortune) is as much a part of the woods as the animals themselves. [As he] wends his way through this soundless maze many are the pairs of eyes turned on him, the furry ears pointed his way and sharp little snouts raised sniffing in his direction. He is continually undergoing the inspection of senses trained to a hair-trigger delicacy. If in tune with his surroundings he is aware of it. . . .

The article reveals the very essence of Grey Owl's kinship with the natural world. We see through his eyes the endless black forests of spruce,

> stately trees, cathedral-like with their tall spires above and their gloomy aisles below . . . sweeping onward into the unknown distance, flowing in mass-formation over all the face of the earth. This is the last grand army of the forest opposing a black impenetrable barrier to civilisation until they too shall fall before the march of progress, to be a burnt offering on the altar of the God of Mammon.

In such oratorical sentences we hear the cadences of the myth-maker calling men's attention to a world they have lost or have yet to gain.

But the myth-maker would not have won attention unless he had been able to convince his readers that he knew of what he spoke. He is at one with the world he is describing here; and the reader feels it. Comparing the situation of the old-time hunter, who could live in one district and find all the fur he needed at hand, with the modern hunter, who has to go further and further afield, into rougher country with a severer climate, he makes out an historical case for those who choose to follow this hard life.

> The kind of man who follows the chase for a living remains the same; the spirit of adventure, the desire to penetrate faraway hidden spots, the urge to wander, is there as it was in his prototype of two hundred years ago. This peculiarity of temperament, this restless voyaging disposition, is shared by all the wilderness dwellers. Indians are for ever changing present camping grounds for others differing in very few respects from the places they leave. All the animals that live in the forest pass most of their time getting from one place to another just like it, and the rest of it travelling through all kinds of difficulties past good feed to get to another locality in no way different. Movement is life in the bush, escape from the deadly stagnation that must ensue from the constant view of a changeless immovable prospect.

Country Life invited him to send them further work, and it was with this that he was struggling throughout the summer of 1928 before their move to Cabano.

Not until a year later, in a letter dated May 6, 1929, does he begin to build up a description of himself as an Indian "by adoption". He tells the editor, with whom by now he was on chatty terms, that he had been adopted by the Ojibways twenty years earlier. But at this stage he still writes of Indians as "them", not as "we", which was the style he adopted later. Already he is speaking of white civilization as something remote, from the cultural influences of which he has been absent for a long time. One can see him in these letters building up this picture of himself, and not for one moment doing it as a calculated fraud, for there was no personal gain for himself in the transformation he was effecting. He still signs himself A. S. Belaney, and he does not deny his English origins to the editor. But one has the clear impression that he is a white man who has turned his back on the white world and given himself up altogether to his Indian surroundings.

Writing of the frontier took his mind back to the early days. He had married an Indian girl, and had lived with the tribe. All that he had learnt of the ways of the wilderness he had learnt from the men of Bear Island and from the Espaniels at Bisco. All the wrongs he had done since had been because he left that environment. He wanted to merge his identity in the landscape and among the aboriginal inhabitants of Canada.

Writing that summer of 1928 beside Lake Attik, feeling at his knee the slight tap of an uncertain, testing hand, knowing that he was under observation, he was beginning to succumb to the purpose for which these two small creatures had been sent into his life.

Such determined little personalities as the kittens demanded names. To begin with they had called them simply the two Micks. Ahmik is the Indian for beaver, and Mick served as an affectionate diminutive. But as they established separate identities there came the need to differentiate one from the other. Mick suggested Irishmen, and with a total disregard of sex the two kittens were called McGinnis and McGinty. As though they had settled it between themselves, the male, McGinnis, a playful energetic fellow who always took the lead in any joint undertaking, adopted Pony as his special patron and guardian, and the female, McGinty, offered herself shyly to Archie.

But to begin with, when they were very small and strange, and before they had accepted Archie, they both adopted Pony as their foster-mother. In *Devil in Deerskins* she gives a lively account of what this special relationship involved her in. She had always wanted children, and now her prayers, she says, were grotesquely and overwhelmingly answered, and she was presented with the equivalent of twins, who took every bit as much time as babies do. Even the diaper-changing had its equivalent. They had filled their tin tub with water, so that the kittens, who were not yet allowed out of the cabin, and showed no desire to go, could splash round in it and refresh themselves. Every time one of the kittens wanted to "go", he submerged himself to do it, for the beaver will not defecate except under water, and Pony was kept busy emptying and refilling the bath-tub. What life was like in the cabin beside Lake Attik with these two furry dynamos is graphically and amusingly described at length in *Pilgrims of the Wild* and in *Devil in Deerskins*. This humble shack was Liberty Hall.

> These were no cringing, terror-stricken things with feral eyes that cowered fearfully in dark corners, but a pair of very wide-awake, aggressive person-alities who gave themselves completely into our hands and proceeded to levy unceasing demands on our attentions.

The question of selling them was settled when one of the kittens escaped, and they all, Dave included, spent the whole day searching for the wanderer. Darkness had fallen when Archie found McGinnis, cowering in a muskeg swamp and plainly feeling very sorry for himself. By the time he had got him into his arms, Grey Owl had sunk up to his shoulders in the squelchy black mud, and each attempt to extricate himself from its sour embrace only served to drive him deeper into it. He knew this, and so after a few attempts, he stood there patiently, clasping the small beaver to his chin, and calling repeatedly for Pony.

When she came, she took the beaver first, restoring it to its companion, who immediately demanded to know in a series of chattering questions where he had been all day. Pony returned to rescue Archie, who had to be pulled out by his shoulders; and then the four of them were in the cabin together. Archie had to retire to bed, for his clothes were thick with odorous mud, and they could not be washed until morning, or even kept in the cabin.

Meanwhile McGinnis also had a cleaning-up job to do. He had been without rest all day and, after all the excitement, was now ready to sleep it off. But no beaver can go to rest without a complete toilet. He had dipped himself in the bath and was now sitting on his tail, clawing himself dry with the special claw, separate from the others, which beaver have for this purpose. Then he saw Archie in bed, and as though he wanted to express gratitude for his rescue he climbed upon the bunk and, propping himself up against

Archie's reclining figure, completed his clawing. Then he sniffed at Archie's face and nibbled a little at his eyebrows. Finally he climbed on to Archie's chest, heaved a great sigh, and fell quickly asleep.

After that there was no question of selling them. The question instead was how to support four lives on a reduced income that could barely keep two. That was a human problem. Meanwhile, in a log cabin beside a lake, these two small fry behaved just as they would have done in the beaver lodge if mother had been still about, able to supply them with milk from her own dugs, and with poplar leaves from the winter store stashed away at the entrance to the lodge by the provident parents before the ice came.

They were active, lusty feeders, although they did not take much at a time, and on a slightly adjusted diet of porridge, tinned milk, and poplar leaves, they soon showed growth. They were very gentle and trusting, and after feeding showed a desire to be picked up and fondled, which they indicated by standing up in the box in which they slept and were fed, holding up their arms, and making yearning sounds. As soon as they were picked up, they responded like children, warmly and affectionately. After ten minutes or so of play in this way, they would suddenly collapse into sleep, often on the inside of a shirt or curled around Archie's or Pony's neck.

Such was their demand for affection that each little animal always made straight for his or her selected foster-parent when one of these petting sessions was due, or when in trouble or perplexed. They were devotedly attached to one another. But they seemed to require, when a problem was beyond them, the protective presence of someone wiser and stronger than themselves. The mother would have provided this in the beaver house. In the cabin, Archie and Pony were constituted over-all protectors.

They had, when the occasion required it, the pathetic helplessness of little children and, when the circumstances were altered, the aggressive personalities to be expected of the product of countless generations of a species which had triumphed over the forces of nature. They spent much time playing together, wrestling with each other, chattering away volubly in a shrill childish treble with that high-pitched note of excitement one hears in the voices of children at play. They were allowed to roam round the cabin where they would, and in this way went on long voyages of discovery behind and over bales and boxes, and in the dark corners that were sometimes easier to get into than to back out of. In such cases, or when they became separated, frantic cries for help would go up until, when the lost one had been rescued and placed back with the other, a rapturous scene would be enacted, as they threw themselves on their backs with wiggles and squeals of joy, and then they would lie down together, holding tightly on to each other's fur.

It was not long before they had their human captors completely under control. At first Archie had raised his gun to shoot them. Then, when he lowered his gun, he said that they would be sold as soon as they got to town. Then the trip to town was put off, although they badly needed supplies. By this time, two months later, they were spending many hours of the day watching the kittens who, by three months of age—they had been perhaps three weeks old when taken from the water—were showing signs of wanting to see what the world was like beyond the confines of the cabin.

This symptom of growth by no means meant any diminution of the deep affection each small animal seemed to have for its particular patron. They still demanded to be picked up and cuddled; they still wanted to include the adults in their games, hiding behind some object and then rushing out at their friends to upset them; or coming to them, waiting helplessly when some problem, such as getting over an obstruction, was beyond a kitten's solving.

But now they were curious, too, and when the cabin door was open they would gaze wonderingly over the landscape. Then they took to going down to the lake together, then to going for little swims and dives, brushing and combing themselves after a dip with that meticulous care which makes the beaver the cleanest of all animals. Beyond the daily feed of porridge now, they were entirely self-supporting, cutting themselves their own daily food supply from the surrounding forest. But always at sundown they returned to the cabin. And then it was as though they put

162

away the workaday world and became as little children again, demanding to be picked up and cuddled, making purring sounds of satisfaction as they made themselves comfortable on the reclining human frame, expressing satisfaction by nibbling at Archie's or Pony's fingers, or nosing into their necks as though, if they could, they would absorb them altogether.

Archie struggled strenuously against this assault on his affections. How could he contemplate trapping animals again when he had lived with them, as he was now doing, and had seen what gentle, affectionate lives they led? But he was a trapper; he had no other way of making a living. Often with McGinnis asleep on his neck or heavy on his lap, he would be examining maps and trails, searching out places where fur might still be found.

Thus the summer passed, with Archie employed as a fire ranger in a tower, not on the move as he had been in Bisco, so that he was able to come back at night to the cabin and his by now active family. When, with the approach of fall, the job was coming to an end, he ceased spending so much time with the maps in the evening. He had even put away the article on which he was still working. He sat brooding, withdrawn and uncommunicative.

Then one night he came home looking immensely serious, and Pony prepared herself for bad news.

"Well," he said to her, "we've got a new job. I'm off the beaver hunt for good."

How, after much self-questioning, he arrived at this decision is told convincingly in *Pilgrims of the Wild*. It was certainly spurred on by the living examples of McGinnis and McGinty, but other factors had been at work over the years. He had become sick of the constant butchery, especially since the part-time trappers left everywhere evidence of their greed and haste to get what they had come for. The genuine trapper sets for beaver only under ice, so that the animal when caught is cleanly drowned. The part-time trapper, who wants to make a little extra money on top of his ordinary trade, comes into the woods in spring when the ice is gone and the female is held to the lodge by her young. He uses

163

spring-pole traps, which whip the animal into the air and leave it suspended over water while it slowly dies an agonizing death of thirst while hanging only a few inches above what could give it life. The part-timer uses steel traps that catch an animal by a paw and leave it sometimes for days to chew off its paw and then escape to die a lingering death in the woods, or a quick one when it is attacked by some predator. Archie had once seen a mother beaver, moaning with pain while her paw was caught in such a trap, holding in her good hand one of her young and suckling it.

From such painful sights he had turned aside. Life was cruel. This was just a place where it showed. For years he had been walking blindly, and now his eyes were opened. The deserted beaver lodges in their thousands which had once been so busy with life were like ghost towns. An area of Ontario one hundred thousand square miles in extent was dry of beaver. Soon they would be gone altogether. Faced with that prospect he saw that beaver stood for something vital, something essential in this wilderness. Without them it would be a waste, not a wilderness.

The chance capture of these two kittens now made death in the woods seem something else than the workings of inexorable fate. It did not have to be. These were not just rich fur-bearing animals which took the trappers' lures, and when they did, were outwitted and had to pay the price. These were sharers of the universe, and these two kittens

> with their almost child-like intimacies and murmurings of affection, their rollicking good fellowship with not only each other but ourselves, their keen awareness, their air of knowing what it was all about [seemed] like little folk from some other planet, whose language we could not yet quite understand. To kill such creatures seemed monstrous. I would do no more of it. Instead of persecuting them further I would study them, see just what there really was to them. I perhaps could start a colony of my own; these animals could not be permitted to pass completely from the face of the wilderness.*

*Pilgrims of the Wild.

"Yes," he went on to Pony, "I am now the President, Treasurer, and sole member of the Society of the Beaver People. How about a donation?"

"Donations are going to be pretty thin," she laughed, then grew serious. "I never hoped you would do that. What'll you do now?"

He explained his idea. They would find some part of the country where the conditions were ideal for beaver, and start a colony there. They would start with no more than McGinnis and McGinty. On their progeny the colony would be built. He would study them, as he had been studying unconsciously the behaviour of these two tamed ones all summer. He would continue to hunt, for he knew no other way to live. That meant that the colony would have to be situated in good fur-bearing country, which in turn meant that it would swarm with trappers, and he would have to be his own game warden. He had nothing to back up this project but two small beaver and an unpaid bill at the store. But he was determined that he would save the beaver from extinction before they went the way of the buffalo. It was a one-man conservation project, a crazy scheme, but one that had to be tried. He said to Anahareo "It may go hard with us—we might have to pull in the belt a few notches. Are you game?"

"Of course," she replied. "We'll both work at it."

As the story is told in *Pilgrims of the Wild*, there appears on the scene at this point, quite by chance, a character who shows the mark of being a literary invention, introduced to the story for the sake of motivating the plot. This is Joe Isaacs, a Micmac Indian, and a born liar, but so amusing and outrageous a one that his tales are half-believed. He tells them of a fabulous part of the country in New Brunswick where the beaver are—well, so thick there is not room for them all in the lakes and rivers available. Overpopulation has forced the emergence of a new species of land beaver, distinguished from your ordinary water beaver by having grown short hair on its tail like an otter. Joe Isaacs is portrayed by Archie as a constitutional liar whose wondrous tales need ninety per cent knocked off them to get down to the truth. Nevertheless, he fires their imagination with his report of the country around the Touladi River in Quebec, which runs into Lake Temiscouata, not far from the New Brunswick border. They look at it on the map. It seems ideal country, with its lakes and rivers, in which to start a beaver colony, and sufficiently well-stocked with other game to provide them with a living.

The writer in Archie, sharpened by practice all summer with the as yet unfinished article, makes Joe Isaacs seem quite real. No doubt someone like him did exist. Travellers' tales of distant territories were dropped at every campfire, and sometimes half-believed. They wanted to get away from this part of the country. Touladi beckoned from eight hundred miles away. New resolutions such as his, not to take the life of a beaver ever again, were fortified by the sense of going on a pilgrimage. Joe Isaacs disappeared from the story never to return to it. Dave White Stone did too, temporarily, for there was not enough money among them to pay three fares. He would join them later. The beavers were placed in a tin-lined box, with a dish of water secured in one corner of it. Until they reached the railroad, Archie carried this on his back, holding it steady by a tumpline wound round his forehead. Along with their canoe, snow-shoes, skis, guns, cooking utensils, and a large bundle of poplar, they boarded the east-bound train at Doucet. Every-thing, including the beaver, had to go in the baggage car, but Archie and Pony had to go in the day coach.

In Quebec City, where they had to change trains, they took the opportunity to feed the beaver on the station platform, thereby attracting a large crowd, not all of it friendly, for such was the outcry of the two Micks that these two be-fringed Indians were thought to be escorting the beavers against the beavers' will. At Rivière-du-Loup, where they again had to change trains, civilization seemed to be closing in on them once more. Towns and small farms lined the railway tracks, and the forest had receded to the horizon. But as the train followed a southward course the country looked more promising for the project, and then big Lake Temiscouata, flanked by mountains, hove into view. Into this the Touladi River ran, and the country east of it looked wild and rugged, just the place for his purpose. They got off the train finally at Cabano, a small town in the 1920s, with one local industry, a sawmill, which employed all the employable male inhabitants. Archie, who had a feeling for small, sturdy, homely places, took an immediate liking to it:

> The very appearance of its tree-shaded, broad sidewalks and unpretentious but neat wooden dwellings somehow suggested a spirit of good will and hospitality, as houses and clothes not unusually reflect the personality of those who occupy them.

On the main street he stopped a young man with a frank, friendly face to ask him where he could find a teamster to move their baggage and equipment down to the lake. The young man's name was Bernie Graham. He could hear the kittens now in their tin box on Archie's back, and he asked what they were. To be stopped by an Indian carrying beaver kittens on his back on the street of his home town at dusk excited Bernie so much that he went home and collected his parents, some food, and a bottle of wine, and in the family flivver took the dirt road down to the lake to interview the newcomers.

The teamster with a pair of horses carried their baggage down to the lake. Archie counted what remained when he had paid off the teamster. His worldly capital consisted of one dollar and forty-five cents. He had his army pension of fifteen dollars a month, a wife, two beaver, and the winter before them. He was to know some of the hardest times of his life before he got through it. But on this golden evening they were all in good heart. Released from their box, the two Micks took in eyefuls of the surrounding scenery, then like two elderly gentlemen paraded solemnly down to the edge of the water to take their initial dip. It looked like a good spot to them all.

CHAPTER **11**

THEY WERE both taken for Indians, and this, as it had always done, pleased him. The project of bringing back the beaver required public support. It would attract much more attention if an Indian rather than a white man were to start it.

He had formed no detailed plan for his beaver colony at this stage. But his references to it in letters show that his imagination had leaped ahead, to see not only the beaver put under a closed season until their numbers were restored, but the timber operations held in check, and the Indians restored to their villages. With his showman's instinct he knew that the proposer of such a project would be listened to more keenly if he bore the badge of suffering himself. Indians and beavers, they shared the same plight. The civilization of machines was overwhelming them. He, an Indian, would be their spokesman. He would stand with his back to the green wall of the forest and defend them.

He had the true actor's response to the expectations of his audience. Even at this moment, before this handful of habitants, he was becoming instantly more Indian. I was to see the same miracle often in London some years later, when a tired, drained man who looked incapable of any further effort would respond to what was expected of him. It was a self-hypnotic power, exercised instinctively.

The hills rising on the far shore of Lake Temiscouata, crowned with spruce and dark-blue in the evening light, seemed to hold their arms open as if to embrace them. This was a good omen. He had with him all his gear—canoe, traps, tent, skis, snowshoes, stove: all that a man needed to live in the world. While Pony was busy with the fire, arranging their evening meal, and talking with her charming ease of manner to the women who gathered about to watch her preparations, McGinnis and McGinty were enjoying their freedom, disporting themselves in the water, putting on diving exhibitions and wrestling matches, then suddenly floating with only their heads visible above the water while they regarded the excited crowd solemnly. Archie stood at the edge of the water, conscious of all this going on behind and before him. If he had not been there the beaver kittens would not have been so carefree. He was the rock in the centre of this excited crowd of animals and humans, a gaunt figure in a buckskin jacket and moccasins, his long hair falling to his shoulders, the primitive northern man facing the great rim of rock-bound earth that was his home.

The next day the beaver were listless and off their feed. Archie and Pony put it down to the confinement of the journey. But all that day the kittens would not go near the water, nor on the next. They scratched themselves a great deal, pulling out in the process handfuls of hair, and looking as a result very unhappy. Sitting there, bowed and solemn, with their balding pates and hooded eyes, they looked like two shrunken and senile old men, instead of the bouncing humorists they usually were. Archie and Pony were reminded of the pictures of Indian warriors, with their heads shaven for battle, and called them the Little Iroquois. But the kits did not share the joke as they usually did when their human companions laughed heartily, throwing back their own heads, baring their teeth in imitation, and shaking with what seemed to be uncontrollable mirth.

They could not start the journey to the Touladi Lakes with the kittens in this condition. It was already growing late in the season, and ice was forming in little pools beside the lake every morning. They had some way to go into unknown country, and a cabin to build, before winter set in. Meanwhile Archie used the enforced delay to good purpose. He had to establish a line of credit with a local store for a winter's provisions, and here miraculously the two sad invalids helped him.

They took them to the local doctor to see if he could provide a salve to relieve the itch. The doctor wrote out a prescription, refusing to take a fee from an old soldier, he and Archie having exchanged some reminiscences of the war while he was examining the beavers. Just as well, for after paying the teamster, Archie had less than a dollar and a half left.

The local storekeeper, to whom they took the prescription to be filled, proved to have the same generous disposition. News of the Indians with their beaver pets had spread around the town. He was quite ready, not only to charge the prescription, but to open an account for stores when they explained they were going into Birch Lake, which was on the Touladi River, for a winter's trapping. They returned to their camp on the shore with the ointment, $150 worth of supplies, and still with a little more than a dollar cash in hand. Who needed cash in the woods? They had what they had to have, their supplies, and a load of worry was lifted from their shoulders.

"Let's open up the champagne," said Pony exuberantly.

Vigorously on their return they rubbed in the ointment, and the two Micks finished the job by having a thoroughly good scratch themselves, which made the ointment penetrate beneath the skin. Almost immediately they began to pick up, and to eat again. Within twenty-four hours they had made an almost complete recovery.

While in Cabano, Archie had sent off a postcard to the

editor of *Country Life*, giving his new address as Poste Restante, Cabano, P.Q., and saying that he was going into the woods until Christmas. He did not want the editor to think that he had abandoned his writing, and he had it on his conscience that he had done nothing now for nearly a month.

Then, on a cold morning three days later, with a touch of frost in the air, and the thin ice formed overnight in the puddles cracking beneath their moccasins as they loaded the canoe, they began the long journey.

A shock was in store for them. When they reached the Touladi River, it did not at all measure up to Joe Isaac's estimate of its virtues. It was a sluggish, shallow stream, incapable of being navigated by a canoe as fully loaded as theirs. There was only one way to get over the difficulty. The heaviest of their supplies would have to be carried by a teamster to a point opposite Birch Lake, while they and the two beaver made their way in the lightened canoe as best they might up the narrow river. The teamster asked ten dollars for the job and with little more than a dollar now in his pocket the Pilgrimage might there and then have reached its end, but out on the lake that night they saw a red fox swimming across the bow of the canoe. The animal could not swim as swiftly as Grey Owl could handle a canoe. They cornered him and captured him alive, and sold him that night at the hamlet at which they landed for the ten dollars needed to carry them on the next stage of their journey. But as he pocketed the money, Grey Owl felt a twinge of remorse. "It seemed somehow like a betrayal," he wrote later; "he had been free like us, and the money no sooner changed hands than I wished I had killed the poor beast outright, and sold the hide instead."

A narrow and quite unnavigable creek led from the Touladi up to Birch Lake, the end of their journey. They would have to walk and carry the entire load of more than eight hundred pounds, including the canoe. The distance by water was only ten miles, but as the country was full of fallen timber, some of it lying nearly breast high from the ground, and there were impenetrable areas of rampikes and muskeg and pieces of marshy land they had to dodge, the distance they actually covered was something more like thirty miles.

All this had to be done carrying this immense burden. The situation was made worse by the fact that the first snow had started to fall, and as a result of the bitterly cold nights pools of water everywhere became coated with ice, making treacherous footing.

On some days they made as little progress as a quarter of a mile. The potatoes they were carrying, a whole winter's supply, froze into a solid mass and had to be thrown away.

"Well," commented Grey Owl later, "that was about two hundred pounds that we didn't have to carry any more. We got considerable consolation from figuring how this helped us. Allowing five more days to get in [to Birch Lake], at the rate of two hundred pounds a day saved, we had made a net gain of a thousand pounds. . . . In the woods a man has often to turn reverses to what good account he may, but this was the first time that I had ever figured myself out of trouble by means of arithmetic."

The loss of the potatoes was a serious enough matter, but worse was to befall them. Each day more snow fell. A heavy fall could have made the use of snowshoes possible, which would have made progress easier, though heavily loaded as they were it would have ruined the shoes. But the fall was light; it came in little flurries blown on gusts of icy wind, and stung the face and made the eyes water before it drifted to the frozen ground. When they made camp at night and lit a fire inside the tent the snow on the canvas surface melted and the tent became as damp as though it had been plunged in the river. When the fire went out the tent froze again, this time as stiff as a board, and the business of re-rolling it in the morning with bare hands became a refined torture that made them whimper with pain as they went about the work.

Following behind Grey Owl, the tump-line pressing into her forehead and the weight of her pack pressing into the small of her back, Anahareo recalled the day she had made that easy journey from the railroad into Pony Hall. Then, as now, a pair of long lean legs in buckskin trousers had kept up an automaton-like progress ahead of her. Then she had carried less than a hundred pounds. She had thought it hard, and had been weary. She could have cried aloud with resentment as she remembered that. Now with hands that ached and eyes stinging with the snow, with the pain of the tump-line searing her forehead, so cold that even the breath in her lungs seemed to press against her chest like cold iron, she was tempted to cry out to make him stop, so that she could fall on the hard grey surface of the earth and feel the blessed relief when the cruel leather of the tump-line no longer pressed into her forehead.

But the long legs ahead of her hardly ever stopped or stumbled. Relentlessly, tirelessly, they went onwards, seemingly oblivious of everything as well as of her.

Though he could see her only when he did pause, Archie was aware of the strained face and the small bent figure that followed him. As each hour passed, and each fresh obstacle was overcome, his lips grew tighter, his face more mask-like. He could have hated the trail for the suffering it was bringing to Anahareo. But the discipline it required of those who followed it, and which would allow no turning back from a task undertaken, fired him to keep on. He tried in every way he could to lighten her burden, but she fought like a wildcat to share equally with him. That devil of pride that lived in both of them could not admit defeat, and she cried out at him in a thin, tired voice, and stamped her feet and would not move until on her slender shoulders he had loaded as much as a man could carry.

Then, though he spoke to her fiercely, and glared at her to bring her to submission, he loved her more than ever; and she, answering him with venom, sometimes turned her eyes away from him lest he should see in them an admiration for him she could not conceal. And while sick with weariness, and oppressed with the thought of the cold unknown that lay before them, they made this slow and painful journey, the beaver, as though they sensed the struggle that was going on, grew silent, watching it all with bright and speculative eyes but keeping very still and out of mischief.

For two weeks they carried on, eating nothing but frozen food, sleeping in blankets that seemed as cold as the ground on which they lay, until one night Archie got up from the fire and with his gun sloped off into the darkness. They had left the river behind for many days owing to the circuitous path necessary to avoid obstacles. He knew that they must be somewhere near the lake by now, and he thought that if he could get to the top of a high knoll near their camping ground he might, under the light of the bright moon which flooded the sky, see an easier approach than the one they were following. At least he could confirm the position of the lake.

An hour's arduous walk brought him to the eminence he was seeking. The whole country lay at his feet, white and silent in the light of the moon. In the distance he could see the lake frozen and motionless with the newly fallen snow drifted into graceful mounds around its edges as the wind got a clear sweep across its open surface. His eye, practised in these things, surveyed the country and saw a lie of land that would provide a good trail. Making his way down from the hill he followed this and satisfied himself that it afforded good footing.

But as he approached the lake he saw signs that confirmed Joe's status as the champion liar of all time, and boded ill for their future. There was a beaver lodge at the head of it, but no sign of mink or otter. And the surface of the snow, untrampled and unmarked, showed no indication of lynx or marten. Joe had said that here they would find the ideal hunting ground that every trapper dreams of, and at the same time a safe place to raise the beaver. On the first count he was wrong, and on the second likely to be wrong too. For he couldn't raise and protect the beaver if there was no fur which he could trap to provide them all with a living.

He returned slowly and thoughtfully to the eminence from which he had descended, and there leaning on his rifle gazed down on the distant tent, aglow with the fire that burned inside it. He saw in his imagination the group that would be about the fire; the woman sewing at a buckskin jacket, the two kittens wearied with play lying fast asleep in one an-other's arms. There in that little radiance set in this white silence was everything that he loved in this world, and he was bringing them to ruin, maybe to death. All for a crazy scheme.

The silent figure, bowed over his rifle, reached in that hour the depth of despair. It seemed to him for a little while, as he stood there thinking back over the past, that the trail he had always loved had now betrayed him; that here with no money, with little food to keep them, and under a self-imposed vow that he could not break without dishonour, he

174

was likely to meet a mean and tragic end, and betray at the same time this woman and the two beaver who had put their trust and their lives into his hands.

He went down with a heavy heart to the little tent. But when he drew back the flap and entered, such a glow of warmth met him and such an air of cheerfulness seemed to irradiate the close atmosphere, that he smiled a little and put his troubles at the back of his mind. He told Anahareo that he had discovered the lake and a good trail leading to it, and that one more day's packing should see them at their journey's end. With that announcement, which even the beaver seemed to understand, the atmosphere of cheerfulness seemed to glow brighter, and for the first time for many nights they laughed and told stories, as they had done the winter before at Pony Hall. And at the sound of human laughter the beaver roused themselves, and with the air of those ready to oblige with a number, commenced to wrestle and do little tricks, as though they too could see a joke and appreciate it. If at times the man's heart was heavy with foreboding that night he did not show it, for he loved the living things that were in the confined space of this little tent, and it lightened the weight of worry that was pressing on him to see them cheerful and happy once again.

When the last packload had been stacked beside the shore of Birch Lake, and they knew that whatever difficulties still lay ahead, the back-breaking burden of the trail was not among them, they heaved a sigh of profound relief. But a job remained that must be quickly dealt with. It was by now the second week of November, and what promised to be a cold winter had settled down in dead earnest. Before the timber froze too hard they must build a cabin, and they now set themselves to this task with high-spirited enthusiasm.

It took eleven days to build, and when it was completed and the first fire had been built in it, they stood at the lake shore looking with proud eyes at their new home. "It was quite a proud looking place when it was all finished," said Grey Owl, "with its smooth red spruce logs with green and yellow moss between them, and its white plume of smoke streaming up like a banner from the stove pipe, to spread in a blue shifting haze far overhead amongst the dark boughs of the pine trees."

This was to be their home for three years. This, the House of McGinnis as it came to be called, was to remain always in the memories of each of them as the house of their dreams. Years later, when he was writing *Tales of an Empty Cabin*, Grey Owl returned there, and the noble and imaginative picture he draws of it in the opening pages of that book tell more than anything can how much the House of McGinnis meant to Anahareo and him. He found it "tenantless and lonely". But, though the inside reveals its humbleness, "Happiness had been there too, for within it, in a corner, there stands a little withered spruce, the strings that once had held some gifts still hanging from its brown and withered branches. Neglected and abandoned, now mouldering to slow decay, it once had been a place of life and movement, of hope, ambition, and adventure."

That had been in their first winter at Birch Lake, the winter of 1928–9. When the cabin was completed, Grey Owl set out by himself to shoot some fresh meat which they badly needed after living on a diet of frozen bannock for several weeks, and to see in daylight what prospects of fur the country around could show. A deer was quickly killed and brought back to camp, and the immediate problem of food settled. Of that, he saw, they need have no worry all winter. But each fresh expedition that he made from the camp confirmed his first suspicions that fur-animals were practically non-existent in this territory. If he proposed to pay off his store bill by a winter's trapping, he was plainly proposing the impossible, and both he and the storekeeper were out of luck. The situation would be exasperating for the storekeeper, but for him it would be worse.

Money would have to come from his writing if they were to survive, but he was having difficulty with that. His pen seemed to labour, ideas were slow in coming. "The Falls of Silence" was not yet in print, but it had pleased the editor, and he took the copy of it and reread it aloud to Pony to see what the secret of its success was, so that he could repeat it. It seemed to them both very good. He was surprised at his own powers of evocation. He had not unrolled it from his pack for two months. It brought back the great North with an overwhelming rush.

Yet at the same time there was something distant and cold about it, a schoolmaster's precise voice saying thus it was, and thus. Pony did not notice this. His voice when, as here, he dropped the drawling idiom that men use for language in the woods fascinated her. She heard, and heard correctly, the voice of an educated Englishman, using language beautifully....

The edges of frozen fens and marshlands and the shore lines of lakes provide a hunting-ground for foxes and lynx, where live the snow-shoe rabbits and partridges, their prey. Back off main routes in lonely ponds and on dammed-up streams, in hidden gullies, communities of beaver labour thriftily all summer against the coming of winter, passing the cold, dead months as a reward for their prodigious labour, well fed and in comfort and warmth. Here is the last stronghold of the trapper.

He had written this before the coming of McGinnis and McGinty. It had taken him nearly a year to grind out this travelogue of the North, this poetic delight in the joys of the trapper's life. What is this he wrote?

One year, I remember, some Indians left a good [trapping] ground because the beaver were so plentiful they even chewed paddles left at night near the lake shore. The thing seemed so unnatural they were panic-stricken and moved. It has been my aim and desire to strike such another spot, but so far have been unsuccessful.

So patronizing, the white lord laughing at the Indians for their superstition! The contrast between his thought then and now was shocking. He could hardly believe that he had written this. He was determined never to write that way again.

He made a trip into Cabano to cash the two monthly pension cheques which had accumulated for him at the post office.

It was the week before Christmas, and he bought a bottle of wine and a Christmas pudding to take home to celebrate the season, some candy sticks for the beavers to mark the day, and as a present for Pony a length of cloth to make a dress. He returned in a blinding, whirling snowstorm to find his little family snug and secure, and very pleased to see him. This was the first Christmas they had spent alone together in the woods. Like all other trappers they had gone into town for the week of Christmas and New Year, partly to renew supplies and have some fun, partly so that Pony could make her confession and go to mass. Even Archie and other trappers like him, mindful of their early years and of homes long gone and far away, refrained in a rough, respectful way from taking life at that season.

Besides, they did not then have the children. This was McGinnis's and McGinty's first Christmas, and they made up their minds to make it a memorable one for them. Pony who, unlike Archie, came from a happy home always reverberating in unison to the joy or woe of some member of it, or united in festive celebration over Christmas or a birthday, probably missed her home most at this time of the year, and grew a little sad.

Archie was aware of this. Nobody could be funnier or more entertaining when he wanted to be. "How We Made Christmas" is one of the most moving chapters in *Pilgrims of the Wild*. Unlike the rest of the account it is full of literary artifice, but none the worse for that. Not since Dickens wrote *A Christmas Carol* has the spirit of Christmas been celebrated so wholeheartedly. After dinner they came and stood together outside the cabin. "Listen," said Pony, "the bells of Christmas." Up above them the wind from the lake rustled the tops of the pine trees, and a sound of distant music seemed to stir the air.

Memories of other richer times, contrasted with the poverty of what they could celebrate with now, brought these two more closely together than they had been at any time before. In this the two beaver played no small part. They were just at the age, like puppies or kittens, when they spent most of their waking hours in the pursuit of fun. But unlike domestic pets they had no moments of mindless abstractions, as when a puppy stands panting, his tail wagging mindlessly, or the kitten in the middle of a game starts washing herself and seems lost in thought. The beaver kittens could suddenly fall asleep, passing out through sheer physical weariness in the act of doing something. But the games always had a purpose, a mock battle between them of immense shift and subtlety, a journey of discovery over bales and under furniture demanding as much co-ordination and communication as would be needed to advance a battalion over a minefield in preparation for an attack.

It was possible to see in every calculated move a little brain at work, and to see mirrored in an entirely expressive face the passage of thought leading to the decision. One saw cunning gathering itself together for something that would outwit the opponent, whether it was human or simply an inanimate piece of furniture, obstructing the passage. Or humour accumulating in quivers of the solemn little face until it burst its bounds, and the small body would rear itself upwards, balancing against its flat tail, and shake, throwing back its head, showing its teeth in a wide grin, and giving the impression of being about to roll over in an uncontrollable fit of laughter.

What they loved, like all animals and some children, was the unexpected. This, on its appearance, they always weighed up solemnly, blinking like two small owls. Then, assured that its intentions were not hostile to them, they approached every novelty with the eagerly expectant air of those who have never been disappointed yet. They had regarded the preparations for Christmas with the intense curiosity of intelligent inquirers anxious to inform themselves as to some complicated procedure. Pony had taken two empty white sugar sacks, cut them at the seams, bordered them with some red fringe she had, and had hung them as curtains. Fortunately they were out of reach of the kittens or they would certainly have been pulled down, thoroughly examined, and then drawn across the floor to line their sleep box against the draught. Archie had cut out with his knife wooden pelmets and had painted these with Indian signs. They had lit many candles, so that the little room was dazzling with light. A saddle of deer's meat was sizzling in the pan atop the stove, and the Christmas pudding bubbling quietly in a pot of water alongside it. The presents were laid out; an air of expectancy hung in the room as tense and exciting as the stage when the curtain goes up at the beginning of a play. Scurry, snuffle, the sounds of low murmuring as one kitten communicated to the other his observations or conclusions on this startling scene, all gave meaning to this lighted tableau in a log cabin lost in the winter snows. When, exhausted with tidbits and the unaccustomed pleasure of wrapped-up candy bars which demanded ingenuity before succulence could be reached, the two beaver fell sound asleep, Archie and Pony were left with their bottle of wine and the remains of the feast to talk until dawn. It was a Christmas night that neither of these two was ever to forget.

They had put up their cabin at Birch Lake in November. To begin with, all was quiet: not a sound or sign of animal life anywhere. Every animal was lying low and listening, watching for hostile moves. By Christmas-time this trapper's cabin must have been unique in Canada for not having nailed to its outside walls the skins stripped from the carcasses of trapped beasts.

Soon the forest moved. The whisky-jacks came first. They would have come anyway, their curiosity and greed, as well as their desire for human company, being insatiable. The next to appear were the deer. Then a great lumbering moose, knee-deep in snow, hung his huge head and stared for hours at the log cabin. At first when Archie or Pony appeared, these visitors would turn and fly. But when no movement was made towards them, they stopped running away, and stood and stared. Then they ventured closer, some of them coming into the yard and eating the tidbits put out for them, but evidently prompted more by curiosity than hunger. Their instinctive fear of man still held them a little in check, but they attached themselves to his presence, and soon were feeding quite peacefully, only stopping to look up when he passed by.

He now spent nearly all his time writing. He was still at work on his second article for *Country Life*, having begun the piece in response to the editor's invitation to show them something more, laboured over it all summer at Doucet, and packed it in to Birch Lake with all the freight on that unforgettable journey. The composition, so protracted, had been much altered to keep up with the dramatic changes in his life and outlook, and so that the transition should not prove too painful a shock he had begun, and craftily kept going, a lengthy correspondence with the editor.

He saw that if he was to draw attention to the approaching extinction of Canada's national animal, the beaver, and along with it the degeneration and decimation of Canada's original inhabitants, the Indians, he could do this better if he spoke as an Indian who was a trapper and woodsman himself. Quite consciously he began now to establish the Indian identity which had long been loosely connected with him, and to abandon the white identity which had been wished on him by his birth.

He saw that a short cut to his goal of gaining wide attention would be to convince the editor of *Country Life* that the true identity of the man known as A. S. Belaney was Wa-Sha-Quon-Asin, Grey Owl. At the same time he had to get the editor to accept that the man who wrote the measured prose of "The Falls of Silence" was really, in his native capacity, a much more colourful character, with a more spontaneous and racy style. He had to strengthen in the editor's mind the impression of authenticity which his stories about wild life must make if they were to succeed. A. S. Belaney had written about animals as an observer: Grey Owl would write about them as a co-dweller with them in the wilderness.

So in writing to the editor he developed a colloquial, chummy style which must have been startling when read in the Covent Garden offices of that famous journal, but also to the editor must have seemed very much like the genuine thing. A mixture of shy naïveté, splashes of local colour, fascinating observations of wildlife around the cabin door: here was a discovery, all the more delightful when he interrupts himself to say with charming simplicity: "I guess I shouldn't be talking so personally to you, Mr. Editor, being a business man."

Dave White Stone, who, after Christmas, had appeared one day with the same nonchalance with which he had first joined them, was a little mulish only when the limelight threatened to veer in his direction. Archie introduces him to the editor:

> My partner is a full-blooded Indian, and he can make his meaning clear on a given subject in fewer words than any man I ever met, Red or White. He thinks this writing business is a mild form of insanity, and getting him to pose for a couple of pictures was like coaxing a horse to climb a steep ladder.

He goes to great lengths to read the editor a lecture on the importance of preserving the atmosphere of the woods and the men who work in them by using language and colloquialisms unrestrained by grammatical laws.

This article, the title of which he does not mention, is the one referred to in *Pilgrims of the Wild* which, when written out,

> resulted in a production about six thousand words in length, very meaty, and in which I covered the greater part of Northern Canada, and touched with no light hand on nearly every incident and animal common to that region. The beaver were in it, and all our other dependants that lived out in the yard and in the lake, so I felt I had done my duty by all of them.

It was not to be published. Either the colloquialisms and the disregard of grammatical laws in this particular piece were too much for the editor to swallow after the stylistic purity and the neat interest of "The Falls of Silence", or the article, being three or four times the length of those appearing in *Country Life*, was incapable of being cut without losing its sense. No copy of their answer exists, but evidently they suggested to him that he should consider writing his life story, for this is what he next set to work to do.

But that is to jump ahead. Well satisfied with this six-thousand-word piece when he had done, and leaving Dave in charge of matters, he and Pony went out to mail it.

It was a pleasant spring holiday after being shut up all winter. At the post office in Cabano they found a cheque from *Country Life* for "The Falls of Silence", published at last nearly a year after they had accepted it. This was the first money he had ever earned with his pen. And with the cheque came a letter from the editor, asking how he was getting on with his writing, and reminding him that he would like to see something more. It is easy to understand the editor's interest. "The Falls of Silence" had shown a unique knowledge of animals and an ability to describe them and their psychology in a prose style as compelling as Henry Williamson's. A. S. Belaney must be a man of education. It was the sort of non-committing, encouraging letter which editors are accustomed to send out, casting their seed on what proves to be generally stony ground in the hope that a grain or two of it might take root and flourish in a pocketful of soil. When they received the ungainly six-thousand-word article shortly after, they must have felt their hopes had as so often been misplaced. They little guessed what a vigorous plant was just waiting to spring up.

They returned, greatly excited, to the cabin, only to find that in their absence McGinnis and McGinty had been behaving strangely. The kittens were now almost a year old, and were at that stage where in their natural surroundings the young male would be beginning to wander a little, and the young female to assist her mother as the mother prepared to have another litter.

It was the onset of spring fever which attacks every living organism, animal, as well as human. McGinnis and McGinty had been showing signs of it by coming to the open door of the cabin, and sitting there gazing in a puzzled way into the distance.

It seemed time to move, which is the human way of expressing spring restlessness. Dave wanted to take a job in the sawmill in Cabano to bring them all in a little money so they decided to go and camp by the Touladi Lake for the summer. A government official gave them an empty cabin on the shores of Lake Touladi to live in. This was christened by them "Half-way" because it was on the road to wherever they were going, and none of them knew at that time where that was. Here the little beaver built themselves a beaver house, not far from the cabin, so that they could run in and out at all times of the day and night. Archie describes the commotion:

> They built themselves a funny little beaver house a short distance away where the water was open and the soil clear of snow. They cut and slashed small poplars and willows in all directions, and their cries and slashings and other uproar could be heard at almost any time. Just about daybreak they would scratch and call out at the door, and being let in would come into our beds and go to sleep. They awoke about noon, and, without waiting to eat, scampered off to the big doings outside.*

Then an old trapper came to live nearby, and they decided to move still nearer to Cabano, where Dave would find it easier to reach his work, and the beaver would be safer. They set up camp this time under some old elms and beside a big abandoned beaver house. This McGinnis and McGinty examined in a state of great excitement. Something in this old house moved them, prompting instincts which were evidently ignited by some primitive scent still hanging about this dilapidated dwelling. They came once that evening when called, jabbering in excitement as though relating all the wonders they had found inside the old house. Then

> they headed for the lake, two gnome-like capering little figures that alternately bounced and waddled side by side down the water trail, and we followed them to the landing as we always did, and somehow wished that they were small again.
> We watched the two V's forging ahead towards the ancient beaver lodge until they disappeared into the dusk. And in the star-light, the wake of their passing made pale rippling bands of silver that spread wide behind them, and touched the shore at last, and so were lost. Once, in answer to a call,

*Pilgrims of the Wild.

184

a long clear note came back to us, followed by another in a different key. And the two voices blended and intermingled like a part-song in the stillness of the little lonesome pond and echoed back and forth in the surrounding hills and faded to a whisper, and died.

And that long wailing cry from out the darkness was the last sound we ever heard them make.

We never saw them any more.

CHAPTER 12

A T FIRST hope persisted that they would return. But as the days passed and there was no sign of them the atmosphere at the camp became strained. Pony showed the most emotion; she grew pale and gaunt, cried a great deal, and could not sleep. She insisted they must search every creek that ran into the lake back to the source. Dave, who had regarded the kittens rather superciliously, knew a measure of loss too. He devoted all his time to the search. "To hell with the job," he told them. "A man can always get a job. But them little fellas—they never meant to go away—we can't forget them like that."

But the loss fell heaviest on Archie. It made the future seem purposeless. Without his fully realizing it until they were lost, these kittens had changed the whole of his life.

Not only the manner of his life, but the mixture of thoughts, desires, hopes that keep a man going. They had been the bridges over which he could pass from the hard, selfish existence he had known to the one he had always yearned for but had been unable to reach. Through them he was becoming a natural man, in tune with nature as they were, sharing with them their emotions, sad and gay. Their disappearance showed him the brutal face of the world again, for he was sure that they had been stolen; being tame they could so easily have been captured alive. This conviction, settling on him because no trace of them could be found, sparked his own brutality, and he was ready to do murder if he could find the man who had taken them.

Dave, seeing this, clucked his tongue sympathetically. "You know," he announced, as though reporting a surprising discovery, "I kinda like to see beaver around here myself, some way." Then he disappeared, taking Pony with him. They tramped twenty-five miles through the bush to some distant hills where he had heard there were beaver. It was the time of the year when the young would have been born. From a beaver house that had four kittens in it, he took two. They weighed not more than a few ounces each. They walked back the next day, Pony carrying the two kittens in a bag on her back. One, a male, barely survived the journey, dying within a few hours of their reaching home. The other, a female, seemed also to have little hope of survival. But she was to turn out to be a determined young lady, and the first evidence of her obstinate will was her defiance of death. She took a hold on life, drank milk greedily, and within days was starting to show signs of bottled-up energy that could only be relieved by action. Archie called her Jelly Roll, a name under which she was eventually to become famous. Archie, with the help of the others, had saved her life. Once, some years later, when he himself might have died of pneumonia, and was too ill to get out of bed and tend the fire, she crept in beside him, and never left him until the crisis was over.

The early summer of 1929 passed uneventfully, but they were becoming strapped for money. They had been sustained by a second cheque Archie had got from *Country Life*, who must have written to say that the six-thousand-word article could not be published in its present form, and urging him to get on with the book, and use this material in it. The cheque was an earnest of their firm intention to publish, but no contract was drawn at this stage.

Naturally their talk was all of the future. The beaver sanctuary was the main aim, but the disappearance of McGinnis and McGinty showed that it could not be established here. Steady work, even if he could get it, was not to Dave's taste. He shared Anahareo's dream of finding gold. All a man (or a woman) needed to go prospecting was a prospector's licence (which cost five dollars) and there was all Canada, except that part of it already being mined, open for the pickings. Like all enthusiastic amateurs they had acquired some of the jargon, and spoke to each other of geological strata, faults, veins, assays, and prospects in particular areas with a professional air which barely concealed their hope of just being lucky and stumbling over a pot of gold.

They were getting nowhere at Temiscouata; at least there was a chance of striking a lucky claim in the country north of Rouyn. Jelly Roll would thrive there as well as here; Archie could write there just as easily as he could here. The argument for moving was unanswerable. The only problem was how to raise the train fares. At this juncture came a suggestion from a friend in Cabano, almost certainly Mr. Graham, the father of the family which had befriended them on the night of their arrival. He had read some of Grey Owl's sketches, and he said they would make very good lecture material. There was a fashionable summer resort over two hundred miles away, Métis-sur-Mer, widely known as Mateece, patronized mainly by wealthy Montrealers and Americans, where it would be easy to pick up some lecture fees by giving talks about the beaver and showing Jelly Roll as a living example of what gentle treatment and affection could do with a wild beast.

It was a long and expensive journey, involving a change of trains at Rivière-du-Loup, and a further journey of a hundred and fifty miles down the Gulf of the St. Lawrence to this resort. They arrived unheralded, and remained unnoticed for the next two weeks, cowering in a tent beside the

Gulf, where Jelly Roll was very unhappy at the confinement —water, water everywhere, but she was not allowed in, it being salt. Local inquiries about the possibilities of giving some lectures met only with blank stares and lack of interest until a woman, taking pity on their condition, allowed them to camp on her property, where there was a small pond for Jelly's comfort.

Then, through the agency of this good samaritan the local ladies became interested in these Indians with the tame beaver. The president of the Ladies' Club read Grey Owl's sketches, approved of the sentiments expressed in them, and gave the go-ahead sign to her committee. An evening's lecture was arranged at the Grand Métis Hotel, and here at the appointed hour came Grey Owl and Anahareo; he feeling, as he described later, "like a snake that has swallowed an icicle, chilled from one end to the other."

He did not know it then, but he had stumbled over the pot of gold for which they were going to go searching among the rocks of the north country. The audience of several hundred listened quietly to the opening passage of his talk, getting the measure of him the way audiences do with a speaker, making up their minds whether to listen or let their thoughts wander. They found themselves listening; at first almost against their will, ready to abandon the fellow if he struck a single wrong note or went on too damn long. Then some chuckles escaped them; he had such a droll way of making these animals become—well, like living people. You saw what went on in their minds. And suddenly—yes, you firmed up on something you had always felt uneasy about—it was a damned shame to persecute the little beasts, and something ought to be done about it.

But he didn't leave you with that thought long enough for you to begin to feel self-conscious about being an animal sentimentalist. He spoke about the Indians and their natural affinity with the world of forest, rock, and water which, as visitors, his audience were paying substantial sums to enjoy on this holiday. Lots of practical information came over in the talk; how to build a fire in a blizzard, set up a winter tent in a howling gale, track a wounded animal at night, survive sudden hazards that could mean death to the amateur in the woods. Old legends of the Indians, told in that wonderfully warm voice, made them not the wooden figures against a painted landscape that Indians so often were in legend and story; this was the history of yesterday, and might have happened right outside this room.

It was his first public appearance, and he probably stumbled a little in the opening minutes, while Anahareo sat tensely among the audience. But soon he felt himself carried away by his own theme, as the artist often does, and when he came to the end the applause was wholehearted and long. Someone got up to propose a vote of thanks, and said that what they had listened to had been not a lecture, but a poem. Loud applause! No doubt his language had been at times elevated, and read in cold print afterwards, it might have seemed a little inflated. But it was the way of him, a part of his surrender to his adopted Indian identity.

> For we are Indian, and have perhaps some queer
> ideas; yet who among you having a faith of any
> kind, will deny us our own strange fancies and tell
> us we are wrong, or say us no.

In this passage in *Pilgrims of the Wild* he is telling of the long haunting cry which came across the lake in the dusk as McGinnis and McGinty swam away for the last time, abandoning their home in instinctive response to the imperative call of the Wild. The faint echo of that cry went on reverberating.

> We sometimes hear it in the storm, and in the still
> of evening; at dawn in the song of the birds and in
> the melancholy calling of a loon, half-heard and
> distant in the night. It wails in the minor cadences
> of an Indian chant, and swells in the deep notes of
> an organ played softly by a master hand; it mutters
> in the sound of sleepy streams, and murmurs in
> the rumour of the river, in the endless tolling of the
> waves upon a lake-shore—each and everyone a note
> from the composite of Nature's harmony, chords
> struck at random from the mighty Symphony of

the Infinite that echoes forever on, down the resounding halls of Time.

The collection taken up at the hall produced the incredible
sum of seven hundred dollars, more money than they had
ever had at one time, for unlike a winter's fur catch, there
was no bill for a winter's stake to be deducted by a store.

But the lecture did something more than provide the
means for the removal of their immediate financial anxieties.
It gave them self-confidence. They had been ignored; now
they were the centre of attention. Visitors came to see Jelly
Roll, who treated the curious with studied disdain. The local
Scoutmaster asked Grey Owl to give his boys some talks on
woodcraft. They had arrived penniless and ignored; now it
was difficult to get away. Other local organizations wanted
him to speak, people were coming round with all sorts of
suggestions for improving their lot, and to get their scheme
for a beaver sanctuary going.

What they wanted now was to get back to Dave, and start
on the journey north. They wanted to get away from the
scene of their sorrow, back to their beloved North country
where they could all start a new life.

Within twenty-four hours of their return to Cabano, they
had broken camp, and moved all their baggage, including
Jelly in a well-ventilated box, to the station. And there on the
platform, waiting for the train to come in, those flutters of
an insufficiently firm purpose began to assail them. They
were held to this ravaged, profitless area by the memory of
the two Micks. What if they should come back? After a
summer of wild freedom, what if they were to come looking
for their foster-parents and no one was there? First Pony,
and then Archie, said that they could not possibly leave.
They might come back. Jelly might die on the journey. They
might find no gold. Archie hated prospecting, and he wanted
to get on with his book. Finally Pony agreed that she would
go with Dave, and come back when the freeze-up came. They
divided up the baggage and the stores, and when the train
finally pulled out Archie stood on the platform with one
rolled-up tent, a box at his feet in which Jelly lay peacefully
sleeping, his guns, and some cooking utensils. But for the
first time since he had come to Canada, no canoe. He noted,

with surprise, that for the first time in his life he felt lonesome.

But not for long. This little animal, born wild and now only a few months old, responding with some primitive maternal instinct to a fellow-creature's distress, turned her charms and affectionate ways fully on him. Anahareo had been in the habit of brushing and grooming her every day, an exercise which Jelly plainly found very satisfying. As a result she now had a rich, full-furred coat, dark and glistening. She also had a singular winsomeness, and was altogether very attractive to look at. She was obviously highly intelligent of her kind. Beaver, more than most animals, give the impression of exercising reason rather than responding to instinct; the way they work and build, seemingly estimating with head on one side before they undertake any task what the rest of us would have to take pencil and paper to calculate.

It was not surprising that Jelly should show herself superior in intelligence to McGinnis and McGinty, whose play had often seemed aimless of purpose, and whose demonstrations of affection were prompted by the desire to be cuddled and made much of. They were like helpless little children; what they missed was their mother. But Jelly at the same age was fiercely independent. If she missed her mother she didn't show it. The man to her was a companion; they were on equal terms. There were times when she wanted to be brushed and cared for, and afterwards to lie with her head on the man's knee resting and dreaming. But the rest of the time she treated him as McGinnis and McGinty had treated each other, keeping up a running fire of conversational mumble to which he gave answer in another language, to the satisfaction of both of them.

Without a canoe he had to walk in to the new camp he had found during the summer about ten miles from Cabano on Elephant Mountain. It was well-built and was beside a small lake where they were not likely to be bothered by passing trappers. He could not easily carry the ventilated box he had constructed, designed for train travelling, so he put Jelly in a packsack, with her head and her arms free, and carried her piggy-back this way the whole distance. Around his body he had draped his blankets and hanging from his

192

shoulders were his cooking utensils. He was carrying in addition his basic needs in cooking supplies, slung in a haversack over one shoulder.

Atop all this load, strapped onto the packsack, sat Jelly surveying the scenery, chattering away to herself, calling his attention to passing wonders, pulling his long hair playfully from time to time, or when she wanted to attract his attention to something, or was trying to struggle free. She trusted her man implicitly. He had taken her in her short life on a number of uncomfortable journeys, but he had not deserted her, and as far as she knew this was what life was, a series of arrivals and departures, with uncomfortable intervals of travel always followed by settlement somewhere.

The lake to which they came had everything to satisfy her. She was now five months old, and stirring within her was the beaver's instinctive compulsion to prepare for the long winter's hibernation. There was not another beaver anywhere near. He watched her build little beaver houses at the edge of the water near the cabin, but these did not satisfy her. Half a mile up the lake from the cabin she discovered an abandoned burrow with a roomy sleeping apartment at the end of it, and this she proceeded to make her home. She repaired the ravages which several winters had made on it with mud and sticks and moss, furnished it inside with clean shavings which she trimmed on shore, and let it be seen that this was to be her habitation.

But she wanted the Man too, and to begin with she would leave her own abode several times during the night and scratch at the cabin door to be let in. When ice formed on the lake, locking the beaver house in, he would go down and see her, calling to her as he approached. She would emerge with little squeals of welcome, and wriggles of her body expressing joy, and he would sit on the bank for an hour or more, smoking and watching her. When the cold became too great to sit there, he hit on the idea of putting her in a box and carrying her back to the cabin for a visit. After an hour or two she would slip into the lake and swim under the ice back to her burrow. Anxious for her safety he would follow her progress with a flashlight. He noticed then from time to time she would run her nose into a muskrat burrow to replenish her air supply.

193

One night, after she had gone back, she returned again of her own accord, and when he awoke in the morning she was lying with her head on his pillow. She had decided to settle in with him, and she proceeded to make adjustments to the cabin to suit her particular needs. This was something without precedent, at least on the terms on which this arrangement was concluded. For here was no timorous beast cowering in the habitation of man for the sake of warmth or what food it could filch. Here was a proud and very independent animal shacking up with a man for mutual convenience, and very determined that it should be held on equal shares.

This led to considerable arguments, as it involved her in cutting a hole in the floor of the cabin and digging a tunnel under one of the walls to make sleeping quarters for herself. It also involved packing a part of the floor with mud to make a dry-packed earthy walk from the beaver house to the water supply, which Grey Owl provided by cutting another hole in the floor and sinking in it a galvanized iron tank, which he had to keep supplied with fresh water. That was not the end of the carpentry. Jelly had then to stop up all drafts, by stealing anything she could lay her hands on including Grey Owl's blankets, and so thorough a job did she make of it that it was soon impossible to open the cabin door.

Arguments led to reprimands, even to punishments, but Jelly gave as good as she got. Finally they settled down for the winter, she to sleep and pursue her own modified winter activities, he to try to write the story of his life for which *Country Life* had asked. But for long periods of time he was lost, as he had been so often as a boy, in watching an animal's behaviour. No man had ever lived so long in continuous and close contact with a wild animal. He was not conscious of the scientific value of this extraordinary relationship. He watched, as a doting husband might watch his young wife at her domestic work. He was amazed at her neatness and skills. She abhorred untidiness; everything must be stacked against the wall; even plates were made to stand up on edge, and peeled sticks and poplar leaves were sorted into neat heaps and pressed against the wall until needed, a reflection of her species' habit of keeping a crowded burrow clear of the debris that would otherwise accumulate.

But it was not only her tireless industry and neatness that

fascinated him: it was her awareness of him, and her acceptance of him as her companion, who shared life with her, and must be kept in communication with. Even when she was sleeping in her dug-out he had only to call and a sleepy voice would answer him on a note of inquiry. Thus he was never alone. He saw how superior as a companion she was to a domestic pet like a dog, who gives affection enough but utterly abases himself to the man, doing nothing for himself but conducting mock hunting expeditions and thumping his tail noisily to express his adoration of his master.

There was no question of being a master with Jelly. She was a totally independent person. All he did for her was refill her water tank daily. She procured her own food, drawing it into the cabin, tailoring it to meet the size of the aperture through which it had to be taken. She would bring out her own bedding every day, spread it out on the floor to air and dry, and then tuck it back in again. A beaver in a totally wild state would have discarded its bedding for a fresh supply each time. But Jelly seemed to know that fresh sugar and flour bags were not readily available, that birch bark, procurable in the summer, was not easy to replace in the dead of winter; and she evidently figured out for herself that airing was a good substitute for renewal. These domestic tasks kept her busy all morning while he sat at his table, watched her, and tried to write.

Something of the block which frequently imposes itself between the author and the start of his book, even when the story is clearly visualized and the urge to get it down is strong, bothered him: it was the old question of finding the right tone, and the opening that will engage the reader's interest. Archie could not find a way of giving an account of events in which he had acted not only as an observer but a participant, without what he thought of as an offensive use of the first personal pronoun. It was not modesty which hamstrung him, but the difficulty of combining the marvellous truth of what he observed with the un-truth about himself which he had established: his Indian birth and upbringing. His problem was not the artistic one of finding the right opening, but the moral one of telling a life-story that began with a lie. He could avoid the use of "I" only by the use of "One", which, as he saw clearly, was a mere "substitution of the foremost numeral . . . for the foremost pronoun", and which would succeed

> only [in imparting] to the narrative an air of portentous hypocrisy that was unworthy of so simple and noble a theme as my beloved wilderness; . . .
> So I decided to write, not a personal biography, as requested [by *Country Life*], but a series of essays on the North itself.

And that is why *The Men of the Last Frontier* came to take the form it did. It was a solution to the difficulty, and it worked well enough with that book, but the personal pronoun was essential if such personal adventures of the mind and spirit as are described in *Pilgrims of the Wild* were to be credible, and "a few good healthy unequivocating 'I's', standing up honestly on their own hind legs" were necessary to the book that brought him fame.

But even the decision to make his life story a book of essays did not start his pen running. He was worried about Anahareo: she had always been his critic and his audience, and now the place was silent, and her absence after three years' close contact made the cabin, in spite of the diversions and the companionship offered by Jelly Roll, empty but for echoes. When he was busy about his household tasks or out in the winter woods, even when he returned to the cabin, stoked up the fire, and chattered with Jelly, he was only subconsciously aware that something important was missing. But when he sat down at the table, with the empty white sheets of paper before him, the ache intensified and the mind turned in on itself.

His cure for fits of the black devils had always been a long tramp in the woods. Now he decided to go farther afield. Giving his camp over to the care of the trapper on whose territory it was, he loaded his toboggan and set off for Birch Lake, with the idea that a visit to the House of McGinnis where his first literary aspirations had come to life at Pony's urgings, and where the articles for *Country Life* were penned with such zest and certainty of success, might press the spring of inspiration and start it flowing again.

The distance from Lake Temiscouata was thirty miles,

through the woods in winter and up the frozen creek, where he now made much faster progress over the ice than they had when the water was there. He came at last to the abandoned cabin where they had been so happy. Pushing open the door in the late afternoon he saw in the half-dark the relics of that last happy Christmas: the wooden Indian head he had carved with his knife, and the war-bonnet he had made hanging above it, limp and discoloured. The Christmas tree leaned against the wall where it had fallen, its branches dry and withered.

He sat down on the bench and looked around him. Everywhere he saw marks that brought back memories that lit the now darkened room with those candlelit winter days. The busy-ness there had been with those two small black-eyed contrivers of chaos; the rustle of secret activity, the conspiratorial murmurings of voices like those of children; the scratches they had left were everywhere visible, in chewed chair legs and deerskins, in the teeth-marks on drinking-tins. There in the corner was their redoubt, constructed with such immense labour and engineering, such shoving and vocal consultation; he recalled them now ensconced behind there, peeping out, their eyes shining with excitement, waiting for the next move in an ever exciting world.

As he sat there, at first overwhelmed with longing for the past, the memory of those cheerful little fellows lifted his depression, and the fullness of his feelings started the flow of his writing. When he had made a fire, and cooked himself some supper, he sat down to write. In two nights he wrote the two chapters "The Tale of the Beaver People" and "The House of McGinnis" which were to become the seventh and ninth chapters and provide the backbone of the book he was already calling in his nostalgic mood *The Vanishing Frontier*. One can see how with these two chapters he settled the vexing question of how to begin, how to set the tone that once it is satisfactorily established carries the work forward to its conclusion.

"The Tale of the Beaver People" recounts the familiar facts of the raids for these rich pelts ever since the white man came to the American continent, increasing through the years until the time of Grey Owl's writing when the beavers were almost extinct. It is when he turns from this familiar recital of wrongs done against a species to describing at close range what he had observed of those he had rescued and tamed, that the narrative springs to life, and we see what a unique observer of animal life he was.

What he is showing us is that the beaver has, above the inherited instincts that direct all animals, including men, in their perpetual struggle for survival, the power of reasoning. Instinct, from long habit, tells the beaver how to cut a tree so that it will fall in the right direction. They are by instinct builders of dams, the main objects of which, from the beaver's point of view, are to give a good depth of water, in which feed may be kept all winter without freezing, and to flood the water back into the timber they intend to fell, so that they will be close to the water and to a quick escape route if attacked. All that inherited instinct teaches the beaver. But reasoning power comes in when, having built the dam in the form of an arc, the beaver shapes it in a concave or convex curve, according to the water-pressure. Reasoning power also is employed when they construct a canal between two bodies of water to facilitate the passage of trees to be used in the construction of the dam or for food, but leave a short portage between two branches of the canal, over which they drag the trees so that the water level is not drained from one lake to another.

"The House of McGinnis," which he went on immediately to write in the first rapturous burst of creativity, described how McGinnis and McGinty settled down at this Birch Lake cabin, cutting theselves a hole in the floor, digging a trench, building themselves the rudiments of a beaver house while remaining like trustful children in close touch with their human friends. The independence of spirit exhibited by these two wild beasts, combined at the same time with a vast affection, not submissive, cringing, and blindly adoring like that of domestic pets, but discerning, exacting, and trusting like that of human beings, sets the tone for this book. All that made the wilderness a flowering place, it says, has been destroyed by man: the Indian, the buffalo, and the beaver, whom the Indians call "Little Indians". Before it is too late, see what they were, what they could again be, if we stopped our work of extermination. In the opening chapter of *Tales of an Empty Cabin*, the last of his books, written six years later, he recaptures the mood that seized him when he visited again the deserted cabin at Birch Lake, finding it

> tenantless and lonely, the moss chinking long since fallen from the gaps between the timbers, its door ajar, and its windows staring blankly out at the beholder. A humble habitation it had been, even at its best; yet much care had been bestowed on its construction, and rude but not inartistic ornaments, of which some still remain, had at one time decked its bare and plain simplicity. . . .

How much his literary style had been influenced by the cadences of the tales told by the Indians is apparent in the highly effective recantation of faded sights and sounds that rise up from his memory:

> the grove [in which the cabin stands] had known them all and known them well. None the less, the great pines, ancient, lofty and aloof, their plumed heads remote in contemplation of the valley, could well have been unconscious of those puny short-lived creatures that for so brief a time had had their being at the foot of them.

Indian, too, is the way the past returns, as though aroused by a ghostly drum-beat, a pale wisp of memory drifting across the valley.

> Although so long deserted, so silent and so still, the place yet seems to live, to reflect some strange influence, vague, shadowy and undefinable; as though it held an echo of what had gone before, or resounded, very softly, to some lingering chord of music that thrummed on and on, long after the player had gone and was forgotten.

Keyed up by these awakened memories, he returned to his camp at Elephant Mountain Lake, and settled down to write. Four months later, on February 5, 1930, he wrote

Country Life that he had finished the book. Through his friends the Grahams, in Cabano, he had found someone to type it. By March 19 he was settling down to the pleasant discursive task of writing the long and chatty letter to accompany the manuscript. Grey Owl was never as simple as he sometimes allowed himself to sound, and much that might have seemed in the offices of *Country Life* in Covent Garden novel and amusing in a letter of submission was carefully calculated to set up in the minds of his publishers an acceptance of him as he wished the public to accept him and his work.

> Please find enclosed the typed copy of my manuscript. I sincerely hope that the bad arrangements of the paragraphs, corrections in punctuation and spelling, and a good deal of general sloppiness will not prejudice you against my work, should you find time to wade through it. The typist evidently looked on this as a heaven-sent opportunity to learn some English, trying it on the dog, so to speak.

He is plainly anxious to give the manuscript the appearance of coming out of the genuine backwoods, its appearance at all a triumph of will over impossible obstructions. He apologizes for not enclosing the photographs which are to illustrate the book:

> The gentleman that generally undertakes that work [developing photographs] in Cabano is busy looking for a few hairs of the dog that bit him, and mineral water does not fill the bill. On the arrival of the liquor plane (the moonshiners are quite modern here) he will probably begin to sit up and take notice, and then I will get my photos.

But the success of the book would depend on its having been written by a man of Indian blood, long inured to the woods and knowing very little about civilization, and unhandy with the way in which a manuscript should be presented. He had to get rid in the editor's mind of the picture he thought existed there, of a proud mother sending from

200

her home in Devon a son's account of trapping in Canada. He had to replace it with a picture of an Indian Métis, with an unusual but still crude gift of expression, struggling to deal with an impatient business man.

Was his tongue in his cheek as he wrote, "I guess I shouldn't be talking so personally to you, Mr. Editor"? I think not. It was essential if his message was to be taken seriously that it should seem to come out of the Wilderness, to be the very voice of the Wilderness; and the figure he created for this purpose, simply to emphasize the message, was that of the untutored half-breed, who is now and then conscious of the presumptuousness of such a despised voice carrying so tremendous a message.

Once planted it was going to be difficult to expunge. But that was the least of his worries at the moment. He was torn by pride between what he had done, and anxiety to make it successful by making it appear genuine.

> I do not know [he went on in this long letter] if it is still the custom to dedicate a book to some person or another. I have done so, but maybe this is irregular. Mrs. Scott-Brown it was who first brought my work to the notice of Country Life, thus giving me a chance to make good, whether I do or not. But as a step-mother whom I am not well-acquainted with which, judging by her letter, is my loss, I did not think of her in that respect.
>
> My own mother I unfortunately never knew. An aunt took her place, and it is to her that I must give the credit for the ordinary education that enables me to interpret into words the spirit of the forest, beautiful for all its underlying note of wildness, and to tell of ways and means that better men have taught me. I would much like that tribute to her to remain, should the book itself be worth printing.

The image the reader receives is of some ancient Indian crone in an encampment in the desert where he had been born. It would have been a shock if the unnamed aunt had suddenly appeared as a masterful English spinster of seventy, bustling about the climbing streets of Hastings.

201

How he had hated her! But the pride of the creator broke through the disguise he was adopting. She should know that she had reason to be proud of him. He even believed that she knew something about his parentage which she had not told him. Always tight-lipped, disapproving, commanding. At times he thought he had stumbled on the truth about himself, and out of some misconceived family pride she was unwilling to admit it to him. They had fought each other from the beginning, ignoring the others; and even after all this time, they struggled for the advantage.

Meanwhile Anahareo had been having her own adventures, and these are related in very lively fashion in *Devil in Deerskins*. The prospecting trip on which she had started with Dave, when Archie had turned back with Jelly Roll, had ended disastrously. Someone had jumped the claims Dave knew about. Her money spent, she had worked for a mining company until the depression had put it into bankruptcy. They were apart from September until the beginning of July 1930, when Pony's job ran out, and with enough money saved she was able to return to Cabano. During the summer of 1930, two events of importance to their lives happened. *Country Life* accepted the book, but did not immediately provide a contract, an omission which was going to lead to a grave misunderstanding later on. And Rawhide appeared. Rawhide was the wild male beaver who was to become Jelly's consort.

No one except an unknown editor at *Country Life* had seen the manuscript of *The Vanishing Frontier*, as Archie had named his book, and there can be little doubt that *The Men of the Last Frontier*, the title under which the book was published in England in November 1931, a year and a half later, was substantially altered from the original. Throughout the summer he was sending changes, evidently at their request, at first good-humouredly but in the end far from it. From "I hope the constant amendments do not have the same effect as the amendments, especially the 49th, to the American Constitution have on the people of that country," to very curt and assertive messages a few months before the book came out.

Meanwhile he had stumbled on another market for his

literary output, one that was to prove profitable and fame-making for him in Canada. In Cabano one day he came across a magazine, *Forest and Outdoors*. In this he read an article on "Wolf Control", in which the author, a noted writer on wildlife, discussed a suggestion then being canvassed for keeping down the growing packs of wolves which harassed the newborn of other species moving from one feeding ground to another.

Grey Owl wrote in to suggest that the only way to deal with wolves was to increase the bounty on their skins, and to get Indians, who knew their ways, to deal with them. He then went on at considerable length to describe how the wolf-pack hunts, and his remarks showed such an unusual knowledge of these animals that the editor published his letter as an article, and begged for more of the same thing. From that time, March 1930, until 1935, when he began his lecture tours, Grey Owl wrote at regular intervals for the magazine, twenty-five articles appearing from his pen in that period.

We can see from the first of these articles that Grey Owl was torn by conflicting desires. He wanted to get in everything that he had to say, and for the sake of emphasis to say it at considerable length. He was proud of his knowledge of wildlife, and liked to display it. At the same time he wanted to convert others to the creed that it was necessary to save life instead of taking it if some species at least were not to become extinct. He was anxious to impart to others his discoveries about the beavers' high intelligence and their great capacity for suffering. Everything is in this first article for *Forest and Outdoors*, for instance, including a potted version of his travels in the years since he had left Temagami: the essence in short of what was to be his greatest book, *Pilgrims of the Wild*.

The editor of *Forest and Outdoors* swallowed it all. His readers were not interested in literary style, they wanted facts. The editor at *Country Life* was more exacting; he wanted style as well as content. As a result, Archie was suddenly busy during the summer of 1930 supplying the demands of two markets. Absorbed in his work, he grew, like all writers, uncommunicative with those around him. Anahareo was a young woman of twenty-four, vibrant with life, confident that her expectations of it would be fulfilled, and impatient to get at it. She looked at the prospect of the winter ahead, shut up with this fanatic, without enthusiasm.

In the early summer of 1930, a young wild beaver was caught in a trap which Archie had set for an otter, whose droppings he had found by the shore, and who, if not disposed of, might threaten Jelly's existence. Jelly, at this time, when the leaves were about to burst their buds, was living out in the old burrow, coming only occasionally to the camp to visit her friend.

Rescuing the trapped male beaver, and finding his foot badly injured, Archie had taken him back to the cabin, set the broken bones in splints, dressed the wound, and fed the beast. The injured beaver then showed no disposition to leave him. It was only a question of time until Jelly discovered that someone had taken her place in the cabin, and was even sleeping on the bed with her man. Her jealousy was ungoverned and Grey Owl had much ado in saving the patient Rawhide, so christened because of some bare patches in the fur on his body, the outcome no doubt of previous fights, from destruction at the hands and teeth of a raging, jealous female of his species.

In two long articles he wrote for *Forest and Outdoors** Grey Owl described how Rawhide came to join them, attached himself to Grey Owl, and stood up to Jelly's attempts to oust him.

An enormous rogue male beaver came after to woo a reluctant Jelly; in the subsequent bloody fight Jelly was nearly killed, but Rawhide came to the rescue and in the end became the suitor instead of the enemy of Jelly, and the father of Jelly's subsequent offspring. The same story is told in *Pilgrims of the Wild*, and it is interesting to see in the later version what a few years of experience in writing had done to perfect Grey Owl's style.

Meanwhile in September they were surprised by a visiting party. Archie and Pony had been up at the far end of the lake. Rounding a bend in the shore-line on their return, they had picked up Jelly Roll who often came to greet them in this way, and was accustomed to climbing aboard and en-

*"The King of the Beaver People," December 1930 and January 1931.

204

joying a quick ride home. As they came towards their camp they saw a group of people. They recognized Bernie Graham: he was busy at the campfire which stood about twenty yards from the cabin door. Another man was seated on the ground, winding some film on to a movie camera. At the shore, watching them, stood a short, stocky man of middle age, looking at them hard as though they were the intruders. As the canoe swept in swiftly to the shore, the stranger advanced.

"Which of you is Grey Owl?" he demanded.

"Why, me," said Archie, with an aggressive thrust forward of his jaw. This visit was not really the surprise that he pretended. On July 8 he had confided to the editor of *Country Life* that he was trying to interest the Canadian government in making some movies of his beavers at work, and on July 25 he had written that the films were to be made next week, and that he was busy training the animals.

"My name's Campbell," announced the small man emphatically. "Campbell of National Parks," he amended. "Where are those beavers of yours?"

They had beached the canoe and were tucking the paddles in under the thwarts, and at that moment the Queen, as Jelly Roll was affectionately called by him, anxious to investigate strangers, was preparing herself for something she always hated, getting out of a canoe on to dry land. Out on the lake she simply slipped over the side and swam away. On shore she had to balance clumsily on the gunwale and flop to the ground. As though she were conscious that she did not look her best at such moments, she snarled and muttered to herself. They had learnt to leave her alone, turn their backs on her, and walk away while she recovered her equanimity and came after them. But Mr. Campbell was there on business, and the sight of the Queen letting herself down over the side like a nervous fat lady afraid to jump was too much for him.

"Quick, Charlie," he shouted, "let's shoot."

Turmoil followed Campbell's sharp cry. While Charlie came running with his camera, Pony fell to her knees and threw her arms around Jelly, and Archie pulled his knife and jumped for Campbell.

"Stop, you damn fool," yelled Campbell. "We only want to get a picture of her."

It took a few minutes to sort out, Campbell setting an example to everyone. He shed his truculent manner, and smiled on everybody with the meaningful benevolence of a public relations man.

"Lay by that camera, Charlie," he instructed. "Mrs. Grey Owl, loose her. We mean no harm." He turned to Archie: "Let's sit down and talk this matter over," he suggested courteously.

Released from Pony's arms, Jelly, her feelings still ruffled and her suspicions of the stranger by no means allayed, leant back on her tail, and by little grunts and shakings of the head and by sharp convulsions of her entire body, showed that she wanted no part of any parlay with these people. She took herself off to the water, swam out, slapped her tail hard to show that there was danger, and disappeared in a circle of spreading rings. In a few moments Jelly's head emerged, her native curiosity being too much for her, and she floated there, about twenty yards from the shore; only her head was visible above the surface, and she watched them like a policeman keeping a suspicious group under surveillance.

Campbell explained his purpose—to make a short film of these beavers living with a man in the bush. The film would have scientific value. The showman in Grey Owl, never very far below the surface, rose to the opportunity. He had written to the Parks Department in the first place, but he had more grandiose ideas in mind than just shooting a few rolls of film. He wanted to make a story of it, and that is what he had meant by training the beavers in preparation for this event. He and Campbell were to be good friends in the end, but Campbell had to do it his way. And the resulting films, as good and exciting today as they were when first shown in the 1930s, won the attention of the world because they were made with the imagination and the patience that had gained the beavers' trust and affection in the first place.

The party was there for several days. The weather was perfect Indian summer. Jelly and Rawhide were busy with their last-minute preparations against winter, and could not spare time to sustain animosities. In and out of the cabin they went, opening the door with one hand while carrying a load of sticks in the other. In the lake they dived and swam, and on shore sat squeezing the water out of their fur. Tired out, they surrendered to sleep, with their heads on Archie's knee and with deep-felt sighs of trust in their protector.

Mr. Campbell was beside himself with excitement; the camera whirred and clicked, and the beavers seemed quite unheeding of it. At night, the party talked. Archie told Campbell of *The Vanishing Frontier*, and of the autobiography he now meant to write. What he wanted was peace and quiet, for himself to write, and for the beavers to carry out their peaceful existence. He kept plugging the theme that the beaver was Canada's national animal, and the species was on its way to extinction. Campbell frowned and was silent, probably envisaging officials in Ottawa who would be suspicious of underwriting with public funds one man's idea for saving a species. The film might be the answer. Mentally he was probably already editing it, and anticipating the effect it was likely to make. He had already chosen the title for it: "The Beaver Family".

In November, Pony decided to go to Montreal and find a job. She got one working at a resort at Montebello, later called the Seigneury Club, owned by the Canadian Pacific Railway, near Ottawa on the Montreal line. She was to help with the outdoor sports—skiing, riding, tobogganing, and bob-sledding—and to drive a dog-team for visitors desirous of sampling the thrills of winter while well-covered with blankets. Archie raised no objection to her going; he promised that if anything should happen to Jelly, or if he became ill, he would send for her. He returned, with a certain amount of relief, to spend a second winter alone with Jelly and Rawhide, and with his writing. Encouraged by the editor of *Forest and Outdoors*, he was recapturing memories of the past, and pouring them out in the series of articles. During the winter he wrote ten. Some of these he incorporated in *The Vanishing Frontier*; others, such as "A Day in a Hidden Town" and "White Water", were to appear some years later in *Tales of an Empty Cabin*. Exercise in writing limbers up the style; words flowed from him as he developed his own natural style, which read easily.

During the winter, the long hours spent sitting at the table writing cramped his muscles. He had to hunt to provide his own meat. He was then alone, and so he had fallen into the habit of taking along with him on these excursions the younger son of the Grahams, the bright, open-faced youth who had directed him on the first evening of their arrival in Cabano. Bernie Graham liked nothing better than to get away at the weekend to Grey Owl's camp, and on snowshoes to track a deer which was to provide Grey Owl and the Graham family with meat for several weeks.

Bernie is still alive, and remembers those days forty years ago when he tramped the woods with this Indian. Grey Owl was always good with young people, as he was with animals. Something protective in his nature came out with helpless things, but he not only comforted, he taught; he wanted to show them how it was done so that they could stand on their own feet and do it. He had endless patience with the innocent and the helpless. McGinnis and McGinty, and now Jelly Roll and Rawhide, responded to him, and Bernie Graham did the same thing. He was going through a unique experience, learning woodcraft from an Indian who knew it to the very bones of his fingers. Sometimes Bernie's father joked and said, "That man is no Indian," such times as when Archie's hunger for music overcame him, and sitting down to the Grahams' piano he would allow his fingers to shift from the thumping dance tunes popular at the time to the classical music Aunt Ada had taught him, as though he had fallen for the moment into a daydream. Or such times as when, arguing with Mr. Graham, his feelings would be carried away and a passionate rhetoric burst through the carefully constrained drawling woodsman's talk he usually affected.

But Bernie believed him to be what he said he was; a Métis. He remembers now that Archie's blue eyes used to pierce right through him as he told him circumstantial stories of his childhood in Mexico, of travelling with his parents with Buffalo Bill's shows, of the slow but steady move year by year up to Canada, and of the early days in Temagami. He talked with Bernie about Chibougamou, where the Ojibway had adopted him into their tribe, and about his experiences overseas in the war. He even told him about the girl he had had in England whom he had married. She was called Connie, he said.

208

These confidences came when they would be sitting over the fire at night, after a day out in the woods, often with their wet clothes hung on a line over the stove filling the air with steam. Jelly had accepted Bernie as a regular visitor, but when Bernie's brother Albert came to the cabin one weekend, bringing his girl-friend with him, Jelly was outraged by the perfume she was wearing and attacked the girl. Before Archie could intervene her sharp teeth had cut a tendon in Albert's leg as he stepped in front of his girl to defend her.

When Archie and Bernie were on the trail, the business was too serious for talk. The Still-hunt—stalking the animal to a point where the kill is more or less certain—demands, as the name implies, absolute silence, economy even of gesture. In the chapter on the Still-hunt in *The Men of the Last Frontier* we can hear Archie's voice instructing Bernie. He must "learn to move as a shadow, his actions smooth as oil, and his senses set to a hair-trigger touch; for the forest is argus-eyed, and of an unsleeping vigilance, and must always see him first."*

As well as taking life in the woods economically and not wastefully, one has to take care to preserve one's own. Take care, but be ready with courage too. Once, when they were coming down the western shore of Lake Temiscouata and had to cross it, the ice was on the point of breaking up. They had no canoe, and if they could not cross it they would have to walk nearly fifty miles. Patches of water on the surface of the ice were visible here and there.

Archie told Bernie to cut a pole, as he did himself. Then Archie went first, tapping the ice with his pole to test its strength. It took them several hours to make the crossing of two and a half miles. Afterwards Archie said to Bernie, "Today you almost met your Maker."

These experiences in the woods with this mysterious, fascinating figure gave Bernie a glimpse of a life he might never otherwise have known. Bernie felt very proud when Archie told Mr. Graham that if he could have Bernie in the woods with him for three or four years he would make an Indian of him. When in town the figure became less glamorous, but no less entertaining. He would come in about

*Grey Owl, *The Men of the Last Frontier*.

once a week during that winter, and Mr. and Mrs. Graham began to be a little uneasy about the influence he was exercising on their son. Exasperated, Mr. Graham looked at him one day and said to him, "If you're an Indian, I'm a Chinaman." Archie laughed, but it was plain that this comment stung him.

"Just wait," he told Mr. Graham, seriously, "I'll have people eating out of my hand."

No amount of doubting by people like Mr. Graham could make him drop his claims to be an Indian. But he didn't like the French word for an Indian, a *sauvage*, and to those who called him that he would insist in his halting French: "Je ne suis pas Sauvage, je suis Indien."

Sometimes he would go with the young men of Cabano, Bernie's friends, to Rivière-du-Loup to drink beer. There was no tavern in Cabano. In the restaurant there, where they would take a meal, he would insist on being served raw meat and uncooked vegetables, and he would eat with his hands, scorning the use of cutlery.

"If they think I am a *sauvage*," he would say bitterly, "I might as well act like one." Liquor always stirred his aggressive instincts. But before he was too far gone, he was an amusing companion to these young bloods, and the laughter around him, like that around Falstaff in the tavern of Eastcheap centuries before, was loud and long. In Rivière-du-Loup he began to attract other company, men his own age who took him for what he said he was, a Métis, judging him to have had some education. Two of them happened to be lawyers, argumentative men who loved a good discussion over the beer mugs. Until something someone said touched him on the raw, and he became suddenly silent and moody, he made them laugh with his sallies and responses, his mind as bright as quicksilver.

"We'll have you in jail yet," threatened one of the lawyers.

"That jail looks so poor," countered Archie, "that if a man was condemned to hang there they would make him bring his own rope."

How did he support himself during this time? He had had no money as yet from *Country Life*, but *Forest and Outdoors*

were paying him forty dollars an article, and he had his
pension cheque each month. He never sold his fish or his
deer meat, considering it wrong to do so. He always gave it
away.

When the time came to finish an article promised to
Forest and Outdoors, he would shut himself up in his camp
and write all night, then come into Cabano to mail it. He
always called at the Grahams' for a meal, and to leave some
gift of fish or meat for Mrs. Graham.

His articles in *Forest and Outdoors* by this time were
attracting a lot of attention. "Little Brethren of The Wilderness", a two-part article which appeared in the September
and October 1930 issues, was widely read because of the
animal lore with which it was packed, and because of the
forceful way in which it proved that animals have as well-
ordered lives as human beings, and have the same right to
live. He was getting a lot of letters, and soon visitors began
to come from much farther away than Quebec.

It was after *Forest and Outdoors* published "The Fine
Art of the Still-Hunt" that the Canadian Forestry Association wrote inviting him to be their guest speaker at their
annual convention in Montreal in January 1931.

After some hesitation, Archie agreed. He arranged with
Campbell that "The Beaver Family" should be shown at the
convention for the first time. He felt pretty sure that he
would be a success: the film would ensure that. All the same
he hated crowds and cities; he felt trapped, like an animal,
by hostile surroundings. So just before leaving he tele-
graphed to Pony at Montebello asking her to join him at the
Windsor Hotel in Montreal, but not telling her why. When
she was shown up to his room, it proved to be a suite, and
there was their host, Sir Charles Radcliff. To Pony's look of
bewilderment, he said: "I accepted an invitation to be guest
speaker at the Canadian Forestry Association's annual convention. I figured before I was through I'd be in dire need
of moral support—that's why I sent for you."

The lecture was as great a success as the one at Métis Beach
had been, but this time it was given to a much larger
audience, and it attracted the attention of a Montreal newspaper, which next morning headlined its account of the

event: "Full-blooded Indian gives lecture on Wild Life".

To this description of his origins, Grey Owl made no objection. "Why spoil their story?" he said to Sir Charles. From this moment on, his first appearance before a large audience, his Indian identity was on record. The disclosure that was to come later made it seem as though his intention from the beginning had been to deceive a gullible public. But the identity was thrust on him; the extent of his fault was that he missed the chance to make a protest about it at that moment, and afterwards it was too late.

The Montreal appearance is described at some length, and amusingly, by Anahareo in *Devil in Deerskins*. Success made him bold. Entertained by Montreal society, he played the part of the untutored savage rather too realistically, until he fell ill with a high temperature and a recurrence of his lung trouble. He was removed to Montreal General Hospital, from which he was not to emerge for two weeks.

When he knew how ill he was, his thoughts were of the beavers. He insisted that Pony give up her work at Montebello and return to the lake to look after them until he could get back.

He was back in Cabano by February 2, and was immediately again in communication with his friends at *Country Life*. A contract had been sent to him for the publication of *The Men of the Last Frontier*. He was not interested in money, only in fame, and he noted with uneasiness that the contract was for the outright purchase of the copyright. He had the idea that an author's continuing interest in his literary property prevented the publisher from ditching a book when it had made the necessary profit, and he suspected that the royalty basis was the usual one on which a book was published, and they were taking advantage of his being an ignorant savage. He seemed to forget that he had started his connection with them as an educated Englishman who happened to be a trapper. But by this time he had so thoroughly dramatized his Indian origins that he seemed to believe in them himself. To the same editor to whom he had written only two years before of Indians as "them", he now wrote of "us". He told *Country Life* now that he was giving up the trail because of his foot wound and the effects of gas on his battered lungs. He informed them that he had TB, "the bane of our race", and that the doctor said that he must go to the mountains to live. He asked innocently what royalties he would get, and he signed this letter Grey Owl, not A. S. Belaney. "It is the only name," he said, "by which I am known in this country." He then sent the contract to the Parks Department of the Department of the Interior to ask their advice. To them he was also now presenting his Indian identity, and this was helpful to them in presenting the film of "The Beaver Family". In fact the unquestioning acceptance by the Department of the Interior from the beginning of his Indian identity did much to quieten the scepticism of others.

In the letter to *Country Life* just quoted, Archie had remarked on his growing fame, not in any sense boasting of it but attributing his ill-health to overwork in writing and lecturing. And he was in fact beginning to be well-known. All his life he had this faculty for attracting the support of earnest and active publicists, as I myself was to demonstrate in the years ahead. When one remembers that two years earlier he had been destitute, completely unknown, a broken-down wandering trapper, and now was writing articles of unique interest, lecturing before large assemblies, and reluctant to accept *Country Life*'s offer of $750 outright for a book which he had completed in that time, and that the Government of Canada was impressed with his unusual achievements, one begins to see what a remarkable and original character was hidden beneath the man now calling himself a Métis and insisting that his name was Grey Owl.

Lloyd Roberts, a free-lance writer and the eldest son of Sir Charles G. D. Roberts, the distinguished writer, had followed Archie's articles in *Forest and Outdoors* and had written to the unknown Indian author to congratulate him on them. At almost the same moment, by chance, an official of the Department of the Interior told Lloyd Roberts that they had a lengthy handwritten manuscript by Grey Owl, which had been accepted by an English publisher. The Indian wanted advice on finding an American and a Canadian publisher. The official showed him the manuscript called *The Vanishing Frontier*, and the contract sent by *Country Life*, and according to Roberts' own description later given in a radio talk, he was horrified to find that the contract was an offer to purchase the book outright instead of paying royalties. His account went on:

> I glanced at the contract, and then with audacity born of sad experience, I took the law into my own hands, drafted a cabled repudiation of the contract, signing the cable "Grey Owl". I followed this up with a long letter to the publishers demanding fair royalties for book rights, and reserving all other rights, and enclosing it with an explanatory letter to Grey Owl.

He admits that he breathed easier when he received Grey Owl's reply. Grey Owl, instead of telling him to mind his own business, was full of gratitude, and asked Lloyd if he would not come and visit him and his wife, "only five miles from Cabano".

Lloyd Roberts' account of that visit is studded with priceless detail that shows the impression Archie was beginning to make on strangers. Lloyd Roberts was an experienced and sensible man, not given to colourful prose or romantic descriptions. He found him "the first Indian that really looked like an Indian—an Indian from those thrilling Wild West days of covered wagons, buffalos, and Sitting Bulls. The stamp of his fierce Apache ancestors showed in his tall, gaunt physique, his angular features, his keen eyes, even in his two braids dangling down his fringed buckskin shirt."

After a call at the Grahams' where Archie's loaded toboggan was parked they were off, Archie in the harness dragging the toboggan, Lloyd Roberts following behind. They crossed the ice on Lake Temiscouata, and beyond the lake struck a bush-road, which dwindled into a hard-packed trail, winding between snow-packed evergreens and naked white birches down to the shores of a little lake. Here stood a beaver lodge, the residence of Jelly Roll and her consort. Archie cut some poplar and birch brush and thrust it through a hole in the ice for feed. Uncovering the blow-hole on top of the lodge he called into it "How Kola", and from the sleeping beaver came a murmured cry.

They continued their trip in snowshoes up the ice on this

214

lake, until Grey Owl halted, lifted his head, and hooted three times. Across the white silence drifted the call of the owl. And presently the call came back. They went on, and rounded a point, and there beside the lake was a cabin, a boyish figure dressed in riding breeches and leather jacket standing at the door.

"Meet my wife, Pony," said Archie.

Dusk was falling when after a meal of bannock and bacon, beans and molasses, they made up the fire. Lloyd looked about him and took in his surroundings. There was just one room, the one they were sitting in. The marks of the beavers' presence were to be seen everywhere in gnawed posts, boxes, table legs. There were just two bunks, a rough-hewed table between them, covered with paper and pencils, and a couple of chairs. Over one of the windows there hung two tiny skulls of beaver kittens, in memory of McGinnis and Mc-Ginty. The small room, which looked very untidy, was crowded with blankets and bags, and the benches and corners were cluttered with hunting and fishing tackle.

Grey Owl squatted on the floor, Indian fashion, arms clasped round his knees. The flame of the kerosene lamp shone on his parted black hair and darkened the deep hollows of his cheeks and eyes. Outside on this first evening a blizzard started to moan and fling spring sleet against the windows; the old rusty stove became nearly red-hot.

It was perhaps seven o'clock in the evening, with supper over and the washing-up done. Grey Owl stoked up the fire, and while Pony stretched out on one bunk and Lloyd Roberts at his host's insistence took the other, Grey Owl squatted down on the floor and began to talk. He talked of the old days, of the woods, of the Indians and the animals, and of what must be done if the beaver were to be saved. He told tales without number of their adventures with McGinnis and McGinty.

Around midnight Pony fell asleep, and Lloyd could hear her gentle, steady breathing from the other bunk. He rarely had to speak himself. He listened, fascinated. From time to time Archie got up to throw another log in the stove. It was not until five in the morning that, having got up for the fire, Archie looked at the clock and said "Ah, brother. It will soon be dawn. What about a snack?"

He cooked more bacon and bannock, and boiled some tea, and as the dawn light was coming in the eastern window Lloyd Roberts stretched out on Grey Owl's bunk, while Archie rolled himself into a blanket on the floor, and soon they were asleep.

When they awoke near noon it was snowing steadily, and it hardly let up for five days. They went out each day on snowshoes, but were glad enough to return to the roaring fire and the hot cabin, and the talk that went on endlessly.

Pony confided to Lloyd Roberts at the end of the visit that she would not spend another winter in the bush. "It's all very well for Archie," she told him. "His whole soul is taken up with his beaver and his writing. But I want to be doing something useful, prospecting for uranium or gold, or else driving a dog team."

On his return to Ottawa Lloyd Roberts lost no time in seeing the Minister of the Interior and reporting his experiences. The Department was well aware of the growing reputation of this Métis. They knew of his articles in *Forest and Outdoors*, and the film about the beavers which they had made was attracting wide interest in the United States and Britain. They were in a receptive mood, and Lloyd Roberts' recommendation that Grey Owl and his beaver colony should be moved to one of the National Parks where they could be afforded proper protection, and that he should be put on the payroll as a government naturalist or Park Warden seemed a reasonable one.

But government departments move slowly. Minutes have to be passed, the adamant treasury softened up. It was late autumn before the arrangements were regularized, and Grey Owl had a letter telling him of the change in his and the beavers' fortunes.

The Park settled on was Riding Mountain National Park near Neepawa, in Manitoba. Grey Owl was to go on salary, so his financial worries would be over, a cabin was to be built for them, and adequate quarters were to be provided for an extensive beaver colony. By the time these arrangements were concluded, it was too late to move; the ice was beginning to form, and Jelly and Rawhide had settled down for the winter. The camp could be constructed during the winter months, and all would be ready by the following May or June when the beavers emerged from their winter quarters, no doubt this year with beaver kittens.

Meanwhile the announcement that an Indian had been appointed by the Parks Department to this interesting assignment stimulated the imagination of the London *Times* correspondent in Ottawa who cabled home to his paper a story headed "An Indian Thoreau in Canada".

Beginning by reminding his readers that H. G. Wells, in the *Outline of History*, had remarked on how little had been done since the Bronze Age in taming, using, befriending, and appreciating the animal life about us, he added that even when attempts had been made to save a species from extinction, what prompted the action had generally been financial calculations, not the rights of the animals themselves or their claims on us.

He went on to tell Grey Owl's story, adding that in the pursuit of this single-minded purpose to save the animals he loved, he had developed an unsuspected talent for writing, and his articles on wildlife were now sought by magazines, while the Dominion Government with his help had been able to secure one of the most interesting moving pictures of the beaver ever taken.

This article appeared in August 13, 1931, a couple of months before *The Men of the Last Frontier* was published. *Country Life* were quick off the mark, publishing in their next week's issue an article entitled "Little Indians" extracted from the 6000-word piece which they still held, and announcing that his first book would be published by them in the early autumn.

There had been stormy weather in the correspondence between the English publishers and their Indian author. They had perhaps taken too much for granted that he would be delighted to find himself published, and had thought it unnecessary to consult him about changes in his style made in the interests of good grammar and English usage. But they were not dealing with a semi-literate half-breed, although he had taken pains to present himself to them as such; they were up against an impressionist using words in unfamiliar forms and altering accepted sentence structure in order to obtain effects which would colour the reader's mind as the artist wanted it to be coloured. The first explosion came with the proofs:

> Capitals, for instance, I have replaced in some cases. Inverted commas I have in many cases removed, as they give a word an apologetic air, as if it did not rightly belong. My words can stand on their own feet. The book is not to be a shining example of English literature—far from it. The book is written by an Indian about his own country, and from his point of view, almost, some of it inexpressible in ordinary English, thus calls for a little poetic license." [July 1/1931]

What he means by "poetic license" is plainly not permissible exaggeration, which it has come to mean, but the acceptance on their part and the readers' part of a half-breed Indian's unfamiliarity with the niceties of English style.

But the full enormity of what they had done was not apparent from the galley proofs. When he received his author's copies of the book at Christmas-time he saw that they had changed the title from *The Vanishing Frontier* to *The Men of the Last Frontier*.

> I was a little surprised to find that you had changed the title without consulting me. As it stands I have written a book about myself, a thing I studiously avoided. Although the critics might say I have written more about the men than the Frontier itself, I care little for the opinion of critics; it is the public I want to please, an entirely different idea. The original title has a greater appeal, it has the lure of the vast, though disappearing frontier, which in the nature of such a work as I tried to produce, dwarfs and belittles that of mere diminutive, short-lived man. That you changed the title shows that you, at least, missed the entire point of the book. You still believe that man as such is pre-eminent, governs the powers of Nature. So he does, to a large extent, in civilization, but not on the

218

Frontier, until that Frontier has been removed. He then moves forward, if you get me. I speak of Nature, not men; they are incidental, used to illustrate a point only. [Jan. 14/1932]

That point was growing in emphasis all the time. What had started out as a half-formed plan to save the beaver in one small corner of the North had broadened now to encompass the salvation of all wild animals. He had seen only himself as the persecutor. But now after five years of wandering along the edge of the vanishing frontier he saw that the trap, the rifle, and poison were working on the inside like decay in a hollowed tooth, and that some day, unexpectedly, the Dwellers in the Forest would come to an end too. If there were absolute protection for all fur-bearing animals, temporarily at least, until the situation was got under control, then we should all see the almost human response to kindness on the part of many animals. With a little patience and tact he had proved that they could be taught to overcome the fear of persecution inborn in them by contact with human beings; and he had shown that they could be made to look on man as a friend.

The force of this conviction shook him so much that he could end a plea for conservation, with law to support it, with the apostrophe: "This is not the voice of Grey Owl that speaks, but the voice of a mighty and ever-increasing army of defenders of the Wild, voices that will be heard. Let your ears be open."

That the urgent and passionate account of the extreme pressure being exerted against the old Frontier and its inhabitants should be turned by *Country Life*'s change of title into an extravaganza of adventurous men seemed to him contemptuous of the character of the true North, a wilful act of misunderstanding, a commercial ploy. From this time on he ceased to correspond with them. He was already at work on his second book, *Pilgrims of the Wild*, and this time he was to take care that the message was not overlooked.

CHAPTER **13**

T HEY LEFT Cabano in April 1931 in very different circumstances from those which had surrounded their
arrival two and a half years before. When they had
paid off the teamster then, Archie had had just over a dollar
left in his pocket. When they had camped that first night
beside Lake Temiscouata, they would have gone hungry but
for the gifts of food and wine from the few townspeople who,
drawn by curiosity, had come down to the lakeside to see
those *sauvages* and their tame beavers. Now he was an
accepted local figure, on the whole well-liked, although there
were a few who were not sorry to see him go. His fame as an
author had spread. Everyone knew about the films the government had made of the beavers. It was a matter of local
pride that the Dominion Government had taken them up.

Cabano felt some glory reflected on them. Archie had been made a Park Warden, and he and his beavers, the latter travelling now not in the old stove-box in which McGinnis and McGinty had arrived, but in a specially constructed four-foot-by-six-foot tank with bath and drying-off platform, and an upper tier for living quarters, were being transported to the West, where a cabin had been built for them, and a beaver colony was to be established.

They were going to Riding Mountain National Park in Manitoba, 276 miles north of Winnipeg. When they changed trains at Toronto, Pony left the party, and Archie travelled on alone with Jelly and Rawhide. In his account of this separation Archie, protective as always towards her, says that they parted in Toronto so that she could go and see her family. But Anahareo, always frank and honest about herself and her relationship with him, says in *Devil in Deerskins* that she left the train at Toronto to follow the will-o'-the-wisp that she always found irresistible, the report of a gold discovery in the Elk Lake country in Northern Ontario. The prospecting trip was a failure, and several weeks later she joined Archie and the beaver at Riding Mountain National Park.

Archie was anxious to reach his destination as quickly as possible. Jelly Roll and Rawhide had been under the ice all winter, the first winter of their cohabitation. He had had an anxious time coaxing them out and re-establishing his former relationship with them. Jelly Roll had been in contact with him since she was a few weeks old, but Rawhide was a wild beaver who had only temporarily made terms with him, and had hung on at the camp because of his fascination with Jelly. Archie had spoken to them all winter through the air-hole at the top of their house, but had not seen them.

It had taken several days after the ice went before they left the lake and came to him. Jelly was the first to yield; she knew his calls and responded to them. Rawhide had hung about at a distance first, watching his mate jealously but diving, with a slap of his tail, if Archie tried to get near him. But in the end, probably reassured by Jelly, he too succumbed. He was never as demonstrative as she was, and he trusted only Archie. But Rawhide came, and within a couple of days, Archie had been able to get them to enter the stove-box. In this they had been transported to the station where the elaborate government-constructed beaver travelling box, designed to Archie's specifications, was waiting on the platform. The signal was given to the Parks Department in Ottawa, and the journey to the West had begun. The beavers travelled quietly, comforted by Archie's presence near them, and the constant sound of his voice murmuring reassurance. When a change had to be made to another train at Winnipeg, he remained with them on the platform. They still had a train journey of two hundred miles ahead of them, then a drive of forty-eight miles in a truck, followed by another fifty miles in a wagon to reach the lake selected by the government for Archie's experiment.

A palatial building, by bush standards, had been built for them, a log bungalow with a verandah all round. At first Archie was delighted with it and the setting, most of all with the novel feeling of financial security induced by the assurance that on the 1st and 15th of each month a salary cheque would be his. He wrote to Lloyd Roberts:

> Well, Lloyd, we are very happy here; we have a fine cabin, a real bush camp clumped with moss, and another going up, on a lovely lake about a mile long. The situation is beautiful, heavy timber, deep water; picturesque yet restful; the place to come and rest and sit around evening fires. Try and make it, Lloyd. We will both be here and bid you welcome, so you can share our happiness.

He conveys that Jelly has had her first litter since their arrival:

> three new kitten-beavers. They came out of the lodge for the first time last night, or rather this morning at 2 o'clock. [Jelly and Rawhide] are still building a fair-sized beaver house right in the camp, having free access to the lake. They still work at it by shifts, bringing mud through the door, and sticks, most of the night; we sleep when we can, from about 4 a.m. until noon.

222

And then he goes on, the tone ironic but the matter deadly serious:

> Say, Lloyd, there is a most damnable misrepre-
> sentation going around that I am a college man.
> This hurts me badly, as anything I may have ac-
> complished in the literary line, little that it is, has
> been the result not of education, but thought, ob-
> servation, a sympathetic insight into my life-long
> environment, and an absolute lack of training in
> writing. Had I the time to have contracted a uni-
> versity education, I would have missed many
> valuable years of bush training, and would have
> remained in the mediocre woodsman class all my
> life. I would have been neither the one thing nor the
> other. Now that I have become a little prominent,
> civilization takes to itself all the glory, as having
> educated me, instead of giving me credit for a little
> native intelligence, the most of the credit being due
> to those men amongst whom I have spent most of
> my life, from whom I learned the art of the trail
> and the life of the Wild. An aunt gave me, during
> her own vacations, a ground-work, English, History
> and Geography, and the rudiments of Arithmetic;
> but particularly English, and I have made but little
> use of it until urged by the desire that, having spent
> my life assimilating a host of impressions of the
> Wilderness, I now desired to express them. Civiliza-
> tion has been kind to me, taken my message to
> heart, elevated me to a position above what I rightly
> deserve; but it did not produce me, and it almost
> never evolves my kind. That remains for the Wilder-
> ness itself, and the simple, kindly people who in-
> habit it, to do.

But in the end Riding Mountain National Park proved a disappointment. In the summer drought the level of the lake sank, the water became stagnant, and the beavers were unhappy. So was he. When the first raptures of being a salaried man subsided, he said to Pony: "What are we supposed to do now—just sit in a void for the rest of our lives?

I'm afraid, in fact I'm scared stiff, I'm not going to be able to take it; this inactivity will kill me. The way I'm feeling right now I hope it does."

When the beavers became listless and unhappy, he set out to explore for a better spot. He did this with the approval of the Parks Department, who suggested that better conditions might be found in Prince Albert National Park, 450 miles to the north-west of where they were, in the neighbouring province of Saskatchewan. He took an immediate liking to Major J. A. Wood, the Superintendent of this Park, who was enthusiastic about the prospect of having the beaver colony, and to the site Major Wood thought would be ideal for it.

And so they came to Lake Ajawaan on an early autumn day. The moment that he saw it, Archie knew that he had found the spot he had been dreaming of ever since they had set out for legendary Temiscouata. Part of its attraction was that it was difficult to reach. They went by car from Prince Albert to the village of Waskesiu seventy miles away. At this point they transferred to a canoe. Archie was glad to take up a paddle again, and in Major Wood he found a good canoe-man. Together they paddled, with long, vigorous, even strokes, the length of the lake, which was fifteen miles, stopping occasionally for a rest, a smoke, and a talk. Not a sign of human life did they see, but there were plenty of signs of animal and bird life. Fish jumped, spreading wide rings on the glassy surface; they saw a moose once, feeding at the end of the water. It raised its heavy-antlered head to watch them pass, but hardly stopped its feeding. They saw many white-tailed deer, and once a beaver house by the shore. The country was well-timbered and rolling; it smelt cold and clear, the true woody scent of the North. His lungs filled to the keen air. He could sense the animal-haunted silence of the land. He knew without question that he had come to what would be his home.

At the north-western end of Lake Waskesiu, they made a short portage, and then launched the canoe again at Kingsmere Lake. They crossed this body of water, a distance of about six miles, and at its northern end came ashore at a warden's lodge. Another short portage led them to Ajawaan Lake, set like a jewel in the evening light, entirely sur-

224

rounded by dense forest, mainly of aspen and coniferous trees, and imbedded near the shore with water-lilies. There was an old cabin, remaining from the days before the Park took in this territory, and here they made a fire, cooked some bacon, and made some bannock; then they lit their pipes and started in talk to lay the foundations of a lasting friendship.

So another move was in prospect for the beavers, but this would be the final one. They reckoned that it would take a couple of months to portage in the necessary supplies and build the cabin, but all should be ready by mid-October, well before the freeze-up. Major Wood undertook to make all the necessary administrative arrangements with the Department. All Grey Owl had to do was to return to Riding Mountain and await the signal to come. He returned to Pony filled with enthusiasm for this new site.

He spent the time remaining until their move dealing with *Country Life*, who were getting ready to publish *The Vanishing Frontier* and, galvanized into life by the *Times* article on Grey Owl, were pressing him for publicity material.

After recounting the story of his remarkable career, and his conversion from trapper to conservationist, the *Times* article had gone on to tell of the truly remarkable advances Grey Owl had made in establishing a special kinship with all creatures of the wild. He did indeed seem from this account another Thoreau, and *Country Life* set out rather late in the day to cash in on their discovery of the man described by the *Times* writer as "a backwoodsman of Indian birth who holds a humane philosophy, whose plan was to specialize in the conservation of beaver and other animals native to this region."

Grey Owl was to show an unusual expertise in the process of what he called "putting himself across", as I was to find out later when publishing *Pilgrims of the Wild*. "This is a book written by an Indian," he continually insists to *Country Life*. "Refer to me as an Indian writer." He now gives his father's name as MacNeill, and his own birthplace as Hermosillo in Mexico. The illusion is complete. He has said goodbye to Hastings, and has assumed the Indian identity. From now on there could be no retreat from this position. Belaney belonged to the past. He signed all letters Grey Owl, and even had his bank account in that name.

The happiest winter of their lives followed. Archie started to write a second book. This was *Tales of an Empty Cabin*, which is very much the same kind of book as *The Men of the Last Frontier*: a series of essays celebrating the things dearest to his memory. *The Men of the Last Frontier* sprang from his recollections of the early days on Bear Island, and at Bisco just before the war. *Tales of an Empty Cabin* springs largely from his later experiences as a riverman and forest ranger, and deals more closely with the coming of McGinnis and McGinty into their lives. The book, I think, was laid aside before it was completed, because he was moved by sadness to write *Pilgrims of the Wild*. This, his masterpiece, was written in the winter of 1933–4. But this first winter at Ajawaan was 1931–2, and the scratch-scratch of the pen which Anahareo heard all day was at work on memories which are recaptured in the early chapters of *Tales of an Empty Cabin*: on getting lost in the woods, on a day in a hidden Indian town like the one at Bear Island, and on drawing portraits like the unforgettable one of Red Landreville, the riverman and the Sage of Pelican Lake. These were stories of the past that he could tell to Anahareo. But *Pilgrims of the Wild* had to be written alone, as we shall see.

In February Anahareo discovered that she was to have a child, and on August 23, 1932, in the hospital at Prince Albert, a daughter was born. The baby was christened Shirley Dawn.

Archie was not new to fatherhood. Children in the mass he loved, and he had a great way with them. But individual claims on him he hated, and on Angele's children he had turned his back. But this newly arrived infant was different. Anahareo was her mother, and that gave the child a special quality of grace. Even so, he struggled rather weakly against surrendering to its claims on his affection. But the struggle was ineffectual.

"Holy Mackerel!" he exclaimed, on seeing her for the first time, "she looks like a maggot," and he was always in her first years to refer to her as "the insect". But it was not long before the child of grace, as pretty as her mother, as deft as Jelly had been at working her way into his affections, had completely captivated him. Dawn was to become the centre of all his thoughts, and the object of all his efforts to make her proud of him.

The Men of the Last Frontier, in spite of the changed title, had enthusiastic reviews in Britain when it was published in November 1931, and in the United States when Scribners published it in the spring of 1932. In England, Bernard Darwin called it "A Romance of Real Life", and other critics marvelled at the power this unknown Indian had at conjuring up the reality and excitement of life in the woods. The book was reprinted in April in England, and letters from appreciative readers began reaching the post office at Waskesiu from all over the world.

When the Macmillan Company of Canada issued a Canadian edition, Grey Owl entered into a friendly correspondence with the president of that company, Hugh Eayrs, and thereafter felt himself on much firmer ground than when dealing with an unknown publisher in England thousands of miles away. Hugh Eayrs was hereafter to be his confidant and friend, and was to write the understanding foreword to the Canadian edition of *Pilgrims of the Wild*. Grey Owl had considered his motives misunderstood ever since the publication of *The Men of the Last Frontier*. He was always sensitive to slights, and reacted fiercely to adverse criticism, not of his writing but of his subject. "And now," he wrote me, "they all seem to get the proper angle, greatly, I suspect, on account of the Eayrs foreword which after all this misquoting, misunderstanding and misconceptions that have arisen, is a most satisfactory state of affairs."

The winter of 1932–3 passed pleasantly, with little Dawn to occupy their attention. When May came Anahareo wanted to take Dawn out to Prince Albert for a change. In the spring when the ice and snow is going, travel of any kind is impossible for a few weeks, and she was afraid of the child becoming ill during that time.

One has the impression in the very honest account Anahareo gives of the next year in their lives—Archie says nothing of this period in his writing, and he ceased for a while to correspond with anyone—that she is like a bird fluttering against a hand that prevents her from being free. Of course she would have liked to stake a claim that would turn out to be a bonanza. Such was every prospector's dream. But what she wanted was freedom to move across the face of the country, to feel the surge of hope as one approached the unexpected, not the flat monotony of the unchanging day following day, to the sound of a ceaselessly scratching pen.

She had to make a bolt for it, and that is what she did. She took Dawn into Prince Albert for a few weeks in the summer of 1933, planning to spend the winter months there with the Winters family, with whom she had lodged in the weeks preceding Dawn's birth. This family were to become great friends of both Archie and Pony, and were to be in a sense foster-parents to Dawn in her growing up.

But in the spring of 1934, when Pony had said that she would return to Ajawaan, she found that she could not do it. There had to be one more trip—out there. Leaving Dawn in the care of the Winters family, and not telling Archie of her plans, she loaded her canoe and set off on her own, a last trip through the Wilderness, the fluttering bird escaping for a moment from the restraining hand.

It was to be nearly eighteen months before she returned. Her own adventures are recounted in *Devil in Deerskins* with the utmost frankness, and we see, not from anything she says of herself, but from the scope of these adventures, why Archie spoke so frequently of her courage. It is a quality she has which springs from her unquenchable vitality; if you know your life cannot be easily quenched, invariably you have little to fear.

It was then that he put aside *Tales of an Empty Cabin*, and in less than a year wrote *Pilgrims of the Wild*, which is the story of Anahareo and himself, and of the coming of McGinnis and McGinty into their lives, and of the tragedy of their loss. Of the coming, then, of Jelly Roll and Rawhide.

It is now the Moon of Snowshoes. Anahareo and the small new daughter are spending the Winter

228

out in town. The beaver are safely stowed away within their fortress. . . . And I am lonesome for them all, and so I spend my time with them on paper.

The manuscript was finished at Christmas-time in 1933, and without waiting to hear from his publishers what they thought of it, he immediately started to write a children's story which was completed by the autumn of 1934, some months before *Pilgrims of the Wild* was published. This children's book he called *The Adventures of Chilawee and Chickanee*, but when it was published in the summer of 1935 it was called *The Adventures of Sajo and Her Beaver People*. This time the change of title met with his approval.

It was when he had the manuscripts of these two books in his hand that Grey Owl's next English publisher, a restless and ambitious man, gave a twist, quite unconsciously, to the fate of all these actors, calling Anahareo home from her wandering, and Grey Owl to the theatre halls of England.

It was to be the death of Grey Owl. But it gave a remarkable flowering to his last years. If, like Henry Thoreau, he had remained in the woods, he might have been remembered as no more than what Henry James called Thoreau: "a sylvan personage [with a] remarkable genius for the observation of the phenomena of woods and streams, of plants and trees, and beasts and fishes, and for flinging a kind of spiritual interest over these things." But Grey Owl is remembered for something much deeper and more lasting.

The urge to escape from the constrictions of our workaday lives is constantly nagging at us, and Thoreau reawakened in men a longing for mysteries that their forefathers had known, when men desired to live, as Henry James puts it in analysing the "slim and crooked" nature of Thoreau's genius, "for the ages and not for Saturday and Sunday; for the universe, and not for Concord." Grey Owl was reminding them of a world they had lost—the world of Nature patiently waiting our return—as *Walden, or Life in the Woods* reminded New England society in 1854 of the simplicity and rural purity of a world being lost to them by the onrush of commercialism and the harsh imperatives of Puritanism.

CHAPTER **14**

I HAD BEEN publishing in England for only two years when the mere chance that I had come from Canada turned the manuscript of *Pilgrims of the Wild* my way. *Country Life* had offended the author mightily, not so much by what they did as by what they failed to do. In the view of the author of *The Men of the Last Frontier*, they had missed the whole point of the book by giving it that title, thus putting the emphasis on men and not on Nature. He would have no more to do with them, and when Hugh Eayrs told him that I was a Canadian who had set up on my own in England, he appointed me *Country Life*'s successor. I could not help feeling that it was ironic that I should have come so far to make my fortune, and found my first money-maker in a book by an unknown Métis from the adjoining province to mine in Canada.

230

One does not have to be an expert to pick out a great book; it is the not-so-great that demand judgement. Important books have their own authority; something masterful is apparent as soon as one begins to read. *Pilgrims of the Wild* is to life in the Canadian wilderness what *Robinson Crusoe* is to life on a desert island. What holds us in Defoe's work is the courage of man in surviving the fate of being abandoned in an empty world. It is a story of moral courage, and the powerful interest it arouses comes from the thousand details of how Robinson Crusoe "made do". In *Pilgrims of the Wild*, moral courage is also what the characters exhibit, and the interest again is provided by the details of what it is like to live in the woods, to live cheek by jowl with animals, to find a plateau on which existence can be shared and enjoyed with the living things that share the world with us. That Grey Owl had been a cruel trapper once was not important. The past ends with the opening page of the narrative. Grey Owl is in flight from the social order in which we also live, to another into which he leads us imaginatively, and from which, at the end of the story, we withdraw with regret and longing.

When I started to correspond with the author I found him as simple and genuine as I imagine Henry Thoreau to have been. Everyone knows the story of Walden Pond. Thoreau built his hut on the shores of the pond with his own hands, cultivated his vegetable patch, made his own clothes, and lived for several years on the expenditure of a few dollars. The charm of the story comes from showing how happily a man can exist without the aids and comforts men spend their lives in toil to acquire. In reading Thoreau we get an image of a sweet and wholesome man, although we know that in fact he was difficult and uncommunicative, turned his back on society, and was a rebel against the state by refusing to pay his taxes.

There is enough in Grey Owl's story to show that he must have been a trial to local authority. He certainly contributed nothing to peace and order in Biscotasing, and he had to take to his heels to escape a warrant for disturbing the peace. He was continually in trouble in the army for infractions of discipline, and only a very perceptive platoon officer saw that he could flourish best when left alone, and made him a sniper. And yet there was an essential honesty and simplicity in him which came over very strongly in his letters to me, and made me anxious to convert others to share my wonder at the discovery of this unusual man.

But it was an undertaking of a rather large order to bring an unknown Métis from the Saskatchewan bush and hope to put him over in London in the mid-thirties as an unspoilt man. The temper of the English at that time was distinctly iconoclastic, and it was an inauspicious moment for promoting prophets. Times were hard economically, and a sombre pessimism about the future was the prevailing mood.

But I was not so much worried by the cost, which I hoped would be recovered from the extra sales generated by the publicity, as by the effect on so holy and dedicated a man if the crowds were small and the response lacklustre. I was daunted by the prospect of having on my hands for three months a man with a mission, who might regard every minute not spent in advancing the cause as a sinful waste of time. I doubted whether I could fill up a lecture schedule. The English are constitutionally allergic to this form of entertainment. It would mean winkling out schools and women's luncheon clubs and church groups. The prospect was far from encouraging.

What spurred me on was the way in which, after some hesitation, having accepted my invitation, he threw himself into the preparation and planning of the venture. He shamed my brand of professional optimism but practical lack of experience.

He became the leader as we planned the project in an exchange of lengthy letters, and we—I use the plural to include the four or five members of my staff who were involved with me in preparing plans—became the followers. He exhibited a good deal of managerial capacity in instructing us on how to present him to the public, and in this he showed a judgement better than ours. It was hard for us, for instance, to resist the temptation of striking the humanitarian note. But on this point he was adamant: he was not an animal evangelist but a man of action. He was not a St. Francis of Assisi; on the contrary, where he came from he was "considered a pretty tough egg". What he was coming

232

to tell the British about was the Beaver People, the Indians, the North—harsh, savage, yet beautiful.

In this he read the English mind better than we did. He reached unerringly to the instinctive longing felt by nearly everybody at a time of crisis for a way of life uncomplicated by progress, unthreatened by war and poverty and hunger. The world depression of the thirties was at its worst. No ray of hope showed on the gloomy horizon. There seemed no reason why unemployment, the dole, hunger and fear, and a bad conscience among people who did not suffer these things to the same degree, should not become a permanent feature of modern life. *Pilgrims of the Wild* told of the same economic forces desecrating a noble prospect elsewhere, and driving not only people but animals to hunger and flight. It also showed how a man of moral courage turned and stood against these harsh pressures. As our plans developed under his energetic prompting, we saw this really was not stuff for schools, Boy Scout troops, and church groups, but for every man jack struggling for survival in a shifting world. This book and its author offered no cure, but they offered hope. Grey Owl grasped it all in a single phrase when he told his audiences: "You are tired with years of civilization. I come to offer you—what? A single green leaf." Once that message got across, we were to have no trouble filling his schedule. We were nearly swamped in the flood of public enthusiasm that acclaimed him.

I speak of his simplicity and genuineness, although I am now aware of what I was ignorant of then, that his claim to be of mixed parentage, Indian and white, was false. It did not really matter. Long years had passed since his birth and schooldays in England, and he had truly assimilated himself to the Indian way of life. He had willed himself into believing the fantasy about his birth. He had never known his father, and he had seen the woman who claimed to be his mother only infrequently. The tight-lipped, disapproving silence about his father preserved by his grandmother and aunts, and the attitude not very far above contempt his Belaney relatives had for his disorganized mother, combined to form in his imagination the idea that something was being kept from him. From that it was an easy step to imagine a more romantic origin for himself. His schoolfellows had believed his story, and from the age of seventeen on he had lived the life that he had dreamed of and longed for since he had first been able to read for himself. To be an Indian! What he laid claim to, some at least of his English audiences also longed for imaginatively. Through him they could live that existence momentarily. If his love for that life had not been so genuine and wholehearted, he could never have inspired them. The secret of his success was his genuineness and his simplicity. These terms are the right ones.

I collected him at the boat at Southampton, and we got to know one another as, through a wet and windy night, we drove up to London together. I brought him up to date on our plans. These were not impressive, but they were daring. We had managed to book less than a dozen lectures, so I had taken a small theatre on Regent Street for two weeks, and he was to appear twice daily there. He looked a little nervous at this revelation.

I had been thrilled with his appearance. Without any attempt to "dress up" for the part, he looked a romantic figure. He was over six feet in height, with a straight but very spare figure, and he held himself well. His face was ascetic, the skin stretched tight over the bones. He was dressed in a blue serge suit and a wide grey sombrero-type hat, with a black neckerchief knotted loosely round his throat, and he wore moccasins. One could imagine him in a monk's robe, a rope round his waist, a cross suspended at his knee. His hair was long, and parted into two plaits. His eyes were a piercing blue, but the pallor of his face, the black hair, the aquiline nose gave him the look of a fanatic, except when he smiled, but even then the face relaxed very little. He did not seem in the least nervous or overcome by his surroundings. I was reassured by his looks and his calm manner, and I cheered up a lot more when I heard him make witty answers to the rather obvious questions the newspaper reporters surrounding him were asking when I came up and introduced myself.

I had booked him into one of those gloomy private hotels, as they are called in England, which throng the streets of South Kensington, and I had picked this place because it was managed by the father of a young man employed by me. He was a very nice, even a brilliant young man, subsequently killed in the R.A.F. over Norway, and I had commissioned him to be a night guard over my captive. The place was stiff with respectability; its furnishings and its patrons were of the late-Victorian period, and I felt the gloom of it myself when we went up the creaking stairs and along a passage that smelt still of old Victorian chamber-pots, and were shown into a room in which there was a bed, a dressing table, and about six chairs.

When we were left alone by the garrulous manager, who meant to be kind, Grey Owl looked at me and said, "Have a chair, brother. Have several." He himself stood with one hand on the dressing-table and gazed fixedly at the wall.

I was dead-beat after a hard day at the office, and a drive down to Southampton and back, and besides the gloom of this place was affecting me profoundly. I wanted a drink, and, with the old myth in my mind about Indians and whisky not mixing, I didn't want him to have one. I wanted to go home. So I said with forced good cheer, "I'll leave you to get unpacked. Have a good night's sleep. I'll come round for you in the morning about ten and drive you down to the office to meet the staff. We have a press conference arranged for eleven."

He barely looked at me, just nodded his head. I hated leaving him in this gloomy room.

When I opened his door next morning he was standing exactly where I had left him ten hours before. His pack still lay on the bed. The straps hadn't been undone, or the bed slept in. I could not believe that he had stood there all night, but I had to believe it. His face was white and strained. Without any other greeting he said to me in a low tense voice,

"Get me out of here, brother."

"Yes, we'll have to get you some other place, something more cheerful."

"I don't want another hotel. I'll bunk in with you. You've got a home, haven't you?"

"Sure, but . . . Well, we will have to ask my wife. Come along, we will go there right now."

I took him home to our little house in Chelsea which opened its hospitable arms to receive him. It was a fine small place, spick and span at this moment with new curtains and carpets and fresh with paint, for we had been married only this year and had not long moved in. My wife had not expected a lodger, but I soon began to see that somewhere in his forest fastness this particular Indian had learnt how to handle women, and soon not only my wife, but the domestics in the house, and even my new dog—a wedding present, formed a protective custody against my tendency to monopolize my find, and push him too hard.

I drove him down to the office to meet the staff. His gloom gathered through the long night barely lifted. In due course, and with deliberate unpunctuality, a few reporters and some press photographers arrived, and took over the office in their customary condescending way. I guided the questions. Grey Owl gave monosyllabic replies. The flashlight bulbs flared, the cameras clicked. The reporters didn't look bored, but they looked mischievous, like children teasing an animal. The conference was not being a success. Then one of the photographers asked Grey Owl to come down into the street outside the office, where at noon in Covent Garden the market carts with the little ponies in their shafts were being packed up at the end of the market day, which had begun here at two a.m. He wanted him to be photographed patting one of the ponies.

"Why?" asked Grey Owl ominously.

"People will lap that up. They go for anything about animals in England."

"I think you've got me wrong, brother," said Grey Owl in a very quiet voice, rising from his chair and padding across the room. He seized the photographer by the biceps of his right arm, which held his camera. He was not perceptibly putting out his strength, but the photographer winced with pain and looked alarmed. After that, not surprisingly, the conference broke up.

Then we got under way. In spite of the inauspicious press conference, Grey Owl caught on with the press. He photographed magnificently, and the fiercer and angrier he looked the more Indian and exotic he looked. Day after day his picture appeared in one or other, sometimes in several, of

236

the London papers, and by the time we opened at the Polytechnic Theatre, it was nearly half-full for both performances of the day.

In the course of a week I had got to know him well. I could see that there was a wild streak in him somewhere. It became apparent when he was pushed too hard, and I noticed that when certain subjects were touched on—for instance, if one talked of *Red* Indians, or if domestic pets were thrust forward to his notice, on the assumption that he was an animal lover, or if one ventured too closely, out of sheer interest, into his past, a cold and steely gleam would come into his grey-blue eyes; and one felt oneself suddenly the object of his dislike. The gust passed like the riffle raised by a cold wind over water, swift and sudden. But unmistakably there had been a chill wind, and one could not forget it. I put it down to nervousness over the frightening task ahead of him, and blamed myself for being too intrusive. But for most of the time he was excellent company. He told stories with all the skill of a trained raconteur. I urged him to throw away his lecture notes, which were rather stiff and formal, and talk to the audience as he talked to us at home. In the beginning he had come alive on the platform only in the protective darkness when the films were being shown and he was commentating from the side. Then with increasing confidence his natural humour broke through, and the roars of laughter from the audience punctuated the showing regularly.

It took no more than a week for him to find his feet. After that he was as much at home on the stage as though he were talking to visitors around the campfire at Ajawaan.

"When I stood on those platforms," he recollected afterwards, "I did not need to think. I merely spoke of the life and the animals I had known all my days. I was only the mouth, but Nature was speaking."

Yes, Nature was speaking, and to huge crowds. We had opened to half-filled houses, but the word spread rapidly, and by the end of the first week policemen were needed to marshal the queues. The public came in busloads from schools, in Rolls-Royces from Mayfair, by underground and bus from the suburbs. We had booked the theatre for only two weeks, and as his fame spread, had filled up the rest of

237

his days in the great towns outside London, from Edinburgh in the north to Bournemouth in the south. A return engagement in London was imperative, so we booked the theatre for a further two weeks at the end of December, and extended his tour throughout January and February in the country.

The crowds everywhere were immense and enthusiastic. In the four months he gave just over two hundred lectures and addressed nearly a quarter of a million people. He had arrived in England with a knapsack and a small piece of hand luggage; he departed at the end of the tour with a trunk and eight large pieces of luggage, six of them stuffed with gifts that had been given him for himself, and for Anahareo and their little daughter, Dawn.

By this time, of course, there were two Grey Owls, the public one, and the private one who revealed something of himself (but by no means all, as the future was to show) when he was alone with me on occasional evenings after the show.

During those late evening talks, especially when he was tired and dispirited, he would start to worry about Jelly Roll and Rawhide. The beavers were being looked after by Anahareo and a young Indian boy during his absence. I noticed after a time that his concern was always for the beavers, not for the woman without whose particular qualities he would still have been a trapper in the woods, not a famous man. Then I began to get the message. All was not well between Anahareo and himself, and this sounded like a note of doom across our enterprise.

I thought he could not be serious. It was as though Abelard had spoken coldly of Heloise. Anahareo had been the heroine of *Pilgrims of the Wild*: she was certainly the leading lady of those films the government had made. The photographs of her in her breeches and shirt and leather boots, a madonna-like smile on her beautiful face as she watched Jelly Roll falling asleep on her knee, or held out a finger for a whisky-jack to alight on, or bent forward to put something in a fox's mouth, had implanted on the consciousness of the English public an unforgettable image. Grey Owl had created her in this image. She must remain the heroine of this story to the end.

238

And yet I could see why there might be friction. When they were in the woods, they had been passionately in love. Each of them was a strong character inclined to dominate. Passionate love demands surrender, and such characters do not find it easy. There has to be found a way, and I believe that it was found in this great ideal to save animals, no longer to kill them. This ideal had lost its heat when it was commercialized. I could sympathize with what I imagined were Anahareo's feelings, that no longer was this a passion shared with her lover, but an act put on in commemoration of what had in the first instance been a noble impulse springing from pure love. Grey Owl had been the creative artist, and he could still get satisfaction from winning converts to the cause. But she was not interested in converts. *Pilgrims of the Wild* had been the telling of their love story, and now she was left alone while her lover, under my management, stumped the halls with his account of it.

There was something more to it even than this. Grey Owl had the gifts of an actor. He responded to an audience, just as the audience responded to him. There could be no doubt about the genuineness of his feelings for nature. I could think of no writer in Canada who had caught so truly the essential boom-note of this huge, rocky, monolithic land. He made pure Canada, the Canada outside the concrete urban enclosures, come alive. We saw it as we had first learnt about it in story and legend; the illimitable forests, the rushing rivers vigorous still after a million years of biting their way through the antedeluvian rock, gushing finally into the great sea-going tideways of the mighty St. Lawrence, or the Mackenzie, or the Columbia. He showed us the men who challenged these great forces of nature to wrest a living from them, and the animals who had their place in that unsullied, still primitive world.

That is why he drew such a response from these great urban crowds of Europe, trapped once again in the 1930s as so often before in history, in the rivalries of human ambition and power, and being driven like cattle to the slaughter. Europe had not heard such a voice as his since the eighteenth century and the beginning of the industrial revolution. Men and women were of course unconscious of this, only aware of their own uneasiness about the future and dissatisfaction with the present. And suddenly here was this romantic figure telling them with his deep and thrilling voice that somewhere there was a land where life could begin again, a place which the screams of demented dictators could not reach, where the air was fresh and not stagnant with the fumes of industry, where wild animals and men could co-exist without murderous intent. It was threatened by the same forces that had overwhelmed them, but there were places like Ajawaan where there was peace.

I was the prophet's keeper, and I could not have such a man giving way to the bottle, or letting it be known that the great romance which, by his own account, had been the inspiration for his elevation to the rank of prophet had broken up. He saw my point; the cold, steely gleam shone briefly in his eyes, but no word got out. The strain on him must have been intense. I was unknowingly helping to kill this man with overwork, and at the same time I was making his name and fortune. I was only subconsciously aware that he was making mine too.

I do not believe that anyone else could at that time have put into words just what Grey Owl's appeal was. But everybody had felt themselves ennobled by supporting it. It was, in fact, a spectacular precursor of the protest demonstrations that were to be such a feature of life thirty years later. The first intimations of what unregulated progress could do to the environment in which we lived were being uncomfortably felt by the public, who had been satisfied, up to that time, to enjoy the benefits of progress without asking what the cost of it might be. The sprouting factory chimneys belching smoke, the receding countryside as cities spread out, the concrete like a lava flow from some threatening volcano pouring over the land, grander shops and meaner dwelling houses, the choking city air, the growing sense of claustrophobia, all helped to lend enchantment to the view of distant forests, blue lakes, green hills, and clear skies, where animals roamed free and men did not fear for their jobs; the Grey Owl country.

But Grey Owl came to tell them that even the forests were being tainted, and the animals were in flight from the creeping, poisoning, destructive tide of civilization. He did not

240

ask them directly to help to hold back that tide by gestures and sacrifices, by refusing to wear furs; or urge them to press for enactment of legislation to protect the environment by imposing stiffer regulations for licensing the use of the land, by setting up National Parks, by declaring closed seasons on the trapping of animals. When he strayed into these issues in his talks he was always plainly uncomfortable, speaking by the book rather than from his mind.

No, he was a poet, recreating for us dreams of innocence. His lectures sang the glories of the past when the earth was untrammelled by the yokes by which men in search of wealth enslave their weaker kind and hold them captive to their jobs in cities. All his books are laments for the old days, thirty years before, when he had been young. There were giants in those days, and he sings their glory as Homer did the primitive heroes of early man. And to such effect that his readers and his listeners were caught by his vision. They longed to turn aside from the things that plagued them—the threat of war, unemployment, everlasting penury in the midst of plenty—and find such an Arcadia as he described. They knew it wasn't possible; they were helpless as though in a nightmare. He had broken free. He took no more life, lived simply with the animal world in a green glade far away. And because this man had shown it was possible, they could keep their dream.

No one believed more ardently in the vision he created than the creator himself. He knew that life was not really that simple, for beneath the surface as he enticingly pictured it, there were a thousand worries. Anahareo was leaving him, he found it more and more difficult to write, drink plagued him from time to time, women bothered him but he could not live without them and his affairs were endlessly complicated. But once it had been like his description, simple, strong, clean, and happy. He took refuge in the past when he had been young and innocent and keen, and had first come to this Northern country. . . .

> when I roamed at will through the rock-bound Ontario wilderness, all my worldly goods loaded into one small, swift, well-beloved canoe or, in Winter, contained within the four walls of a none

too spacious log cabin, hastily erected on the shores
of some frozen, or soon to be frozen lake.*

Men were men then. He exaggerated their glory only because
he saw it again with the imagination of a youth of seventeen.

Of the two different Grey Owls struggling for dominance,
the showman, after the triumph of this tour, was in the
ascendant. He had been uninterested in money except as a
means to further his cause.

Betty Somervell, a lady of infinite resource, patience, and
charm, saw him safely back to Canada. She had been an
important part of the organization managing Grey Owl's
travel arrangements and public appearances. In fact, he
hated trains and was driven everywhere the length and
breadth of England; it was Betty Somervell who drove what
he always referred to as the canoe, teasing in this way our
earnestness in guarding the Indian myth.

I had instructed her not to give him the cheque for his
half-share of the lecture receipts until the ship was at sea.
The amount was so large that, on hearing what it was, Betty
reported that Grey Owl went white as a sheet. He was suddenly, by his standards, a rich man. He was completely
disinterested in money, and had never once inquired how
we were doing. In addition to his share of the lecture fees,
there were the royalties on his books. *Pilgrims of the Wild*
had been reprinted five times between its publication in
January and his arrival in October, and it was reprinted
each month of his tour. We were selling about five thousand
copies a month. *Sajo*, which was published in September
1935, was reprinted four times between then and Christmas.
It was selling even faster than *Pilgrims*. From possessing
nothing, he was suddenly making something in the neighbourhood of $30,000 a year. Translations had been con-
tracted for in all the main European languages, and
Scribners in the United States were getting under way with
their editions of the books.

He simply could not comprehend money in these terms,
and his first instinct was to give it all away to any and all

*Grey Owl, *Tales of an Empty Cabin*.

242

who seemed to him to be in servitude, people like taxi-drivers and waiters. But then he sobered up, and on Major Wood's advice made a will, and passed it all over to a trust company to manage for him. And then sat back to dream.

His plan for that summer of 1936 was to finish *Tales of an Empty Cabin*, and to return to England in the autumn of 1937 for a second lecture tour to coincide with the publication of the new book. The number of disappointed applicants, towns all over England which had not been able to book him in the first tour, made a second one imperative. Besides this, there was another matter, which did not appear to impress him, but had impressed me, and thus made me urge him to undertake a second tour.

The first one had coincided with the serious illness of George V, and this had prevented Queen Mary, who had read his books, been captivated by them, and pressed them on the two princesses, her grandchildren, from hearing him lecture. I heard through Vincent Massey, the High Commissioner, that there would almost certainly be a Royal Command if Grey Owl revisited England, and as the entrepreneur of this enterprise, this seemed to me an additional laurel-wreath which should be added to his glories.

For a second tour he wanted new films, and as the new lectures would be based chiefly on the material in *Tales of an Empty Cabin* he wanted to go back to the Mississauga and recreate the early days and his life on the river. The plan he proposed was that there should be a summer film and a winter film, that he would write the scripts and Hugh Eayrs and I, as his British and Canadian publishers, should put up the money.

We agreed to do this for the first film to be shot, the summer one, but it took so long to arrange for cameramen and crew, for rivermen and canoes, and for all the paraphenalia involved in film-making in the bush that the summer film could not be made until the summer of 1937.

But by the time it came to put up money for the winter film, in the summer of 1937, I had to draw back from the investment. All my funds were invested in a publishing firm now issuing seventy-five books a year: I could not spare the capital, and wrote frankly to Hugh Eayrs to tell him so.

Eayrs fully sympathized with my position, and put it tactfully to Grey Owl, at the same time promising to see what he could do to get federal government support. Eayrs was a friend of the Prime Minister, Mackenzie King, whose memoirs he hoped one day to publish. There was also a neighbourly connection. King's famous rebel grandfather had lived in a house on Bond Street in Toronto which adjoins the Macmillan publishing offices, and Eayrs had been active in saving this building as a national monument. Also King was M.P. for Prince Albert, and Ajawaan lay in his constituency. He had a cottage on Kingsmere Lake, but he visited it only once.

On the surface there was much to attract Mackenzie King and Grey Owl to one another, but beneath the surface accord there was much that set them poles apart. Grey Owl had an innocence and a directness of purpose which Mackenzie King could only have found naïve. King invited Grey Owl to dinner at Sussex Drive, and listened sympathetically to his appeal for government support for the making of this film. Probably King had already made up his mind to see that the money was not given, but he told Grey Owl that he would have to refer the proposal to the Minister of the Interior, and that he would hear the decision very soon.

Poor Archie! He was entering the last desolate stretch of his life when, having reached spectacular heights of success, he was to tumble to temporary neglect. Shining with purpose and convinced of the success of what he was doing, he was to move into the penumbra that surrounds prominent men of great influence. Human imperfections such as jealousy, suspicion, envy, and distrust, of which—for all his main deceit—Archie himself was perfectly innocent, play in these shadows. As Lester Pearson's fascinating autobiography shows us, Mackenzie King thought that his High Commissioner in London, Vincent Massey, played up too much to the aristocracy, and Massey's report to him of the kind and extent of the patronage accorded to this half-breed, I suspect—there can never be any proof—troubled Mackenzie King. When the big fish flips her tail the minnows are in an uproar. A report was asked for on Grey Owl. I saw only one tiny end of this: a letter from the Indian agent at Chapleau to his master next above disclosing that on his

244

first appearance in the Northern woods, a slim, handsome young Englishman, of the name of Archie Belaney, had appeared, relating even then that his father had been an Indian fighter in Mexico and his mother an Indian woman. But he spoke like an educated young man, not a fugitive from the Wild West when the Indians were being subdued.

The shadows were beginning to form in the sky over him. The brightness was going out of his life.

In September 1936 Betty Somervell accompanied her husband on a business visit he was making to New York, and went on to Ajawaan to stay with Grey Owl and Pony. She was an unwilling witness of their parting.

As Pony says in *Devil in Deerskins*: "I don't know when it began, but Archie and I had grown pretty far apart. I guess he saw the writing on the wall long before I did, because several times when I was planning on a trip, I remember Archie saying, 'The only way I can hold you . . . is by letting you go.'"

There was a difference of eighteen years in their ages. The difference is important because Anahareo in 1936 was only thirty. When they had shared everything, no hardship mattered. But now he was preoccupied. He hardly looked up from his writing. When he wasn't at work on his book, he was answering the quantities of fan-mail reaching him in sack-loads every time a Warden passed his cabin. Or he was planning his film, or sending off lengthy telegrams over the Forest Ranger's telephone concerning his coming lecture tour in Britain and the United States.

She felt shut out from his life. She might have felt less so if she could have seen a letter he wrote to Hugh Eayrs in October 1934, when *Pilgrims* was finished, but not yet published. Recollecting the events which make up the story of *Pilgrims of the Wild*, he tells Hugh Eayrs,

> Those days will never fade. The half of it is not recorded; the privations, the starvation, the slavery and the hardships, not the honest hardships of the Northern Wilderness that a man might fight against and be a better man for it, but the real suffering, more mental than physical, that two, or rather four, exiles underwent, when civilization, like some

all destroying master, as it seemed to us, had us with our backs to the wall, stripped, unhappy and alone. Yet we do not forget that same civilization took us by the hand and helped us to better things. . . .

No shadow can fall between our lives, now that we have seen those desolate, yet somehow glorious days together, when each did his part to the best of his ability, when we were brothers in tribulation and were so close together, when what hurt one hurt the other more, when we shared our scanty food between the four of us, almost ate out of the same dish. Such things can never be quite forgotten. . . .*

But here, two years later, the moment of parting had come. It did not come suddenly, or angrily. Betty Somervell and her husband were staying in the camp. There were two cottages at Beaver Lodge now, the original lakeside one, where Jelly and Rawhide had their beaver house, and an upper cabin where guests slept.

After supper on that last evening Grey Owl and Anahareo withdrew to the lower cabin. The Somervells were going out next day on their return journey to England, and Anahareo and Dawn were to accompany them as far as Prince Albert, where they always spent the winter.

Grey Owl and Anahareo talked all night. Then when the new day had dawned, they came out toegther to the boat landing. This was to be their last hour together, although the party would not be leaving until after breakfast when the sun would be well up. The date was November 15, 1936, and ice was already forming along the shore. They said their solemn goodbyes then, and each promised to come to the help of the other if the need ever arose. Then, after breakfast, when the canoes were loaded and Pony was in the stern of one with the paddle, she turned the canoe swiftly, looked back once over her shoulder, saw him standing there, and lifted her paddle in salute. Then she turned to face the other shore. She never saw him again.

*Letter dated Oct. 17, 1934. What I have quoted are extracts from a very long letter.

246

Yes, the light was going out of his sky. Hugh Eayrs wrote to tell me of this break, and of Grey Owl's intention to marry a French-Canadian girl, Yvonne Perrier, and I answered him on December 4, 1936:

> The news you give me of his matrimonial intentions is—I don't know what to say—amusing, appalling, amazing: one would have to know the lady to pick the right adjective. We shall *not* announce a fresh marriage, if there is one, in England, for Anahareo is just as much a hero to the English public as Grey Owl.

A second tour was necessary, not only to meet the many demands for it in England, but to provide Grey Owl with the necessary capital to make the winter film. By now his great success in Britain had washed back on to American shores, and the lecture circuit there was clamouring for him. Colston Leigh, the American agent, booked him for three months from the beginning of January, when he would have completed his three-months English tour. Could any man stand six months of such a life without a break, especially one used to the solitude of the woods?

I had published *Tales of an Empty Cabin* in October 1936. In some respects it is the most delightful of Grey Owl's books, for it deals exclusively with the characters, both human and animal, who were always the subjects of his best anecdotes, calling forth that warm, ironic humour which his literary style needed as an anchor against the tug of his rhetoric. The mighty Mississagi River is at the heart of the book, and Beaver Lodge and its inhabitants, "all things both great and small", are at the end of it.

The second tour was an even greater success than the first, but it was not such great fun. We had started from scratch then; we had to make Grey Owl known. The venture might have been a resounding failure, and in that event would almost certainly have been the straw to break the camel's back of my young publishing business. The success of the tour, and the sales of Grey Owl's books, had transformed Lovat Dickson Ltd. just as much as—perhaps even more than—it had transformed Grey Owl. We had nothing to do this time but pick out the most profitable engagements for him, make sure the booksellers had plenty of stock of his books, count up the money and divide it, and make sure that Grey Owl didn't get into trouble.

Some of the happy excitement had gone out of the venture. The new Mrs. Grey Owl, whose Indian name was Silver Moon, which unfortunately carried with it a hint of theatricalism missing from the splendid Iroquois syllables of Anahareo, proved to be a charming, pretty, quiet, self-contained girl who appeared to manage Grey Owl very competently. He not only had a new wife now to care for him and accompany him on his travels, but I had found an excellent young man, Kenneth Conibear, a Canadian studying in England, and I had appointed him watch-dog in place of the two old Etonians who had functioned magnificently in that office, with that happy mixture of ad-hoc-ery and mild mockery which gave the first tour its appealing amateur touch. Ken Conibear was the son of a Hudson's Bay factor in the Far North. He had been taught entirely by his mother, and had then had a brilliant career at university. He knew as much about the North as Grey Owl did.

All should have been well. And it was. The success was never in doubt. But there were disturbing symptoms which, as the doctor in charge of the case, worried me privately. Take myself. I felt more like a theatrical promoter now than a keen young publisher pushing his author. Grey Owl, I could not help noticing, behaved more like a successful dramatic impresario than a man with a mission. There was more than a hint of professionalism now in an undertaking which at the beginning had the appealing earnestness of a struggle to maintain in a sinful world an essential and primary truth.

The climax of the second tour was the expected Command to Buckingham Palace. Grey Owl and I went alone, accompanied by the projector and its operator from the Polytechnic Theatre. Vincent Massey, the High Commissioner, who was diplomatic guardian of our little party, was in a great state of fuss, and I was nervous, not knowing how one got out of the Palace if Grey Owl should break down, overcome by all the dazzle, or worse still, seek relief for his nervous tension by becoming indelicate in some of his stories. The party was really for the two princesses, Elizabeth and Margaret Rose, but such was Grey Owl's fame, the whole royal family turned up, including the King and Queen, Queen Mary, and the Queen's parents, the Earl and Countess of Strathmore. The audience also included several rows of what were, I imagine, palace staff—secretaries, ladies-in-waiting, and so on. According to Mr. Massey's solemn instructions, we were all supposed to be in our places, including Grey Owl, when the great doors to the drawing-room were to be thrown open by two footmen, and the King and his family were to enter. Whereupon we would all stand up, and then when the royal party and we had taken our seats, Grey Owl was to advance to where a cinema screen had been erected and there deliver his address.

But Grey Owl would not have it so, when Vincent Massey patiently unfolded the procedures to him. No, the way he wanted it, the royal family and everybody else would be seated in their places, and when the footmen threw back the great doors, he, Grey Owl, would enter.

You would have thought we were suggesting something that outraged decency. Hissed explanations and persuasions were exchanged, for the second row of seats was already occupied by palace officials who had been invited to attend, and none of us, except Grey Owl, wanted this dispute to become public. Grey Owl was adamant. Either that, or the lecture was off. I could see that he was in one of those obstinate moods that are really a shield for inner tension, and after a few minutes of expostulation Massey saw this too.

So the monarch was seated when the great doors were thrown open, and there, a dramatic figure in his buckskins and leather, stood Grey Owl.

He flung up his right arm in salute, and addressing the King directly, said "How Kola." There followed a few words in the Ojibway tongue, then his arm was lowered: "Which, being interpreted, means 'I come in peace, brother,'" he said to the King. A smile spread over the King's face, he bowed his head slightly to acknowledge the message, and Grey Owl walked to the spot where he was to give his talk.

Like an experienced actor, he found the point in his audience most sympathetically inclined to him: it was where the two young princesses sat, and from then on he addressed himself exclusively to them. He gave one of the most masterful talks I had ever heard him give, and showed the films; and then, on an arranged signal from me, he drew his talk to a close. But Princess Elizabeth jumped up, and cried, "Oh, do go on!" and with a triumphant glance at me he spoke on for about ten minutes more.

Afterwards the King came up to him, a daughter on each side of him. The King asked more questions about the beaver; his interest had plainly been caught on the subject of their threatened extinction. I was admiring Grey Owl's attitude; he was more than ever the Indian, proud, fierce, inscrutable. Those fringed buckskins, the wampum belt, the knife in its sheath at his side, the moccasins on those polished floors, the long dark hair surmounted by a single feather, were all in such contrast with the trim, neat figure of the King, with the fair, reddish hair characteristic of the House of Windsor, the morning coat, the gleaming shoes. The drawing-room sparkled as though set with thousands of jewels, this illusion coming from the crystal chandelier and the crystal lamps on side-tables. There was silk everywhere, in the dresses of the ladies, in the curtain hangings, and in the lampshades. Shifting colours as people moved, sparkling light as the crystals reflected this movement, and the sound of thin, amused, distant, well-bred English voices in a great drawing-room in London: what a long way it all was from Beaver Lodge, with Jelly busting open the door and advancing purposefully with an armload of sticks and mud to repair some rent in her domain. Grey Owl was never disturbed when she did this while he sat talking to visitors. He seemed no more put out by the wonder of finding himself the centre of interest in these very different surroundings. When it came time for him to leave—we were to have tea with some of the palace officials—he put out his hand to the King and touched him on the shoulder with the other, in which he carried his beaded buckskin gloves, as brilliantly decorated with coloured beads as this room was with its light-reflecting crystals: "Goodbye, brother," he said to the monarch. "I'll be seeing you."

250

He gave 140 lectures between October and December 19, and during that time he never missed an engagement, or was late for one, except when he was involved in a motor accident between Oxford and Southport. A crowd of over a thousand had waited for him an hour and a quarter when he climbed on to the platform at the Cambridge Hall, to receive one of the greatest ovations of his career.

He was haggard with fatigue when I saw him off from England. I suspected that he had been fighting off the strain with the bottle. I knew that he was only a casual sleeper, never lying down for more than an hour or two during the night, and taking cat-naps during the day. Lines that could have been dissipation or fatigue creased his dark face like scars. He said that he was never coming back to England; that next year he would make the winter film of the Mississauga, and he urged me to come and join him there so that he could show me the country. I agreed, but somehow I knew that it would never happen. I had a conviction that Grey Owl and I were parting for ever. Although on the last night before he sailed we talked of the future as well as of the past we had shared, we each spoke as one would speak to a dying companion from whom one was about to part forever.

I heard of him only at intervals as the American tour progressed. He was not in good health, but the lectures were a success. I had few details. Not all these were reassuring, and my imagination could not help filling in sombre tones to the picture. The American tour must be a let-down after the English one. The English have kept their romantic eighteenth-century picture of the Indian, but it was my impression that the Americans had largely lost theirs in the subjugation of the West at the end of the nineteenth century. What Longfellow and James Fenimore Cooper had earlier pictured as noble had to be depicted as unreliable and cruel savages being herded into enclosures for their own good. Dee Brown's *Bury My Heart at Wounded Knee* gives a very good picture of that.

I could guess that to half of Grey Owl's appeal the Americans would be deaf. And I knew that this would enrage my friend. And when enraged, he was inclined to be aggressive.

I heard indirectly of one or two fights. I heard that he had lectured at Columbia University and at Harvard, and had travelled east and west to meet his engagements. But there were not lectures twice a day, as there had been in Britain. That was not possible in a country the size of the United States. Days of idleness for him in hotels in strange cities were dangerous. I knew that he was to give a last lecture at Massey Hall in Toronto on March 26 before returning to Beaver Lodge. I heard that he had said to a friend just before that, "A month more of this will kill me." As the time of the final lecture drew near I felt an increasing anxiety about his state of mind.

Far away as I was, and not hearing from him directly at this time, I thought I knew the struggle that must be going on in his mind between the shownman and the conservationist. As I have said earlier, he did not use the word conservationist about himself in its modern sense; hardly anybody did at that time. He had a set of simple ideas, that the beaver should be protected in every province in Canada, that all wildlife deserved some degree of protection from wholesale slaughter, and that the Indians were the people best fitted by nature and tradition to be the custodians of the wilderness, and should be trained to act as caretakers of the nation's wild heritage. He could only state these principles; he could not organize them into being. He knew that only the government could introduce these measures and force them into being. The knowledge that he was meanwhile making money out of their advocacy really worried him, and when the agent Colston Leigh offered him a three-year contract to lecture in the United States every winter, he refused.

"It is hard to keep one's mission in perspective," he wrote in his last article in *Forest and Outdoors*.* He felt himself caught in a trap, held there by the power of public admiration. He longed for escape. "If I am to remain loyal to my inner voices, I must return to my cabin in Saskatchewan . . . and take time to think."

After this last lecture he took the train to the West. It was Silver Moon whose health then broke down, not his. When

*"My Mission to My Country," February 1938.

252

they reached Prince Albert, she had to return to Regina for an emergency operation. When he was sure that she was out of danger, he hurried on ahead, for he was anxious to see Dawn in Prince Albert, but even more anxious to get back to his cabin, and see and hear Jelly Roll and Rawhide again.

A government truck drove him to within a mile of the cabin at Ajawaan, travelling over the ice, which still held. He made his way by snowshoe the remaining distance, a journey that could not have been easy in his debilitated condition. He found everything well at Beaver Lodge.

Major Wood had kept a man at the cabin all winter, so it was warm and there was a good stock of wood and food supplies. When he left Prince Albert in the Park truck, Major Wood had told Archie that he was under no circumstances to let this man go for at least two weeks, and Grey Owl had nodded, but had said nothing.

He wanted to be alone there, and next morning he told the man to go. That was on Friday morning, April 8. Making his way back to Prince Albert, the man stopped at the ranger's cabin at Kingsmere Lake and mentioned that Grey Owl had told him to go. The next morning the Kingsmere ranger went to Beaver Lodge. Grey Owl seemed all right, and very happy, he said, to be back.

But the next morning Grey Owl telephoned the Park office at Waskesiu and reported that he was feeling ill. This information was relayed on to Major Wood, who immediately instructed the Waskesiu ranger to go in and pick him up and bring him in to the Prince Albert Hospital. The rescue party arrived in Prince Albert at eleven o'clock on Sunday evening. Grey Owl seemed all right for twenty-four hours, but then he developed a temperature. At midnight on Tuesday he sank into a coma, and at eight o'clock on Wednesday morning, April 13, he died without regaining consciousness. X-rays taken immediately after his death showed nothing that could have killed him. There was only a slight congestion of the lungs, but his powers of resistance had gone altogether. The cause of his death was exhaustion, but it was exhaustion of hope and purpose which are born in the imagination and signal to the heart when to stop.

News of his death came to me at seven o'clock in the evening when the B.B.C. rang me to ask if I would broadcast at ten o'clock that evening on his life and work. I spent the intervening time preparing something to say. Slowly, after the first shock of sorrow over the sudden obliteration of such a man, I was beginning to realize what a difference his sudden death had made to my fortunes. In April 1938 the coming European war seemed very close. Germany had just annexed Austria, and was now threatening Czechoslovakia. Hitler was already master of Europe in the sense that all statesmen seemed to dance to his tune. With Anthony Eden's resignation and Neville Chamberlain's assumption of the direct control of foreign affairs, we seemed likely to fight sooner than later, for it was beginning to be clear that nothing was so deleterious to peace as fawning upon Hitler. I had published Sir Robert Vansittart's poems. He had been removed from the control of the civil service and given the empty office of Diplomatic Adviser to the Government. His advice was not even asked for, much less taken, and seeing a man as demented as Chamberlain in pursuit of peace had driven him nearly mad. His views were expressed with great force but with charm. They were anti-German only because Germany at that moment was Europe's enemy.

I therefore believed that war would come before the autumn, and Grey Owl's death, and the removal from my list of its most distinguished author, seemed the signal for the closing down of my business. Together we had conquered the English public. But our relationship had been more than that of author and publisher. We had been brothers. I spoke of my friend that night with deep feeling, engendered by this sense of sharing in his withdrawal, and conscious that I spoke to an audience of millions who had been moved by what he had written.

Within a few hours of my speaking, the dam burst. My friend Matthew Halton, the London correspondent of the *Toronto Daily Star*, telephoned to tell me that that evening's issue of the *Star* carried a long story by the noted Canadian nature writer, Gregory Clark, asserting that Grey Owl was not a half-breed but had been born in Hastings, England, the son of someone who described himself on the birth certificate as a "Planter" named George Belaney, and an English wife with the ordinary English maiden name of

Katherine Morris. The boy had been christened Archibald Stansfeld Belaney and he had come to Northern Ontario when he was seventeen. He had worked as a trapper and guide in the Mississauga area, had married an Indian wife, and had fathered several children. He had been a bad hat, and had finally to leave the area to escape a warrant that had been issued for his arrest. Suddenly everything that had been built up—the hope, the moral compunction people had felt for the first time—seemed empty and foolish. We had been duped. There was no Arcadia. The machines were our masters, and we had been deluding ourselves in thinking that we could defy them.

CHAPTER **15**

THIS DESPAIR was only momentary. Vigour returned when the campaign waged by circulation-seeking newspapers, quick to urge on the public that their sympathy and innocence had been taken advantage of, reached such a pitch of calumny, with "disclosures" and "interviews" with figures out of the past, that those who could not forget him or cease to love him, were drawn together in defence, shouting back as hard. Old Hastonians came forward to say that they had always thought that he had Indian blood. But two maiden ladies of advanced age emerged as aunts, and English aunts living respectably in English seaside towns are difficult to denounce as imposters. The *Times* published a long letter from me asserting the truth of what

Grey Owl and Anahareo had told us. They also published prominently a cable from Anahareo confirming that she had always believed him to be Indian. The *Times* even provided on the subject one of its famous "Fourth Leaders", leading articles in which perceptible truth lies below a slight vein of irony—a style which, when applied to an ideal subject, as it was in this case, can be very effective. Grey Owl, said the *Times*, "seemed to have had as many birthplaces as Homer, as many wives as Solomon, and as many aunts as Sir Joseph Porter." Fortunately, the *Times* went on, the public in general will soon tire of this supremely unimportant topic. What would remain was what he had achieved:

> He gave his extraordinary genius, his passionate sympathy, his bodily strength, his magnetic personal influence, even his very earnings to the service of animals, and of man through the right understanding of animals. "He prayeth best who loveth best"—if ever a man lived in the spirit of the last verse of "The Ancient Mariner", it was Grey Owl in his later years. There lies the truth about Grey Owl, inseparable from the truth of Grey Owl.

When the truth had been established, and it was no longer possible to doubt that the boy born in Hastings as Archie Belaney had been buried in Saskatchewan as Grey Owl, it was possible to see that an eccentric of an unusual kind had passed across the scene. England has long been a breeding-place for this rare species, which seems often to require several generations of inclination towards the unusual to produce at last the notable specimen which, by chance mutation, seems to have in just the right proportions unusual intelligence, a quickened sympathy with life in whatever form, an instinct towards self-dramatization, and a suppressed energy, all of which when released produce results often of a salvationist nature. Some cause, some oppressed people, some persecuted species, has to be rescued. The names of Sir Richard Burton and Lawrence of Arabia spring automatically to the mind, partly because they adopted other beliefs and dress to achieve their goals.

257

But we are reminded too that Darwin, when he set out to voyage in the *Beagle*, was prompted by the same need to escape the oppressions of mid-Victorian society before proceeding by sympathetic observation to discover in the world of nature the origin and meaning of life.

Grey Owl, to use the name by which he will always be remembered, came to Canada at a time when the natural world was beginning to show the scars inflicted on it by the unregulated pursuit of wealth. At first he was only uneasily aware that the bright, romantic image he had treasured for so long was not altogether there in reality: animals writhed in their death-throes in traps, some Indians wore European clothes, got drunk, could be wastrels. Timber-fellers were infiltrating the big woods, and the detritus of the sawmills and the prospectors' dynamite was beginning to foul the rivers. Life was not perfect. Yet to be alive in this setting was paradise. His writings about those early days all sing the joys of the great forests, the mighty rivers, and the men and animals who live along them.

It was the First World War that changed him utterly. He came back to the woods to find that destruction had left desolation even here. High fur prices had brought in men evading military service who had had to live by trapping. They had introduced wholesale methods of slaughter, and the animals had retreated to remoter places. The timber. cruisers and the prospectors had scarred and blackened the woods. The Indians' old hunting grounds had been taken over, and fights for prized territory were not uncommon amongst rival factions. Prohibition had come in, and with it the moonshiners and the stills. Men, Indians and white alike, had been degraded.

Sickened by these things, the tough *hombre* in him, which had always been part of the romantic image, took over from the poet and dreamer. Part of Belaney's trouble was, in the opinion of Factor Woodsworth, that he never grew up. Mr. Woodsworth was right. But it was also the quality of Belaney's particular condition that he did not submit to the repressions which we accept as we grow to conform to society. Saint or sinner, he could be either. But never the good, grey, steady hue that Mr. Woodsworth liked to see in a man.

For those few years from 1918 to 1925 there is no trace in his record of that close and sympathetic observation of and accord with animals which everyone had noted in him from the time he was a little boy. His mother, on one of her two widely separated visits to the Belaney household in his childhood, was told of the "menagerie" which he had been allowed to have in one of the rooms on the top floor.

"He kept all kinds of things in that room," she wrote to me in that breathless unpunctuated style in which all her reminiscences, verbal or written, were conveyed. "I or others seldom ventured without his protection, but they were all quite tame and would come to him even the reptiles."

She remembered on the occasion of this visit the trouble he had given over St. Helen's Woods:

> He would knot his sheets to get to the ground from his window and it was high—One morning I went into his room early and behold a rope was tied to the bedpost and out of the window he had climbed hours before

It was on that visit also that

> going upstairs to bed a snake was lying along the stair I was to tread upon—I was of course terrified —his only worry was in case I had wounded the little beast.

The same thing was remarked by Bill Guppy in Temagami, and by Angele and the Bear Island band when he first came among them. And Mrs. Sawyer noticed it too, in the early days in Bisco, because it was so unusual. People took it for granted that boys should go after birds and squirrels with catapults and that dogs should be tied up, sometimes without water. It attracted attention when a man was kind to animals.

But after the war he was a changed character; a ruthless trapper, a hard drinker, quick to draw his knife. No longer does he amaze them with his skill on the piano; he never touches it, and he consorts much more with Indians than with white men.

259

"He took a fancy to the Indian people, I think," says Mrs. Sawyer, "and let his hair grow and then he coloured it, dyed it black, and then he used this alum in the water. He bathed his face and arms, and it gave him a real, real brown tan. Then he used to braid his hair and tie it with little buckskins. That was just the way he was, you know. He took a fancy to them and he liked their ways."

At first a kind of self-abasement seems to prompt all this. He takes upon himself the humiliation he sees the white man as having thrust upon the Indians. In towns he will not use the sidewalk but walks in the gutter instead. He eats with his hands, professing disdain of cutlery. He likes his meat fly-covered. But when he is with the Indians he is like St. Paul among the early Christians; arousing them to a self-awareness of their proud history, of the wrongs that have been done them, of the old customs and religious rites with which their ancestors had marked the passage of their lives. Once, long ago in his English boyhood, he had invented the romantic tale of his half-Indian parentage, and of his birth in an Indian encampment in Mexico. Now he asserts the truth of this, and of his upbringing by Indians and his training in their ways.

There is just enough truth in this for it to be half-believed. He had married an Indian, although this he did not openly admit in Bisco. He had lived for some years with the Bear Island band, and all his woodcraft had been learnt from the Indians with whom he had hunted and worked. As much later, in 1936, he was to write in reply to a letter from Chief To-To-Sis, "the Indians taught me the very things that are now making me famous." And he reminds him that what he is doing for them is not done for any reward, "but because I love you—because Indians were my very first friends, because the Indians took me and made a man of me."

Confronting the white man, he is for the underdog, as symbolized both by Indians and by animals. What he comes in time to say to white audiences is, in effect, "I can prove to you that these people—and these beavers—are articulate in their own right," and he does it by showing them in their natural environment, behaving as moral creatures leading purposeful and useful lives, until the white man's itch for domination and possession persecutes and scatters them. To

260

the Indians he is not the defender but the catalyst, the stirrer-up of pride, the evangelist pointing out their only road to salvation. Get education, he urges them, *but do not forget that you are Indians.* Do not become just poor imitations of white men. *Be proud to be Indian.*

The metamorphosis, the Indianization of Archie Belaney, was gradual but steady. By 1925 he was in appearance and behaviour what he claimed to be, a man of mixed blood, who earned his living by trapping, lived rough, and behaved toughly, and was a constant thorn in the side of authority; a bad man to get mixed up with in a drinking bout or a fight.

He might have ended as George Belaney had done, and been killed in a drunken brawl, but for the accident of circumstances. He fell in love with Anahareo, carried her off to the woods with him, and found in her revulsion against the cruelty of a trapper's work the key that opened again the locked doors on his lost childhood, now over thirty years away. It had been screened behind the horrible years of war, and the struggle since for a living in these desolate woods. The two beaver kittens he rescued at Anahareo's plea appeared to him as emissaries from a hunted band suing for mercy, appealing to him as the dreaded hunter.

From that time on his life changed, although, as this account has tried to show, the change was not sudden and dramatic. Surrender to his own true self came only slowly. But when it did it was complete. And, because of the intensity with which he always felt things that touched him closely and the genuinely great gift he had for observing and describing the behaviour of animals, this surrender made him, the outcast Métis without training but with what were thought to be inherited primitive skills, the most famous and certainly the most admired field naturalist of his day.

He seemed to be quite unaware of what he had achieved. "Nothing to it," he wrote to Lloyd Acheson, his old fire-ranging boss on the Mississauga, "but a little kindness and patience."

I wish you could spare a month [he wrote from Ajawaan in 1934] to spend up here and see these animals. They are all free and wild and do as they like, but spend a lot of time around the cabin, that is the deer and moose and muskrats, etc., who are very friendly. They wander all over the country and return at regular intervals, except the beaver who have built their lodge inside the cabin, half inside and half outside, and are here all the time. The young ones, of course, go away in the Spring, when a year old, and mix with the native beaver throughout the Park. It took me two years to tame the moose, and he is as familiar here as a horse, and sleeps alongside the cabin about once a week. It has taken a lot of work, all at night, to get around these creatures and have them become attached to the place, but it has been a worthwhile accomplishment in the cause of conservation, and it gives people an opportunity of studying Canadian wildlife at close quarters in its natural state. All I do is keep the animal visitors interested so they stick around.

You've got to be on the square with them [he concludes], or you don't get along.

He became a man with a mission. Those who have had to live closely with someone so imbued will know that nothing can be more difficult. Grey Owl could change his name, his habits, even his mode of speech; the metamorphosis could in the end be so complete that no stranger meeting him would suspect him to be anything but an Indian, and at the same time he could mesmerize himself into believing that he was what he claimed to be. But one thing he could not change, and that was the complexity of his inherited cast of mind. Belaney upon Belaney, generation upon generation, back to those who had walked behind the plough, or ridden with falcon on wrist in the misty hills of the Scottish lowlands, had contributed to that pattern, and nothing in a short life-time could change it.

So he could be two things at once, and not be conscious of the ambivalence. Anahareo as an Indian could recognize only directness. We stand back amazed at what we consider to be her frankness about herself and her courage. But this

262

is the Indian in her, just as the complexity of motives and impulses were the inexpungeable Anglo-Saxon in Grey Owl. At certain points they could not meet; their concepts had different aims. Progress towards understanding was impossible because the course these concepts took was tangential, away from understanding, not towards it.

On the voyage to England for his first lecture tour Grey Owl had been greatly attracted by an intelligent young Toronto girl, Laya Rotenberg, crossing after graduation from the University of Toronto for her first visit to Europe. What surprised and gratified him was her feeling that it was required of her that she should give something to the world, and she was waiting expectantly for the demand to be made. He had not encountered this attitude in someone at the beginning of active life before. It reflected his own strong feelings at this stage. She was frequently at our house during that tour, and I saw him watch her with the same intense interest with which I could imagine him watching an animal as he established confidence and trust between them.

Long afterwards she wrote to an eager and intelligent young historian who was seeking to draw from her who had known him so well some explanation for the co-existence in Grey Owl of such contradictory qualities. Here was a man whose honesty was not in question, and whose pioneer work in wildlife preservation was to be of immense significance in forcing government action to protect our environment, going out of his way to delude the world about his parentage. The historian was honestly puzzled. She replied:

> It is almost thirty-five years since I met Grey Owl and assisted him on his first lecture tour in the British Isles. I still see and feel the almost magical impact his presence and message had on audiences, large and small, wherever he spoke. I literally saw him capture the attention and often the hearts of the very people he criticised and often scolded for their indifference or hostility. . . .
>
> In this his honesty was above suspicion. Therefore it never occurred to me to doubt his statements about his father being a Scotsman and his mother

263

a full-blood Indian. Nor did I make any connection, then or since, between that detail and the authenticity of his being what he became and what he is remembered for.

If as later investigation showed he was not part Indian, well I for one am reluctant to describe him as an imposter, or put any pejorative label upon him. After all, an imposter is a hypocrite or a quack with devious ulterior motives, a person who misleads knowingly or is without qualification to advise. Certainly where his life and work were concerned he had earned the right to be respected and cleared of either epithet.

Long before pollution and the needless killing of wild-life began to worry the world as is today the case, Grey Owl strove to keep our Canadian Spring singing. In the end, that's what counts most, is it not?

I catch again in memory the thousand glimpses I had of him in those years, hear the very echo of his voice, the soft shuffling sound of his moccasins on the carpets of an old London house.

Ah, did you once see Shelley plain,
And did he stop and speak to you,
And did you speak to him again?
How strange it seems, and new!

I never went with him on the trail. We were to go down the Mississagi together, but I never got there. But once we went to Epping Forest, a green glade hanging just beyond the arid stone wilderness of east-end London, and made camp and lit a fire with sticks, and broiled steaks on a hot stone.

I crossed a moor, with a name of its own,
And a certain use in the world, no doubt.
Yet a hand's-breadth of it shines alone
Mid the black miles round about.

264

For there I picked up on the heather,
And there I put inside my breast,
A moulted feather, an eagle feather . . .
Well, I forget the rest.

SOURCES & ACKNOWLEDGEMENTS

Donald Smith, a Ph.D. candidate in Canadian history at the University of Toronto, has been my mainstay in writing this book. His field of study is early nineteenth century Indian-white relations in Upper Canada, and in the course of his work he made an extensive series of taped interviews with Indians and whites in Biscotasing, Grey Owl's "home town" for fifteen years. These provide a cross-section of opinion of the inhabitants of what was once a small frontier town which must be unique in Canadian historical records. He has generously put his records at my disposal, providing the basis for much of my depiction of Grey Owl's life at this period.

Donald Smith has also been able to enlarge on the researches of Archie Belaney's life in Hastings which G. L.

267

Campbell and I made at the time of Grey Owl's death in 1938. These historians have a nose for the important clue, where the biographer has only the trick of applying the evidence to his narrative.

The Green Leaf, published soon after Grey Owl's death in 1938, was designed as a tribute to his memory. It contained an introductory essay, a summary of the press commentary (particularly of the controversy about his origins then still raging), extracts from his letters, and an article called "Grey Owl's Philosophy", taken largely from a diary kept by Betty Somervell of the long conversations he had with her as she drove him around England. In addition, there was the text of "Grey Owl's Farewell to the Children" of England, a broadcast which he was invited by the B.B.C. to make. A fuss blew up when he was pressed by the B.B.C to withdraw from his script a reference to the evils of fox-hunting. Grey Owl refused. The broadcast was never given. *The Green Leaf* closed with a picture record of his life. His handy publisher, who seems never to have been at a loss to turn everything to account, printed 100,000 copies of *The Green Leaf* as a pamphlet at, I think, threepence a copy: they melted away within a day or two. Because the little book has been out of print all these years, yet recaptures so well the mood of those days, it has a bibliographical importance, and I give this extended note of it.

My own biography of Grey Owl, *Half-Breed*, written hastily in 1939 under the shadow of war, appeared a few months before Europe capitulated to Hitler. It was a lop-sided book, a passionate defence of Grey Owl's integrity against the charges of "fraud" and "impostor", and in its single-mindedness, it missed the essential man. The success it had was entirely due to Grey Owl's fame, not to the biography, which was in that class condemned by Harold Nicolson in his 1927 lecture on "The Development of English Biography" as "impure", suffering from "the undue intrusion of the biographer's personality and predilections, or an unrestrained desire to celebrate the virtues of the subject."

Anahareo's *My Life with Grey Owl*, published in 1940, is a rich source of knowledge about him, written from a personal angle. Her autobiography, *Devil in Deerskins*, published in 1972 by New Press, Toronto, and Peter Davies,

London, is an essential book in the study of Grey Owl, and I have drawn from it quite largely in presenting Anahareo's point of view in *Wilderness Man*.

From other sources I have obtained enlightening details of Indian and white life in Northern Ontario seventy years ago: particularly the unpublished recollections of Vince Crichton of Chapleau, from which I have quoted with the permission of his son Vince Crichton, and also the notes made by Agnes Belaney, the daughter of Grey Owl and Angele, of conversations Angele had with her Indian grandmother, Old Lady Cat.

The many quotations from Grey Owl's letters and published books are made with the permission of the Trustees of the Grey Owl Estate, The Macmillan Company of Canada Limited, Peter Davies Limited, Charles Scribner's Sons, Paul Hamlyn Ltd., *Country Life*, and Dodd, Mead Limited.

Finally, to the many scores of people whose recollections have helped me, and to the resources and archives of the Canadian Broadcasting Corporation, the National Gallery of Canada, and the Writers' and Speakers' Research Bureau of London, my ever grateful thanks.

Toronto   LOVAT DICKSON
March 1973

BOOKS BY GREY OWL

The Men of the Last Frontier (the original title, his own, had
   been *The Vanishing Frontier*)

Country Life	LONDON	1931
Macmillan Canada	TORONTO	1932
Scribner's	NEW YORK	1932

Pilgrims of the Wild

Lovat Dickson	LONDON	1935
Macmillan Canada	TORONTO	1935
Scribner's	NEW YORK	1935

The Adventures of Sajo and Her Beaver People

Lovat Dickson	LONDON	1935
Macmillan Canada	TORONTO	1935
Scribner's	NEW YORK	1935

271

Tales of an Empty Cabin

Lovat Dickson	LONDON		1936
Macmillan Canada	TORONTO		1936
Dodd, Mead	NEW YORK		1936

The Tree (an extract from *Tales of an Empty Cabin*)

Lovat Dickson	LONDON		1937
Macmillan Canada	TORONTO		1937

A Book of Grey Owl (selections from *The Men of the Last Frontier, Pilgrims of the Wild, The Adventures of Sajo and Her Beaver People,* and *Tales of an Empty Cabin*)

Peter Davies	LONDON		1938
Macmillan Canada	TORONTO		1938

SUGGESTIONS FOR FURTHER READING

ACKERNECHT, ERWIN H., "White Indians". Bulletin of the History of Medicine, Vol. XV, 1944.

ANAHAREO, *Devil in Deerskins*. Toronto: New Press, 1972.

ANDERSON, J. W., *Fur Trader's Story*. Toronto: Ryerson, 1961.

BARBEAU, MARIUS, "Indian Captivities". American Philosophical Society, Vol. 94, No. 6, 1950.

CANTWELL, ROBERT, "Grey Owl: Mysterious Genius of Nature Lore". *Sports Illustrated*, December 1963.

COCKERELL, T. D. A., "A Visit with Grey Owl". *Natural History*, March 1936.

DICKSON, LOVAT (ed.), *The Green Leaf*. London: Lovat Dickson Ltd., 1938.

History of Hastings Grammar School 1619–1966, The.

RADDALL, THOMAS H., *Footsteps on Old Floors*. Toronto: Doubleday, 1968.

RASHLEY, R. E., "Grey Owl and the Authentic Frontier". *The English Quarterly*, Fall 1971.

SPECK, F. G. and F. I., "The Ojibwas, Hiawatha's People". *Home Geographic Monthly*, December 1937.

WALLACE, A. F. C., "Culture and the Beaver". *Natural History*, November 1965.

ZASLOW, MORRIS, *The Opening of the Canadian North*. Toronto: McClelland and Stewart, 1971.

INDEX

275

Barry, Mr. (name assumed by George Belaney), *18*

Bax, Clifford, *2*

Bear Island band, *46–7, 59–60*

Bear Island camp, *55–6*

Beaver Lodge, *252*

Belaney, Archibald Stansfeld (also known as Wa-Sha-Quon-Asin, He-Who-Flies-By-Night, Grey Owl). His own statements about his origins, *3*; Hastings upbringing, *25–42*; emigrates to Canada, *43*; early years with Bear Island band, *50–8, 68–9, 71–4*; meets Angele Eguana, *64*; returns to England for a visit, *74–5*; marries Angele, *77–8*; lives as Indian, *78*; abandons Angele and moves to Biscotasing, *84*; becomes Forest Ranger, *89*; traps from Bisco, *95–6*; winters in woods with Marie Girard, *96*; leaves Bisco to escape warrant for arrest, *98*; joins Army, *99*; sniper in Flanders, *101*; wounded and returned to England, *101–2*; marries Connie Holmes, *102*; returned to Canada and discharged, *103*; meets Angele again, *106*; son Robert Bernard born, *107*; returns to Bisco, *107*; trying post-war years, *108–11, 113–20*; rejoins Forest Ranger Service, *112*; desecration of the wilderness, *112–14*; is divorced by Connie Belaney, *115*; Bisco evenings and Belaney legends, *115–20*; meets Anahareo, *124*; visits Anahareo and her father, *126*; falls in love with Anahareo, *130*; sends for her to join him, *131*; first winter together, *133–44*; turning-point in their lives, *144–6*; teaches Anahareo the secrets of animals' lives, *146–7*; searches for unscarred territory, *4, 148–9*; the late spring hunt, *150*; the coming of McGinnis and McGinty, *150–1*; first attempts at writing, *154–6*; Dave White Stone enters their lives, *154*; *Country Life* accepts "The Falls of Silence", *156–7*; the myth-maker emerges, *157*.

The Indianization of Archie Belaney, *158*; gives up beaver hunting, *163–4*; plans a one-man conservation project, *165*; the vision of Touladi, *165–6*; the move to Cabano, *166–7*; Temiscouata country, *169*; journey to Birch Lake, *171–6*; building the House of McGinnis, *175–6*; winter at Birch Lake, *176–80*; the forest moves in, *180*; communicating with *Country Life,* *181–3*; the move to Half-way House, *183*; McGinnis and McGinty return to the Wild, *184*; the coming of Jelly Roll, *187*; the lecture at Métis-sur-Mer, *188–91*; Archie and Jelly settle for the winter at Elephant Lake, *192–5*; commences *The Men of the Last Frontier, 196–9;* creating Grey Owl and killing Belaney, *200–1, 225*; commences writing for *Forest and Outdoors, 203–4*; the coming of Rawhide, *204*; first films of beavers, *205–7*; a winter alone, *208–11*; lecture in Montreal, *211*; correspondence with *Country Life, 212–13, 217–18*; Lloyd Roberts' visit to Cabano, *214–16*; appointed Warden of Riding Mountain National Park, *216*; commences *Pilgrims of the Wild, 219*; moves to Ajawaan in Prince Albert National Park, *223–5*; starts writing *Tales of an Empty Cabin, 226*; birth of Dawn, *226*; finishes *Pilgrims of the Wild* and *The Adventures of Sajo,*

228; comparison with Henry David Thoreau, *229, 231*; accepts invitation to lecture in England, *5, 232*; instructs English publisher how to "put him across", *232–3*; arrival in England, *234*; moves in with his publisher, *235–6*; secret of his success, *237*; first signs of break with Anahareo, *238*; success of *Pilgrims*, *242*; financial success, *243*; second tour agreed on, *243*; making new films, *243*; increasing tension with Anahareo, *245*; the parting, *246*; success of second tour, *247*; marries Yvonne Perrier, *248*; Royal Command Performance at Buckingham Palace, *248–50*; leaves for American tour, *251*; returns to Ajawaan, *252*; death, *5, 253*; shock of disclosures about origins, *5–7, 254–5*; controversy, *256*; the defence, *256–62*; judgement, *263–4*.

Belaney family:
—— Ada (Grey Owl's aunt), *7–11, 15, 30–2, 33–43, 80, 201, 208*
—— Agnes (Grey Owl's daughter), *124*
—— Archibald (Grey Owl's grandfather), *10, 13, 15, 24*
—— Juliana Jackson (Grey Owl's grandmother), *15, 26, 31–2, 80–2*
—— Carrie (Grey Owl's aunt), *7, 15, 26, 30, 43*
—— George (Grey Owl's father), *14, 15–23, 261*
—— Mrs. George (Grey Owl's mother. Also known as Katherine Cochise, Kitty Cox, Katherine Morris, Mrs. Scott-Brown), *18–24, 29, 155–6, 201, 259*
—— Hugh (Grey Owl's younger brother), *11, 22, 29*
—— James Cockburn (Grey Owl's great-uncle), *13, 14*
—— John (Grey Owl's great-grandfather), *13*
—— Robert (Grey Owl's great-uncle), *14–15*
—— Rose Ethel (George Belaney's first wife), *17*
—— Shirley Dawn (Grey Owl's daughter), *226–8, 238, 253*
Bernard, Gertrude, *see* Anahareo
Bernard, Mr. (Anahareo's father), *128–9, 130, 137–8*
Big Elk, Chief, *27*
Birch Lake, *171, 175, 180, 196*
Biscotasing (known as Bisco), *6, 45, 82, 108–13, 146, 153, 260*
Bolton, Joe, *114*
Both-Ends-of-the-Day, *46, 68, 71*
Brown, Dee, *251*
Burroughs, Mrs., *65*
Burton, Sir Richard, *257*
Bury My Heart at Wounded Knee, *251*

Cabano, *45, 184*
Campbell, J. C., *205–7*
Canada, S.S., *43, 44*

Lovat Dickson was born in Australia and brought up in Central Africa and Canada. In England he founded his own publishing firm which published the books of Grey Owl. Subsequently he was with Macmillan & Co. in London for 22 years. His previous books include *The Ante-Room, The House of Words,* and *H. G. Wells: His Turbulent Life and Times.*